OUT FROM THE SHADOWS

Studies in Austrian Literature, Culture, and Thought

OUT FROM THE SHADOWS

Essays on Contemporary Austrian Women Writers and Filmmakers

Edited and with an Introduction by
Margarete Lamb-Faffelberger

ARIADNE PRESS
Riverside, California

Ariadne Press would like to express its appreciation to the Austrian Cultural Institute New York for assistance in publishing this book.

Library of Congress Cataloging-in-Publication Data

Out from the shadows : essays on contemporary Austrian women writers and filmmakers / edited and with an introduction by Margarete Lamb-Faffelberger.
        p.   cm. -- (Studies in Austrian literature, culture, and thought)
    Includes bibliographical references and index.
    ISBN 1-57241-037-X
    1. Austrian literature--women authors--History and criticism. 2. Austrian literature--20th century--History and criticism. 3. Women motion picture producers and directors--Austria. 4. Women and literature--Austria--History--20th century. 5. Motion pictures--Austria--History.
    I. Lamb-Faffelberger, Margarete, 1954- II. Series
PT3818.097   1997
830.9'9287'0943609045--dc20
                    96-9842
                    CIP

Cover design:
Art Director and Designer: George McGinnis

Dedicated to my parents

Dr. Othmar and Margarete Faffelberger

CONTENTS

Preface

Since the 1950s Austrian women writers and filmmakers have created a remarkably large body of work. These literary and film texts have increasingly become a question of and occasionally also an instrument for emancipation. During the restorative phase of the 1950s and 1960s, initial emancipatory efforts by such authors as Ingeborg Bachmann and Ilse Aichinger scarcely found resonance in the climate of consolidation. During the 1970s, however, the women's movement in Austria gained momentum, and its influence extended to an ever increasing number of women writers and filmmakers. In the 1970s and 1980s and continuing into the 1990s, literature and film by women often reflect and critique Austria's sociopolitical situation. In spite of the authors' doubts that art today can be used as a means for social change, their texts are directed towards social and ethnic consciousness-raising.

Since Austrian women writers and filmmakers were only marginally involved in the process of reestablishing Austria's post-World-War-II cultural identity, their work was hardly recognized as an important contribution until the 1970s. However today, Austria's literature and film created by women is no longer hidden within the shadows of the body of art created by their male counterparts, but receives international recognition. Many of the works are now considered trend setters within the realm of German culture, such as Ingeborg Bachmann's novels and Valie Export's films.

Out from the Shadows is intended for an English-speaking audience as well as for colleagues in the fields of German and Austrian Studies and their students. It attempts to provide an insight into the development and progress of the women's literature and film scene in Austria from 1945 to the present. Yet, the collection of articles does not present a complete picture. While striving to include as many authors and filmmakers as possible, mere pragmatic needs such as deadlines and book size made a number of choices necessary. Twenty articles were finally selected to introduce individual Austrian women writers and filmmakers and the vast body of their work. Many of these texts are available in English. Those that are not yet available in translation are nevertheless presented in English by the contributors. We included a few dialect poems to sample the unique form of artistic expression.

Several colleagues were able to write their studies in consultation with the author/filmmaker whose oeuvre they discuss. For instance, Ruth Beckermann, Anna Mitgutsch, Elisabeth Reichart, and Renate Welsh personally added their input to the respective presentations. Contributors' interviews with Kitty Kino, Doris Mühringer, and Nadja Seelich also enhance the discussion of their work.

In order to fulfill our obligation to the English-speaking audience, a number of manuscripts required complete or partial translations. Particularly Klaus Zeyringer's article on critical dialect poetry proved to be very challenging and required translations from various Austrian dialects into High German and further into equivalent expressions for our English readers. My sincere gratitude goes to Gudrun Bauer for her thoughtful work during long hours converting these texts as well as the study about them into English.

Moreover, I am deeply indebted to my colleagues who have contributed to this project. I would like to convey my sincere gratitude for their willingness to share their expertise in the subject matter as well as their confidence in me as the editor of this project. Still, the book could not have been created without the generous support of Lafayette College's Office of Research. In this regard, I owe special thanks to the Provost, June Schlueter and the Director of Research, Jeffrey Bader. In addition, I would like to express my sincere appreciation to a number of respected colleagues in particular to Donald Daviau, Margret Eifler, Jorun Johns, Dagmar Lorenz, Pamela Saur, and Laura Walls for their willingness to contribute time and effort in order to share many great insights and make valuable suggestions. To my colleagues in my home department I am thankful for all the support provided, for well-meaning insights shared, and lessons learned. From the bottom of my heart I express my thank you to Barbara Young for many hours of helpful discussions, for great advice and sound judgment, for caring and sharing, and being a wonderful friend.

A word of especially grateful acknowledgment belongs to Carey Knox, my Excel Scholar, assistant, and friend. Carey's personal contribution to this project is invaluable—her strong dedication to the editorial process, her outstanding organizational skills, and her amazing computer wizardry. To work together with her was a great privilege for me. Carey's earnest curiosity in the subject matter, her endless patience, and always good-humored words of encouragement have greatly enriched my work. I would also like to extend my gratitude to Stephanie Tolischus for her help in the beginning stage of the project as well as during the final phases of indexing and editing.

I dare say that this book would never have come into existence without the undying support of my family—my children Nikolas, Christina, and Thomas, and my husband Walt Lamb. Thank you! I am dedicating this book to my parents in deep gratitude for their love.

Introduction

Literature and films created by women since 1945 have truly enriched the Austrian art scene. Their contributions, however, were only marginally recognized and remained largely hidden within the shadows of the body of art created by their male counterparts in the process of searching and reestablishing Austria's post-World-War-II cultural identity.

After 1945, the aesthetic and philosophical trends of the "modern period" and the "avant-garde" of the early twentieth century lay buried under the rubble which the years of fascism and national socialism left behind. To define a cultural identity distinctly different from Germany, Austria proclaimed the "Anschluß"[1] to its own great era, —the cultural heritage of the nineteenth century, and the *fin-de-siècle* literature and art.[2] The recreation of art institutions with this nostalgic look back discouraged any artistic expression that voiced criticism against established art forms and current politics.[3]

In this restrictive and discriminating climate—off the beaten path in search for a distinct Austrian identity and culture—progressive and aesthetically innovative artists and writers created provocative statements of rebellion directed against Austria's political and cultural canon. The theoretical foundation for the artistic expression was sought within the avant-garde period of the early twentieth century and the language-philosophical traditions of Walter Benjamin and Ludwig Wittgenstein.[4]

The Generation After the War—*Die Nachkriegsgeneration*

Outside the literary canon as well as the male-dominated avant-garde art scene, the young *Nachkriegsgeneration* (post WW II generation) of Austrian women writers made their debut on the literary stage, for instance Marlen Haushofer, Ilse Aichinger, Ingeborg Bachmann, Jeannie Ebner, Friederike Mayröcker, Christine Busta, and Christine Lavant. Born in the late 1910s and early 1920s and having come of age during the bitter Nazi years, these women searched for their own voice in order to effectively articulate the realities of their lives. Writing for these women became a journey towards their inner self and a search for self-realization, and as such a confrontation with the pain inflicted by the deceit of their fathers and their fathers' generation.[5]

This post-World-War-II generation refused to write explicitly about historical events, and yet their texts imply history. Often, the word-pair "remembering and forgetting" are written into familiar structures of the private sphere.[6] Thus, their literature brings to light the microcosm of arrogance, ignorance, and chauvinistic attitudes which dominated during Austro-Fascism and continued after 1945. Still, an "escape from societal bonds in an ultimately freeing way" was unknown to the women writers of the post WW II generation—explains Nancy Erickson (*Out From the Shadows*, 200).

Ilse Aichinger and Ingeborg Bachmann soon became established as prominent young Austrian poets within the realm of the West German literary canon. This was the result of the Gruppe 47 awards in 1952 and 1953 respectively for their critical writing and innovative aesthetics, as well as the 1954 *Spiegel* cover story about Bachmann and her extra-ordinary poetic talent. The image of the great Austrian lyric dominated the Bachmann-reception until long after her death in 1973. Bachmann's poetry quickly entered standard schoolbooks and reading lists in Austria and West Germany and thus became a part of the Austrian literary canon.[7]

In 1961, Bachmann published the first of several prose texts, namely *Das dreißigste Jahr* (*The Thirtieth Year*, 1963). Unlike her poetry, it was not received favorably. The negative criticism concentrated on the text's seemingly missing reference to a so-called "concrete reality." Bachmann's prose texts were largely frowned upon for their "radical subjectivity," and her 1971 novel *Malina* was "originally rejected as a confused and bitter autobiography"—as Margaret McCarthy points out (*Out From the Shadows*, 40).

While Bachmann and Aichinger became well known, texts by Haushofer, Mayröcker and others were appreciated only within the literary circle. Their literature remained on the margins of acceptance. Bjorklund claims that Mayröcker's texts—strongly influenced by the Wiener Gruppe's avant-garde relationship to form—reject narration and rupture realistic conventions (*Out From the Shadows*, 57).

What unites the work of the *Nachkriegsgeneration* is the radically new use of language—a language with which to express the writers' own realities, a language with which to gropingly approach the realities of their experience, a language that opened up new perspectives for the writer and the reader. At stake was then and still is—as Beth Bjorklund reminds us—"the issue of whether language is an adequate medium for rendering experience; or whether reality instead is not being insidiously distorted by the linguistic means used to evoke it" (*Out From the Shadows*, 56).

The many signs of alienation inherent in the works of the *Nachkriegsgeneration* demonstrate the search for traces and imprints of forceful intrusion onto the female body, and onto the wishes and the dreams of women. Their texts are therefore rich in codes, without suggesting an alternative or even a utopian female image. Thus, readers and critics alike often condemned content and form as unintelligible and stilted. In 1962, *Die Verbannten* (The Banished) was published by Milo Dor[8]—a collection of texts written by the *Nachkriegsgeneration*, whom Dor called "the banished" because at that time there existed no relationship between their literary work and the reading public in Austria.

The Younger Generation

Only during the 1970s, in the wake of the women's movement, the younger generation of women writers, filmmakers, artists, and critics recognized Bachmann's *Malina* as well as the work of Aichinger, Haushofer, and Mayröcker as major contributions and considered these texts important forerunners of an *écriture féminine*. This younger generation of women writers and filmmakers, generally born during the 1940s, emerged "out from the shadows" of Austria's male-dominated artist milieus. They were confronted with the underrepresentation of women in the arts and the indifference of their male colleagues as well as the art institutions as a whole towards their work. Strongly influenced by the political and social agenda of the women's movement as well as by innovative art forms such as actionism, expanded cinema, and the language experimentations of the Wiener Gruppe, these women felt the need to strive beyond the playing fields of artistic indulgence and go "against the horizon"[9]—as Jaqueline Vansant puts it—by asserting their feminist views and pleas.

The Feminist Avant-Garde

Austria's feminist writers and filmmakers reestablished a link with the prewar avant-garde in order to lay the theoretical foundation. They share the same concerns about the material basis of art and pursue the same fundamental goal, namely questioning the traditional concept of the art-object as an organic and autonomous form. Thus, they too attempt to close the gap between art and everyday life.[10]

Two of the most innovative and most prominent representatives of Austria's feminist avant-garde today are the internationally acclaimed author Elfriede Jelinek and the multimedia artist Valie Export. Both, writer and artist, deal with women's representation within the canons of society and the culture of art. Elfriede Jelinek's texts are strongly characterized by her critical relationship to language. For Jelinek language signifies the power structures and mirrors the dominance of logocentrism within a capitalist society.[11] Valie Export's critical analysis of women's position in western patriarchal societies reflects upon Freud and Lacan's notion of "the woman as the other." In addition, she insists "on bringing together two seemingly disparate discourses: [namely] technology and the [female] body"—as Roswitha Mueller explains (*Out From the Shadows*, 244).

Jelinek's and Export's innovative aesthetics is aimed at a strong criticism of the social, economic, and political situation of women in today's Austria. Their literary texts as well as film texts are respective expressions of an *écriture féminine* directed against the traditional writing of "his-story" and the established social and cultural canons. Displaying distinctive features of feminist writing such as anti-linearity, anti-mimesis, and polylogic, these texts are created through the artistic methods of collage and montage. The criticism of the dominance of logocentrism and its phallocratic order constitutes the center of the art-production and is directed at undermining the fundamental concepts of our thinking.

The artistic attempt to jolt the conscience and bring to light the inefficiencies of social and political dicta and their tragic effects on women is not completely new to this generation of female writers and filmmakers. Elfriede Gerstl, born a decade before Export and Jelinek, and therefore considered as one of the *Nachkriegsgeneration*, has been writing her socio-critical and aesthetically innovative work since the early 1950s. Konstanze Fliedl explains that Gerstl's writing against the clichés of femininity and the cultural industry rejects "the solemn moral stance of enraged social criticism" (*Out From the Shadows*, 144). Rather, she applies satirical aesthetics as a means of trivializing reality. Her texts—as Konstanze Fliedl argues—"reverse the satirical process: reality is made to look so trivial that it becomes ridiculous" (*Out From the Shadows*, 144). Fliedl labels Gerstl's satirical aesthetics "understatement"—and rightly so—since Gerstl's art is "quieter, more subtle and more precise than an indignant lashing-out in all directions. That is why Elfriede Gerstl's voice has often gone unheard" (*Out From the Shadows*, 144). It is therefore no coincidence that her novel *Spielräume* (Rooms to Move) written in 1968-69 was not published until 1977. Even though she received a number of awards in the 1970s and 1980s, today she is still considered the "great unknown" of the literary scene.

Following in the footsteps of Elfriede Gerstl, Elfriede Jelinek, and Valie Export, Austrian female writers, such as Elisabeth Reichart, Anna Mitgutsch, Renate Welsh, Marianne Fritz, and filmmakers, like Friedericke Pezold, Käthe Kratz, and Kitty Kino, continue to display gender and sex issues combined with social and historical processes. In the wake of the women's movement with its political activism followed by an intensive theoretical discourse in France and the United States, the self-liberating and emancipatory tendencies of literature and film by and about women, which were largely ignored during the first two decades after the war, became widely accepted as a means of self-realization and emancipation. The act of creating literature and film as a journey into the "self" allowed writers and filmmakers to speak about themselves and to experience their "self" in the act of creation.

New Subjectivity

Some texts by and about women during the late 1960s until the mid-1970s have been viewed in the context of the so-called "New Subjectivity." These writings describe new modes of experience of and for women and—may we say—a new emotional reality. Thus, they entail the possibility of reducing the weight of a restrictive and suppressive upbringing by writing about it. As Klaus Zeyringer points out, "authors created memories for themselves and their readers, in order to find the 'self' by writing against the self-denial thrust upon them by their upbringing. And to that end they had to do what was denied to them during their childhood, namely to speak about the self."[12]

In 1968, Barbara Frischmuth published *Klosterschule* (*The Convent School*, 1993), which became immensely popular. Even though Frischmuth "has shown resistance to the label 'feminist,' many of her books have focused on women's experiences, choices, and constraints, and some contain specific and pointed protests against oppression of women"—as Pamela S. Saur reminds us (*Out From the Shadows*, 100). During the 1970s, Barbara Frischmuth published the Sophie Silber-trilogy; a decade later she created her Demeter-trilogy. Both are intriguing sets of novels in which she thematizes the fundamental question of: What does the female world encompass? Where does it begin and where does it end? Ulrike Kindl calls it Frischmuth's attempt to go back to the roots of humanity by creating a feminine cosmology.[13] Weaving the worlds of reality and fantasy together and moving in and out of levels dealing with human experience and notions of mythology, Frischmuth designs positive models of femininity.

Self-Realization and Emancipation

Since the women's movement in Austria had markedly gained in recognition in the late 1970s, the label "New Subjectivity" should not keep us from recognizing the strong sociopolitical character of the texts. Time and again, women writers and filmmakers display the individual's imprisonment in fixed and inflexible roles, in the rules and norms of conservative, rural, and urban social structures. The private sphere is recognized as a reflection of public attitudes. "Outward conditions are assessed from the perspective of a subjective look inward,"[14] as demonstrated by Brigitte Schwaiger's phenomenally successful autobiographical text *Wie kommt das Salz ins Meer (Why Is There Salt in the Sea?*, 1988). In Elfriede Jelinek's *Liebhaberinnen* (1975; *Women as Lovers*, 1994), Paula and Brigitte try to escape their monotonous life and the vicious cycle that has placed them at the bottom of society in a remote country village, but do not (or perhaps marginally) succeed in striving beyond the horizons of their destiny.

By the 1980s, the search for a woman's position in today's society, the search for identity and self-realization, leads often to the mother-figure. She becomes a symbol for the traditional role of women: the mother who is submissive to the authority of man; but also the mother who constitutes the authority figure for the daughter. Jelinek's *Die Klavierspielerin* (1983; *The Piano Teacher*, 1989), Mitgutsch's *Die Züchtigung* (1985; *Three Daughters*, 1987) and Fritz's *Dessen Sprache du nicht verstehst* (1985; Whose Language You Do Not Understand)— to name a few—deal with the question of "inheritance" of female roles. The issue of the so-called "inherited" notion and attitude towards female sexuality is demonstrated in Jelinek's *Lust* (1990; *Lust*, 1992) and Schwaiger's *Liebesversuche* (1989; Love Experiments). It is the restrictive "fig leaf and the leaf over the mouth"—as Zeyringer puts it— which is the negative legacy that the mothers often leave their daughters.[15]

Women who are psychologically wounded and "deformed" by dominant phallocratic forces in today's society and therefore destined to failure are depicted in Marianne Fritz's *Die Schwerkraft der Verhältnisse* (1978; The Gravitational Force of Relationships). The private fate of Berta Schrei becomes the model of women's failure. Marianne Fritz's powerful language weaves stories and dreams, tales and history into a narrative web of tragic fate. Her female protagonists wounded by oppression and forced into suppression end up silenced in the psychiatric ward. Just like Berta, women have—for centuries— neutralized the propitious as well as ominous potential of their talents into speechlessness, silence and madness. Just like Berta, they were wrong to consider it evident that this potential—when once set free— could or would change the world.[16]

Still, literature and film created by women are conceived as responsibility "to tell the truth" and "to call things by their name"[17] in a society caught up in repressing and forgetting. In the late 1980s, women's writing and filmmaking reflect current social and political developments. Troubling political issues, in particular the Waldheim affair, with the multitude of unanswered questions about Austria's Nazi past infiltrated many texts and films.

Reactivating Memory

Reactivating memory becomes central to a number of authors like Ruth Klüger, Marie-Thérèse Kerschbaumer, and Elisabeth Reichart. Reichart explains in an interview her motive for writing *Februarschatten* (1984; *February Shadows*, 1989) and *Komm über den See* (1988; Come Across the Lake): I "felt compelled by a sense of personal responsibility and duty to give voice to the real victims of Fascism, in particular to the women whose stories have been largely excluded from public dialogue to date" (*Out From the Shadows*, 129). Marie-Thérèse Kerschbaumer's books *Der weibliche Name des Widerstands* (1980; *Woman's Face of Resistance*, 1996) and *Schwestern* (1982; Sisters) deal with the repression and exploitation of minorities and the underprivileged.

Ruth Beckermann's films must also be "situated within the context of contemporary feminist and minority discourse and present a noteworthy contribution to an interdisciplinary exploration of those questions that are related to the ethnic and cultural identity of today's Jewish Austrians from a woman's point of view"—as Renate S.

Posthofen points out (*Out From the Shadows*, 266). Beckermann's critical writings and films force the viewers to rethink and reassess their memory in terms of traditional judgment.

Transforming existing images by creating texts of association that chain the conscious to the unconscious—both in the act of art creation and in the reception process—is essential to contemporary Austria's literature and film created by women. By undermining the fundamental concepts of our thinking, "traditional premises such as logic and causality are confronted critically" to make translucent the "established canons and the limits of their truths."[18] In spite of their doubt that art today can be used as a means for social change, texts created by women are nevertheless directed towards social and ethnic consciousness-raising.

Lafayette College

Notes

1. Walter Weiss and Sigrid Schmid, eds. *Zwischenbilanz. Eine Anthologie österreichischer Gegenwartsliteratur* (Salzburg: Residenz, 1976).

2. Otto Basil, Herbert Eisenreich and Ivan Ivask, eds. *Das große Erbe. Aufsätze zur österreichischen Literatur* (Graz: Stiasny, 1962).

3. Kurt Bartsch and Gerhard Melzer, eds. *TransGarde. Die Literatur der "Grazer Gruppe," Forum Stadtpark und "manuskripte"* (Graz: Droschl, 1990).

4. Hans Christian Kosler, "'Neo-Avantgarde?' Analysen zur experimentellen Literatur," *Theorie der Avantgarde. Antworten auf Peter Bürgers Bestimmung von Kunst und bürgerlicher Gesellschaft*, ed. W. Martin Lüdke (Frankfurt: Suhrkamp, 1976), 254 ff.

5. Cf. Donald G. Daviau, ed. *Austrian Writers and the Anschluss: Understanding the Past—Overcoming the Past* (Riverside: Ariadne Press, 1991).

6. "Gemeinsam ist dieser Nachkriegsgeneration...daß sie sich schreibend in der Verweigerung von Geschichte immer wieder impliziten historischen Rückbezüglichkeiten zuwendet; daß sie dabei oftmals das Begriffspaar "Erinnern" und "Vergessen" in den

privaten Raum und in familiäre Strukturen einschreibt." Christine Schmidjell, ed. *Marlen Haushofer. Die Überlebenden* (Frankfurt/Berlin: Ullstein, 1993), 7-8.

7. Kurt Bartsch, "Früh kanonisiert und heftig umstritten. Ingeborg Bachmanns Werk in Literaturkritik, Literaturwissenschaft und Schulbuch," *Die einen raus, die anderen rein: Kanon und Literatur*, ed. Wendelin Schmidt-Dengler, Johann Sonnleitner and Klaus Zeyringer (Berlin: Erich Schmidt, 1994), 176.

8. Milo Dor, *Die Verbannten. Eine Anthologie* (Graz: Stiasny, 1962).

9. Jaqueline Vansant, *Against the Horizon* (Westport: Greenwood, 1988).

10. Harold Rosenberg, *The Anxious Object: Art Today and Its Audience* (Chicago: University of Chicago Press, 1966).

11. Jorun Johns and Katherine Arens, eds. *Elfriede Jelinek. Framed by Language* (Riverside: Ariadne Press, 1994).

12. Klaus Zeyringer, "Austrian Literature by and about Women in the 1980s: The Feminine Name of Resistance and the Way to the Mothers," unpublished manuscript. The German version of this study was published in David F. Good, Margarete Grandner and Mary Jo Maynes, eds. *Frauen in Österreich. Beiträge zu ihrer Situation im 19. und 20. Jahrhundert* (Vienna/Cologne/Weimar: Böhlau, 1993).

13. Heinz Puknus, ed. *Neue Literatur der Frauen. Deutschsprachige Autorinnen der Gegenwart* (Munich: C.H. Beck, 1980), 146.

14. Zeyringer, "Austrian Literature."

15. Ibid.

16. Bettina Rabelhofer, "Von Steinen, Schmerz und Sprache. Das Textbegehren der Marianne Fritz," unpublished manuscript.

17. Zeyringer, "Austrian Literature."

18. Margret Brügmann, "Weiblichkeit im Spiel der Sprache. Über das Verhältnis von Psychoanalyse und 'écriture féminine,'" *Frauen Literatur Geschichte*, ed. Hiltrud Gnüg and Renate Möhrmann (Stuttgart: Metzler, 1985), 395-415.

Out from the Shadows!—Ilse Aichinger's Poetic Dreams of the Unfettered Life

Edward R. McDonald

Ilse Aichinger is a prominent member of the group of writers who reached maturity in the postwar period.[1] Deeply influenced by social and psychological upheavals wrought by WW II as well as the turmoil following in its wake, their writing is replete with expressions of doubt and marked by a pronounced skepticism about literature's ability to help reshape postwar Germany and Austria into new landscapes of humanity wherein rational and moral principles might prevail. Aichinger was given considerable recognition for her first work, *Die größere Hoffnung* (1948; *The Great Hope: A Play*, 1974), after which she evolved into one of Austria's prominent contemporary writers with an oeuvre consisting of lyrics, a novel, short stories, dialogues, essays and radio plays.[2]

In her diverse writings, Aichinger repeatedly intones her conviction that a great many people born into contemporary civilization are living in dark times and have become alienated; not only beset by a breakdown in true human communication but also living within a world lacking both unity and structure.[3] It is therefore a domain in which people are oblivious to the effects of "Trugbilder," deceptive appearances that conceal the essence of truth in daily life. Therefore, Aichinger's writing is both a challenge and a warning to the reader to step forth from shadows of unawareness that obfuscate true knowledge and thereby enslave the human spirit. Time and again she reflects her desire for a new humanity able to cast off the bonds of ignorance to bring about a continuous renewal of the spirit through critical introspection. In the manifold forms of Aichinger's written expression, the reader readily notes a recurrent theme dominating her work, specifically the issue of existential freedom.

Already in *Die größere Hoffnung*, Aichinger focuses on the quest to attain truth and existential freedom.[4] Ellen's first step toward the realization of this "greater hope" is to relinquish her futile desire to emigrate to America in hopes of evading Nazi persecution. As she voluntarily chooses to publicly acknowledge her Jewish heritage, Ellen sets out on a symbolic journey into hidden recesses of her being. Once she sews the Star of David onto her clothing and joins up with a group of persecuted Jewish children, the Nazi noose begins to coil tighter around her, yet at the same time Ellen seems to become proportionately freer.[5]

Although rarely inclined to offer critical commentary on her work in public, Aichinger nevertheless chose to do so when accepting the annual prize of Gruppe 47 in 1952, notably at a time when bold experimentation with literary form was generating controversy among the more politically engaged postwar writers. These social activists believed that the ever-increasing emphasis on formal artistry only reinforced a growing tendency to avoid sound self-criticism and confrontation with the recent past.[6] Members of "the young generation" felt that advocacy of literary "Gestalt" (form, aesthetics) over literature's "Gehalt" (content, intention) could only exacerbate the problem of *Vergangenheitsverdrängung* (repressing the past) and help foster a social profligacy of psychological repression or collective amnesia. Aichinger stands out among writers who rejected the convenient advancement of a popular notion in the era of *Wirtschaftswunder* (economic miracle), namely that the past had best be forgotten since it hindered the reconstruction of a new world of security. In *Die Silbermünze* (1956; The Silver Coin),[7] a short story in which a war invalid is forced to earn his living by selling "traurige Karten" (sad cards), Aichinger juxtaposes the wounded man's sad sketches of his wartime experiences with "neuere Ernte" (new harvest), the postwar era's opulent harvest of tomatoes, currants and oranges that now grace many tables. Here Aichinger portrays children growing up in her consumer-oriented postwar society and suggests that their young minds are being nourished by a culturally transmitted materialistic attitude that allows them to callously ignore the bitter realities wrought by the war.[8] It is in this context of moral wariness that Aichinger ventured the critical opinion that creative writing should never be reduced to polished virtuosity devoid of risk-taking. Yet it is clear that Aichinger was never opposed to technical virtuosity per se. In her own challenging texts moral issues are frequently accentuated by means of unconventional images and forms. Yet for Aichinger no author should aspire to formal excellence in literature, should such a quest sadly effect the poet's task of depicting the positive vital spirit in human life.[9]

Ilse Aichinger's narrative world has been described as being surrealistically topsy-turvy with plots barely yielding to traditional demands of chronological development. Nevertheless, she consciously avoids the surrealist's predilection to blatantly deviate from syntactical norms for the purpose of heightening overall effect. In lieu of all such contrived linguistic violations, Aichinger's fanciful existential imagination strives to give expression to her overriding concern with the question of human dignity through a carefully controlled idiom that is markedly precise and devoid of bombast.[10] For example, in *Spiegelgeschichte* (The Mirror Story), a tale from the prose collection that appeared in 1953 under the title *Der Gefesselte* (The Bound Man), the tone of Aichinger's heroine, who also serves as her built-in narrator, is remarkably subdued. Aichinger's untraditional narrative logic mirrors memories of the young woman who died after an abortion. Significant events in the span of her life that ordinarily—perhaps by resorting to the more traditional use of flashback—would lead the reader to the point at which the story begins, namely the protagonist-narrator's funeral, are here explicated by her mind that has taken leave of her body; but in reverse chronological order and, with precision and vital immediacy in the narrative present tense: "And the deacon already began, you hear his voice, young and eager and unstoppable...Your grave is open...Your pallbearers do not ask much and pull your casket up again. And then they remove the wreath from the lid and hand it back to the young man who bows his head on the edge of the grave" (DG 63).[11]

Thus, there is an unmistakable nexus linking Aichinger's "Gehalt" to her extraordinary "Gestalt." Her mode of heightening tension is brought about by the subtle stylistic usage of the present tense whereby the dead girl is able to concurrently draw the reader of her story into the dual roles of both detached observer and subjective sympathizer. The normally expected or logical sequence of cause and effect are reversed, and the autobiographical account of the deceased narrator's life, when presented in retrospect, seems as though it were being reflected through a mirror. Nevertheless, the view cast by the mental mirror of the heroine's disembodied mind is clear and unclouded. She is one of the multitude of Aichinger's figures who has emerged from the darkness of the past and gained clearer insight into her own life. In this "reverse narrative" that chronicles the course of a life from the gateway of death to the moment of birth, a calm objective detachment replaces the expressionist's or surrealist's penchant for sudden outbursts of subjective narcissism. Aichinger's essays scrutinize familiar events and objects with the intent of forcing the reader to question their validity.

Aichinger's inquiry into the familiar—the hallmark of her prose—brings into clear focus the existential question of authentic living, of coming to grips with deceptive appearances, conventional behavior and everyday traditions. The private sphere (Aichinger's "Heimliche"), the customary way of living in familiar surroundings, is exposed as being at times scarcely more than an impoverished state of mental adaptation influenced by the power of tradition within that environment into which one happens to have been born.[12] But Aichinger is no naturalist; for her, the forces of time, place and milieu do not determine the character of a human being nor preclude a possible change in one's disposition or Weltanschauung.

Since Aichinger's so-called surrealism manifests deep-rooted suspicion of the established customary situations and familiar objects of daily life, effective hermeneutic investigation of Aichinger's "narratives-of-the-mind" demands that the reader suspend any conditioned predisposition toward social, moral and psychological issues. For the most part Aichinger resorts to utilizing surrealistic elements in order to alienate the reader from the usual or normal way of perceiving things, which for her constitutes the necessary initial step toward self-awareness and authenticity. In *Das Plakat* (The Poster), she characteristically shows through her images how the familiar can be duplicitous and deadly. Despite his fixed laughter, the boy depicted on the poster advertisement laments that he too is experiencing the same drab and dusty reality at the train station as that of the "Plakatkleber" (the worker who pastes posters onto the wall) who is slowly dying from a respiratory disease. As the "Plakatkleber" moves about the dreary area pasting his posters onto the walls, the acerbic remarks of the poster-boy belie an ostensibly wonderful life—he is depicted as standing in a cooling sea spray—and undermine the attractiveness of the poster's beckoning call to youth to join him at the summer camp being ad-vertised: "Come with us!" His rebelliousness notwithstanding, the poster boy seems fated to remain sadly immobilized and locked within a framework of images that falsely display joy. Through the metaphor of an advertising campaign that offers familiar prescriptions, albeit false, Aichinger calls upon us to avoid blind acceptance of the familiar. The falsification here that informs the basis of the naive young girl's everyday reality proves fatal. She succumbs to the "Trugbild," the de-ceptive image. Intent on joining the poster-boy in a dance, she is lured across the tracks to her death by the sirenic dictum, "Come with us!"

Permeating Aichinger's creative prose are images that appear to be linked to ideas by chance alone, many of which are reminiscent of Sigmund Freud's insight that seemingly random mental associations often reveal hidden or repressed realities.[13] Early on Aichinger made copious use of dreams or dreamlike material in her writings, thus leading her reader to query which events find existence in empirical reality and which in turn form the basis of the fantastic occurrence. Here a literary affinity to Franz Kafka's mode of writing is discernible: Aichinger's work demonstrates a close proximity in structure, style and texture to his psychic narratives.[14] We note a Kafka-like willingness to provide the means of access necessary for interpreting the parable and reaching a suitable resolution, yet in this very same vein, Aichinger too is quick to snatch back the key that would allow us access to the meaning of the message, and usually at the very moment when her reader believes it to be within his/her grasp. Aichinger's narratives, like Kafka's, are expressionistic in a very limited sense, for her controlled use of language belies any such straightforward classification. Represented within the body of her work are Kafkaesque characters who have become psychologically immobilized in life. As is the case with Kafka's ambivalent characters, Aichinger's polarized individuals vacillate between the extremes of ardent desire to cross a psychic frontier in hopes of achieving a goal that portends to give meaning to their lives and excessive fear of making such a move. Anxiety causes them to live in a state of psychological arrest, of suspended animation, where life is only half-lived.

In *Wo ich wohne* (Where I Live) (DG 93-98) initially a part of Aichinger's collection of short stories from 1963, the title story traces the descent of the narrator's abode from the apartment building's uppermost level into the cellar laden with coal dust. Here, in the figure of a built-in narrator who is incapable of self-assertion, Aichinger presents her reader with a case-study in mental ineptitude. Her narrator cannot ask other tenants in the building whether he lived one flight higher yesterday and, therefore, pretends that he has always been conducting his affairs as is presently the case, namely while living one floor lower. The abnormal becomes his norm. His failure to try to effect some form of genuine communication cuts him off from any meaningful flow of ideas in the surrounding world. Lacking in inner fortitude like so many of the solid middle-class citizens whom Aichinger saw kowtowing to the Nazis, the "hero" cannot venture a single step toward attaining something that might prove to be better and less threatening to his existence. Since he is no longer capable of taking decisive measures, he cannot alter his symbolic position of sinking into the hellish cellar. He poses no significant question concerning what is happening to him, but simultaneously refuses to give up hope that his old world will remain intact. Yet no consolation is forthcoming. Old doors now appear only halfway open and offer but an occasional glimpse into previously known space lying beyond the threshold. Likewise, the windows seem to have diminished to half their original size and offer a decidedly more restrictive view of the community that is active outside, a leitmotif that plays a key role in other prose pieces by Aichinger, such *Das Fenster-Theater* (The Window Theater) and *Der junge Leutnant* (The Young Lieutenant). Doors, windows and other such familiar reference points are transformed in consequence of the limited field of perception of Aichinger's inept heroes. Familiar, "homey" things become threatening objects that belong more appropriately to the realm of the "Unheimliche" (ominous, dangerous realm).

In *Der junge Leutnant*, a short story that appeared in 1957 in *Stillere Heimat* (Silent Home), the protagonist moves about in a cold, dark village where he is pelted by an escalating icy rain. He reiterates how "das Unheimliche" obtrudes itself upon his consciousness, how the strange village appears with its brightly-colored but securely closed doors that seem to be gradually melting into the darkness. He tries in vain to distribute his visiting card to the villagers who might offer him hospitality and perhaps some slight ingress into their community, yet all their doors remain tightly shut. He echoes the plight of Kafka's *Landarzt* (Country Doctor), the country doctor condemned to move back and forth across a frozen tundra between the communal village and the realm in which he had been dwelling in counterfeit fashion, while calling it his true home. Aichinger's young lieutenant is similarly a fixated professional whose obsessive dedication—here to the military's officer corps—has caused him to neglect life; and suddenly he too becomes a rebel questioning the value of "das Heimliche," the familiar life exemplified in the customary logic of his military superiors who have abandoned him in a strange village. Was it a joke, he asks, for them to sacrifice him in this manner? Towards the story's conclusion, both the double-entendre embodied in the word "sacrifice" along with the narrative's perplexing chronology—for he alludes to the village's strange war memorial as being from a "later war"—cause the reader to wonder whether the young lieutenant is already dead, much like the built-in narrator of Aichinger's *Spiegelgeschichte*, and/or whether he perhaps is struggling against an undesirable descent into the "Unheimliche," the drab realm of the shades. Perhaps too he has been given a premonition of his death in an impending battle, for while the sleet worsens, the young warrior expresses the wish that he had chosen to don his battle garb rather than his dress uniform. No connection span links the ego and the narrow inner realm of Aichinger's introspective built-in narrator's vision to the broader concerns of the external world beyond the pale of his subjective musings. What heretofore had been presumed to be de facto, an unquestionable truism in life, has lost its age-old validity, namely that invariably a door would open to lead the seeker out of the cold darkness and into warm, familiar light. In *Wo ich wohne* and *Der junge Leutnant*, the striking disjunction separating the individual from other human beings in the community-at-large is stylistically symbolized by fading laughter, the disappearance of other voices, and the transition from dialogue to monologue.

In *Die Maus* (The Mouse), a better-known piece contained in Aichinger's 1965 collection *Eliza, Eliza*, the persona narrating her tale also stands in the line of Kafka's traditionally naive anti-heroes. The mouse-narrator perceptibly displays the growing angst that Kafka thematically fused into his mole-hero's reactive behavior in *Der Bau* (The Burrow), a tale of a mind in decay; and Aichinger's deranged mouse is a successor to Kafka' mole. The mouse espies a ray of reddish light penetrating steadily into the tiny domicile, yet he/she cannot take a step that might lead toward a more authentic, meaningful reality within a community and thereby overcome growing existential alienation. Muted sounds coming from without suggest that escape from the constricting situation is indeed possible, yet the narrator anxiously refuses to consider the possibility of probing an unknown reality. Thus, the mouse remains shackled, confined. So intent is Aichinger's mouse on avoiding problematic reality and remaining encapsulated within the more secure realm of the "Heimliche"—which here is the type of consolation offered by a familiar milieu to the naive trusting subject's mind—that the craven creature even attempts to avoid any type of surface that might reflect its external image, be that a mirror, a pane of glass, or even water. The mouse's uncertainty and abject fear of going beyond the realm of the familiar gradually leads to its deformation as a solipsist. The mouse-narrator rationalizes that the secret to its joy in life lies in the fact that no one can find it.[15] In a manner of speaking, the mouse is already dead to the world.

Aichinger illustrates her originality and integrity as an artist as she fuses grotesque absurdities to normal quotidian modes of being. Through her peculiar admixture of elements of dreams and myth with social reality, she mirrors a universal situation in a particular symbolic instance. Her narratives highlight how certain character types run the risk of existential isolation in consequence of their total disengagement from an authentic life. These stories reflect a *Weltschmerz* rooted undoubtedly in Aichinger's personal moral concern about people who readily are taken in by mendacity and, worse still, succumb to self-deception. However, her basic leitmotif of existential bondage versus the existential concept of freedom recurs in diverse ways in various stories. As Aichinger sets about trying to give poetic form to her belief that people are in danger of becoming existentially "gefesselt," her characters evolve into figures who for the most part are symbolic ideas rather than actual beings.

In *Das Fenster-Theater*, also from the collection *Der Gefesselte*, Aichinger satirically delineates a female figure who is representative of her major thematic concern with growing social isolation coupled with an increasing lack of meaningful communication. The woman acts out her pitiable role on a small stage—symbolized by the windows—within a narrow urban theater of life. The ending of *Das Fenster-Theater* remains open, essentially because the future of this woman who felt compelled to report the old man to the police for seemingly strange behavior is also uncertain. Toward the beginning she inadvertently becomes one of the leading participants in an innocent theatrical spectacle, one that equally frightens and fascinates her. The old man's antics, which she sees him perform through his window across the way, momentarily unbind her from her lonely humdrum existence that was pushing her vital spirit down within her subconscious mind: "Everything was too deep down" (DG 83).

Aichinger's twofold repetition of the image of contained laughter applies first to the old man and then to the child, but the juxtaposition is used for more than mere linguistic effect. The image of restricted laughter provokes the reader to ask whether this woman has become an immutable psychological type or whether she one day might manage to come to a better understanding of life after she is offered a geographical change of perspective. We initially witness the motif of contained laughter in its application to the unpretentious old man who takes joy in amusing the child: "Now the old man laughed so that his whole face showed deep wrinkles, then he brushed over it with a vague gesture, became serious, yet seemed to hold his laughter in his hollow hand for a second and threw it out"; and shortly thereafter Aichinger applies it to the child who espies the police led by the woman as they break into their world of innocence: "He laughed, brushed his hand over his face, became serious and seemed to hold his laughter in his hollow hand. Then he threw it with all his might into the faces of the police officers" (DG 84-85). The laughter shared by the old man and the child mocks this society that has lost its spontaneity and unadulterated sense of humor. We learn at the story's end that unbeknownst to the woman who has become estranged from genuine living, the old man is skilled as a mime yet deaf to the world. He had merely been entertaining a child who had moved into the recently vacant apartment above hers which also faced his window.

The themes of isolation and communication recur throughout the tales contained in *Der Gefesselte*, yet Aichinger always gives them a new twist. *Der Hauslehrer* (The Tutor) is an account of an episode that a sickly boy experiences with his tutor. Once again Aichinger's prose draws us into an exploration and examination of the dubious nature of "Trugbilder," familiar objects that offer only false consolation. As a result of having been sequestered within his home, the boy has been conditioned to fear a harmless old beggar, yet he exhibits no sense of apprehension whatsoever toward his tutor. The child, still unable to reach the "peephole" and peer out into the world beyond, has never learned to recognize the extreme danger that uncritical acceptance of "das Heimliche" could pose to his personal welfare, not even when his tutor is seized by a sudden fit of madness. The boy observes the clenched fist and twisted face of the madman through a dark mirror and, therefore, never sees the contorted visage directly for what it really is; so even after he is rescued by his parents from impending mortal danger, he continues to insist that the threatening reality was merely a harmless game. During the tutorial prior to the tutor's seizure, the boy reads facts out of a book that pique his curiosity, yet whenever he seeks information about the mysteries of nature—such as migrating birds, or where the wind drives the clouds—his youthful questions go unanswered. The tutor impatiently bids his young charge to cease his inquiry into life: "'Continue reading!'" said the tutor impatiently" (DG 49). *Der Hauslehrer* concludes with the implication that a young mind is left with a lack of trust in the world of adults. In essence, the boy never truly comes out of the shadows, as symbolized by the mirror that falsely reflects the grimaces of the tutor. Again the reader is made to reflect on whether this developing youth eventually might overcome the growing sense of isolation and cynicism in the adults' non-communicative environment, a world that characteristically refuses to probe the essence of things and is all too ready to accept the familiar as the voice of authority and source of indisputable truth.

In Aichinger's prose, she calls for emergence from a state of being that has been obfuscated by shadows of ignorance into the light of existential freedom. In *Die geöffnete Order* (The Open Order), another narrative of existential bondage contained in *Der Gefesselte*, a soldier who is inclined toward cynicism is given the risky mission of carrying a sealed order from headquarters to the command troops. His suspicious disposition drives him to break the sealed order and read the message contained therein: "The order states his execution" (DG 32). To his horror the order forebodes his death, i.e., he interprets the words literally and denotatively. For him the message is unequivocal and can only mean that it is the message-bearer's fate to be executed at the hands of a firing squad. In a desperate attempt to save his own life, he decides to shoot his younger companion and slip the opened order into the dead man's pocket. However, the route along which they are traveling is wide open and he is exposed to enemy fire. As luck would have it, the plans of the scheming soldier are foiled underway when he is wounded. Nevertheless, he manages to convince his escort to take the order from his person and deliver it personally, lest he fall into a faint or the message become illegible after being bespattered by his blood. Upon reaching the prescribed destination, the bleeding soldier is taken to a room where he falls prey to delusions. Within a brief span of time that seems to him to be the last moments of life, the once incorrigible skeptic undergoes an epiphany and gains clearer insight into the meaning of existence. While lying on a bench in an open space, a symbolic situation that hints at the chance for possible emergence from the shadows of cynicism, the wounded soldier's rebellious attitude gives way to a new sense of cheerfulness. Notably, upon regaining consciousness, he refuses to disavow his true position as the official message bearer; in effect, an assigned role or identity that he had considered life threatening. In a final note of irony, the erstwhile cynic discovers that he had never really understood the real import of the message that he had been asked to bear. He did not have the vaguest sense that the message never placed him in danger, but rather was intended to help to save him and his comrade. Yet he comes to realize that the word-combination in the message, that perhaps approximated something like "To Be Executed upon Arrival" was no more than a code for the attack order that the company had eagerly anticipated, "a peculiar code for the beginning of the action" (DG 38). Unlike the enigmatic conclusion of *Das Fenster-Theater*, the open ending of *Die geöffnete Order* contains the clearly perceptible element of "greater hope" for the salvation of the hero. Despite the soldier's error in judging "the familiar," we are left with a sense of relief that is tied to the hero's ongoing liberation from his former negative self, the result of his acquisition of greater self-knowledge.

Aichinger's symbolic dream images—such as the ray of light in *Die Maus* that finds its way into the frightened creature's hole or the tightly-closed doors in *Wo ich wohne* and *Der Leutnant* that keep aspirants to meaningful relationships with others sequestered—are linked to distinct feelings; in the case of Aichinger's anti-heroic protagonists, these images symbolically reflect the feeling of existential angst. Similarly, Aichinger's array of colors in her fiction concurs with particular sentiments. The color "green" is traditionally associated with the awakening of spring and the rejuvenation of vital forms; in its Christianized form it takes on the meaning of "the greater hope" offered by the doctrine of redemption: the Christian promise of the reborn soul's eternal life within a heavenly kingdom, dwelling gloriously in the presence of the beatific vision. Images associated with "green" reflect optimism in Aichinger's work, whereas the absence of greenery evokes dread and the sense of sterile existence within an expressionistic-like wintry landscape of the soul.

In *Mein grüner Esel* (My Green Donkey), part of the collection *Wo ich wohne*—(contained within the Reichensberger edition in EE 79-82)—the reader becomes aware that Aichinger's reflective narrator is absorbed in introspective acts of self-exploration as she tries to determine the particular relationship she has with her symbolic green donkey. Each day the animal comes to her from a world that seems to be, at least to her, both dark and devoid of meaning.[16] Her donkey traverses a railway trestle, arriving always at the moment when dawn transforms darkness into light, when night fades imperceptibly into day, and shadows begin to disappear. The narrator admits that she lives for the daily arrival of her donkey, yet realizes too that attempts to uncover more of the animal's background by probing into the seemingly dismal world across the bridge will not bring her contentment. She acknowledges that their relationship has its limitations and consciously desists from trying to discover more about the donkey's desolate world with its now inactive power plant, boarded-up windows, and lonely street that, according to her way of thinking, only points one toward a "world-direction" that has never been to her liking: "A world-direction, to which I never could relate" (EE 81). She cannot alter his unique position, thankful for those moments when he parades in front of her creative imagination. Nevertheless, the apprehension that she exhibits concerning her donkey's physical and mental welfare indicates the closeness she feels toward her symbolic creature. Little wonder that she steadfastly refers to him as her own. Why then does she abstain from attempting to cultivate a reciprocally intimate relationship with her donkey? What is revealed by her conscious renunciation of any desire to track him to his lair of safety? Does she perhaps fear that a haunting history might repeat itself? After all, she states categorically that she does not want to fall prey to the old mistakes by demanding too much of him (EE 81).

When the frightful deprivation is finally at hand and her green donkey no longer makes its verdant presence known to her mind, will the narrator become silent, beset perhaps by a linguistic crisis? How can the flourishing green life arouse the creative spirit, protect it from the drab darkness, once the mind's eye is deprived of the colorful element(s) that sustain vitality: "Why should I not acknowledge that I live for that moment when he appears? That his appearance generates the air that I breathe...?" (EE 80). When ultimately stripped of further contact with her green donkey, the final link connecting the real world across the bridge to her mind, will the narrator exist devoid of "Air to breathe," blindly and breathlessly in ever-increasing subjectivity, and removed from the real world?[17] Much like the cryptic writings of Kafka, Aichinger's prose pieces pose more questions to us as critical readers than we are able to answer; and similarly her creative imag- ination reflects the crisis of language for the poet as both articulator and reflector of our hopes and dreams for genuine meaning in life.[18]

In the title story from her collection *Der Gefesselte*, Aichinger's graphic portrayal of inner freedom versus external bondage calls upon the reader to supply cogent answers to the philosophical-psychological question raised. "Der Gefesselte" is an enigmatic tale of a man bound by an external rope. We are charged to determine who he is, what he represents, why he is fettered, and why he chooses to remain bound once he has acquired the skill to free himself. What is the significance of the rope that hampers his every movement, yet simultaneously motivates him to develop his uncanny ability to transcend the mundane by performing spectacular feats with amazing grace?[19] While Aichinger's symbolic language and poetic images beckon us to seek access into her poetic world, they also demand that we first be willing to call customary and generally accepted standards into question.

In this instance Aichinger's hero is a true hero, not a trickster, for by acknowledging his rope, the stamp of his identity, he deceives neither others through some delusion nor himself by acceptance of "Trugbilder," or false appearances. The author sees "der Gefesselte" as a potential force within us. She would have us come to the very same realization to which her hero comes, namely that freedom lies in understanding the amount of "play" that one's rope allows; in other words, learning to accept one's natural-internal and social-external limitations and, yet continuing to assert oneself in the face of encumbrances or restrictions. Aichinger's moral warning remains consistent and absolutely unambiguous: the so-called modern era in which we are living is a somber time, primarily because the narrow-minded thinking of the naive masses has allowed malevolence to thrive. Therefore, Aichinger exhorts us to engage in a practice of continuous self-examination, to overcome our own restrictive ropes.

Aichinger's mosaic of puzzling details in *Der Gefesselte*, in which fantastic and factual elements are juxtaposed, calls for a reexamination of accustomed modes of (un)critical thought. The naive reader is tempted to take the conventional picture at face value and ignore the symbolic value of Aichinger's language and poetic images. Aichinger insists that we distinguish events in her stories that take place on the symbolic plane from those that occur on the real or empirical level by evoking a creative *Möglichkeitssinn* (sense for possibilities) that goes beyond our conditioned *Wirklichkeitssinn* (sense for reality). For Aichinger, the latter may be ossified and relay the erroneous message that the quintessential is always found within the familiar.

The despair that Aichinger symbolically depicts at the conclusion of *Der Gefesselte* is a poignant expression of the man's sudden help-lessness—devoid of his rope, the suddenly unbound hero becomes a craven coward. He takes flight and hides, yet signs are still present that he has not lost his ability to start over once more. The reader senses that his setback is only temporary and that once again his inner voices will drive him to reject the familiar, traditional life in which he no longer can authentically participate. There is no turning back. Thus, as the story of *Der Gefesselte* comes to a close, Aichinger presents the reader with a glimmer of hope for a new beginning, and closes her parable of bondage with dynamic images of inevitable life—"During dawn it seemed to him that the water was covered with ice, as if snow had already fallen over there in the marshes, snow which takes away memory" (DG 29). Unlike the daunting images and voices of faint-heartedness in Aichinger's accounts of existential anxiety—such as in *Die Maus* and *Wo ich wohne*—now that "der Gefesselte" has fled the temporary sanctuary of the encapsulated circus world and gone forth into the world-at-large, the future uncertainty mirrored in the image of the winter world with its snow-covered earth might indeed suggest on the one hand that no protective shelter will be made available to him, yet on the other there is the hint implicit in the metaphor that he will probably survive the winter and be reborn into a reality that is more vital, rich, and genuine than the isolation of the transient and solipsistic circus world that he had fled.

Ultimately the development of "der Gefesselte" as a hero is positive, not at all like that of the deranged psychological types Aichinger portrays in *Seegeister* (Ghosts of the Lake), also part of her collection of prose in *Der Gefesselte*. As a *Bildungsnovelle*, the protagonist's *Bildungsziel* or goal of self-actualization is attainable and will in all likelihood again be realized, despite the calamity resulting from his loss of the rope. In *Seegeister*, however, the goal of self-actualization is far beyond the reach of the character-types whom Aichinger satirizes. They are victims of an inability to move beyond their limited vision or outside their human frailty. Through personal foibles they expose themselves as people who have turned into façade-selves. As "ghosts" or shades they have become mere wisps of an authentic self.

Again Aichinger exhibits her special gift for symbolically representing universal truth in the particular instance, for her *Seegeister* are commonplace people whose sham behavior has made them into pitiable figures. They include a man who is reluctant to acknowledge the slightest mistake; an insecure woman who calls attention to herself by means of fashion sunglasses; and a paranoid sailor on a mail-ferry who feels that everyone is mocking him and finally is driven to self-destruction by his insecurity (DG 86-92). As psychological types, each of these insubstantial shells of humanity unwittingly relates to the other two by excessive psychological dependence on communal sanctions and a readiness to conform, even at the expense of forfeiting what is left of their personalities. There seems to be no escape from the oppressive weight of the yoke that harnesses their minds. The façade-selves in *Seegeister* are prepared to resort to subterfuge in order to survive the summer—Aichinger's symbolic season for the period of maximum potential vitality in a person's life. Yet as summer draws to a close, the inability of Aichinger's "ghosts" to experience any inner-directed life leaves them with no psychological reserves, and they expire miserably in an unenlightened state of being.

Aichinger increasingly manifested the disquieting sentiment in her later work that meaningful communication among human beings seemed to be eroding steadily.[20] The intensification of this disturbing attitude is evident in her twenty-one-piece collection entitled *Schlechte Wörter* (1976; Bad Words), where Aichinger grapples with the problem of the potential of creative language to bring about genuine communication. The author begins to display greater reluctance to present a "story" in the traditional or realistic mode. She questions the efficacy of attempting to express the sense or essence of objects through the medium of language. Issues dealing with anxiety—or freedom from it—to which Aichinger continuously gave form through linked poetic images are here expressed primarily through isolated symbolic images and figures. For example, in her narrative *Flecken* (Spots) (SW 15-18), she alludes to spots on an armchair whose exact essence the reader can scarcely hope to fathom. Words seem to have become "bad" or inadequate for conveying the quintessential. Yet despite her increasingly negative view on the limitations of language, Aichinger never yielded in the struggle to overcome her personal language crisis. Despite the possibility that her written words might prove to be an exercise in futility and, for her, deserving of the appellation "bad," Ilse Aichinger, who early on experienced the corruption of the German language and erosion of traditional middle-class values in her homeland under the dictatorship of the Nazis, never quit warning her readers to be aware that traditional linguistic patterns do not necessarily signify eternal verities. For Aichinger, basic existential truths lie deep within us, yet their light only becomes perceptible as we struggle to free ourselves, transcend our linguistic conditioning, and cease to remain passive recipients of language's traditional and oftentimes spurious prescriptions. Thus, the reader of Aichinger's prose must be prepared to abjure the dictates of traditional linguistic patterns that call for mindless conditioned responses. Aichinger's creative imagination calls upon her readers to become co-participants in a continual creative act of self-discovery so that the ego might become free and remain so in its ongoing pursuit of the unfettered life.

Lafayette College

Notes

1. See Henry and Mary Garland, *The Oxford Companion to German Literature*, 2nd ed. (Oxford/New York: Oxford University Press, 1986), 12; Dagmar Lorenz, *Ilse Aichinger* (Königstein/Ts.: Athenäum, 1981); Ingrid Gomboz, "Bibliographie Ilse Aichinger," *Ilse Aichinger*, eds. Kurt Bartsch and Gerhard Melzer (Graz: Droschl, 1993), 249-293. Most quotations of Aichinger's prose for this article come from *Ilse Aichinger: Werke*, ed. Richard Reichensberger, 8 vols. (Frankfurt: Fischer Taschenbuch, 1991). Citations are listed with the title in abbreviated form and the page number: DG = *Der Gefesselte*; *Erzählungen I* (1948-52); EE = *Eliza, Eliza*: *Erzählungen II* (1958-68); SW = *Schlechte Wörter*; AU = *Auckland: Hörspiele* (Auckland: Radio Plays).
2. In 1951 Aichinger received an invitation of the Gruppe 47 to read her short story "Der Gefesselte." In 1952 she received Gruppe 47's prize for her story *Spiegelgeschichte*. Other prizes she received are the "Literaturpreis der Freien Hansestadt Bremen" in 1955, the "Immermann-Preis der Stadt Düsseldorf" in 1957, the "Bayerischer Literaturpreis" in 1961, the "Nelly-Sachs-Preis" in 1971, the "Trakl-Prize" of 1979 and the "Kafka-Preis" in 1983.
3. Aichinger's first group of short stories appeared in Austria bearing the title of *Rede unter dem Galgen* (1952; Speech Underneath the Gallows), one of the leading pieces in her

narrative collection. It was then published in Germany one year later by S. Fischer, whereupon it gained fame both in German-speaking lands and abroad under its new title, *Der Gefesselte*. Aichinger wrote "Hörspiele" for the German radio and was active on the staff of several newspapers and literary journals. Her radio plays include *Besuch im Pfarrhaus* (1961; Visit to the Rectory). *Wo ich wohne* (1963) contains both selections of stories and verse, while *Eliza, Eliza* (1965) constitutes another assembly of her short stories. In the wake of *Auckland* (1969), a collection of radio plays, one can detect a transition in Aichinger's approach to storytelling: for example, in *Schlechte Wörter* (1976), a collection of 21 texts including the radio play, *Gare Maritime* (1976). The collection *Meine Sprache und ich. Erzählungen* (1978; My Language and I: Stories) contains all prose written in the late 1970s; the title story is a fitting example of Aichinger's critique of language. *Verschenkter Rat. Gedichte* (1978; Advice Given Away) thematically arranges poems written between 1955 and 1978; an extended edition of *Zu keiner Stunde. Szenen und Dialoge* (1957; At No Time: Scenes and Dialogues) was published in 1980.

4. Early on in her monograph, Dagmar Lorenz takes note of Aichinger's preoccupation with existential freedom, an observation that Lorenz continues to support throughout her book's subsequent chapters. She postulates that Aichinger's thesis, which views freedom in this subjective way, resonates the idea that bondage, hindrances and restrictions in life cannot of themselves prevent a person from being free. Lorenz, 16.

5. With regard to *Die größere Hoffnung*, Lorenz points out that the reader should not make the mistake of classifying Aichinger as a biographical writer who is intent on illustrating symbolically how she had suffered under the Nazi regime. Lorenz, 1.

6. With the introduction of Wolfdietrich Schnurre's innovative *Kahlschlag-Prosa* (Clear-Cut Prose) at the gathering of writers and intellectuals dubbed Gruppe 47, specifically with Schnurre's presentation of his "defoliated" narrative piece *Das Begräbnis* (The Funeral) at the first meeting on September 10, 1947, the practice of reading one's work aloud before the assemblage was initiated. However, despite his stature within Gruppe 47, the respected Schnurre felt compelled to quit "the group" in 1951

because he was rankled by the growing number of writers who were not politically engaged as were those of his own "young generation." For him the excessive focus on formalistic aspects undermined literature's contextual message. According to Schnurre, and other members of the "young generation," new experimental phenomena serving formal excellence for its own sake detracted from their basic aim to cleanse the German language and overcome the willful abuse and degradation to which Nazi bombast, jargon and propaganda had subjected it. Schnurre feared that "Gestalt" in literature was beginning to overshadow "Gehalt," the primary bearer of his generation's sociopolitical and moral messages.

In this regard, see Edward R. McDonald, "Wolfdietrich Schnurre's Manifesto, 'Schreiben heißt registrieren': Die Vorherrschaft moralischen Gehaltes über ästhetische Gestalt," *Er bleibt dabei: Schnurre zum 75.; Erinnerungen und Studien,* Schnurre Festschrift, ed. Ilse-Rose Warg (Paderborn: Igel, 1995), 214-244; for more exact details pertaining to Gruppe 47's origin and its history see Hans Werner Richter, ed. *Almanach der Gruppe 47* (Hamburg: Rowohlt, 1962).

7. *Die Silbermünze* is published in Reclams Universal Bibliothek (8262-8265) under the title *Deutsche Erzähler der Gegenwart. Eine Anthologie,* edited and introduced by Willi Fehse (Stuttgart: Reclam, 1959), 7-10.

8. *Die Silbermünze* was written in 1956 during the energetic economic upsurge of the so-called "miracle" years, but even ten years earlier, shortly after the capitulation of the National Socialists, Aichinger was heard bemoaning the potential of postwar Austrians and Germans to psychologically repress disturbing memories of their involvement in the wartime past in favor of renewed material security. See Aichinger's "Aufruf zum Mißtrauen," *Der Plan* 1.7 (1946): 588.

9. See J.C. Alldridge, ed. "Ilse Aichinger," *Modern German Authors. Texts and Contexts,* vol. 2. (London: Oswald Wolff, 1969), 7. Alldridge also finds it interesting that Schnurre observed a striking "contrast between the enthusiastic and uncritical acceptance of her readings by non-writers, and the equally enthusiastic but very critical reception accorded them by her fellow writers"; cf. Alldridge, 45.

10. Brita Steinwendtner, "Sammle den Untergang. Zu Ilse Aichingers Kurzprosaband *Schlechte Wörter*." Bartsch und Melzer, 141.

11. *Spiegelgeschichte* was originally printed in 1952 in the journal *Merkur* and one year later appeared in the short story collection, *Der Gefesselte*. It is also anthologized in *Deutschland erzählt*, ed. Benno von Wiese (Frankfurt: Fischer, 1962).

12. Wolfschütz notes that Aichinger's "Sicht der Entfremdung" (Visions of Alienation) stems in great part from her early disillusionment at developments in the world about her. Therefore, for Wolfschütz it is no coincidence that Aichinger's first literary production in 1946, which bears the title *Aufruf zum Mißtrauen*, derives its tone of impassioned pleading and sense of psychological engagement from the early unsettling socio-political developments to which Aichinger bore witness. Hans Wolfschütz, "Ilse Aichinger: The Skeptical Narrator," *Modern Austrian Writing. Literature and Society after 1945*, ed. Alan Best and Hans Wolfschütz (London: Oswald Wolff, 1980), 157.

13. Sigmund Freud delineates the dialectical terms "heimlich"/"unheimlich" in his essay "Das Unheimliche"; the reappearance of the uncanny in daily life is associated with the disclosure of hidden or psychological repressed elements; Sigmund Freud, "Das Unheimliche" (1919), *Freud-Studien-Ausgabe*, ed. Alexander Mitscherlich, et al., IV (Frankfurt: Fischer, 1970), 241-274, see 248.

14. Some members of Gruppe 47 referred to Aichinger as "Fräulein Kafka." However, when awarded the Kafka Prize in 1983, Aichinger stated that she had not been privy to Kafka's entire literary opus despite the fact that most critics attributed a direct influence of Kafka on her parabolic style and her combination of precision, irony and humor.

15. Wolfschütz considers the introspective built-in narrator of *Die Maus* to have a meditative approach to reality so absolute that it is self-destructive. The narrator's withdrawal is "not merely a decision to renounce greater knowledge of the world but a disavowal of individual wishes and preferences; it is a conscious attempt not to seek self-knowledge and self-realization." Wolfschütz, 170.

16. Jürgen P. Wallman thus surmises that the donkey is a somewhat grotesque representative of the subjective realm outside objective

and empirical reality, and Aichinger's narrator finds personal reality to be more vital and rich than the desolation of the so-called real world from which she has defected. "Ilse Aichinger und ihre Dichtung," *Universitas* 28 (1973): 42.

17. In this regard, Hans Wolfschütz interprets "breathlessness" as a threat to the narrator's well being. No longer having "air to breathe" is directly linked to a possible loss of language facility, especially in the creative sense. He notes that as Aichinger's narrators lose contact with the world, they also lose fluency, verbal organization, and the ability to use words to convey the essence or meaning of objects. Wolfschütz, 171.

18. Aichinger echoes here the anxiety expressed by Hölderlin whose growing awareness of his dementia induced him to give form to the language crisis at the beginning of the nineteenth century in his poem *Hälfte des Lebens* (1803; Mid-Life); or at the beginning of the following century by young Hugo von Hofmannsthal in his *Brief an Lord Chandos* (Letter to Lord Chandos).

19. Bedwell rightly asserts that "as in Kafka's, the reader must be prepared to enter a different world, a world whose superficial divergence from what we know to be real only serves to emphasize what we feel to be true." Using symbolic excerpts from Aichinger's text, Bedwell deftly interprets *Der Gefesselte* as a type of "Bildungsgeschichte," whereby the hero is seen progressing from a symbolic (re)birth through childhood into a compressed (symbolic) adolescence. Most of the narrative action concentrates on ensuing adulthood which is accompanied by the Bound Man's professional career. At this time he demonstrates the acquired mastery of the trained, disciplined and consummate artist who knows his natural limitations and effectively works within them. Carol B. Bedwell, "Who Is The Bound Man? Towards An Interpretation of Ilse Aichinger's 'Der Gefesselte.'" *The German Quarterly* 38/1 (1965): 30f.

20. Already in *Knöpfe* (Buttons), her radio play that was first broadcast in December 1953, Aichinger showed signs of lamenting the dehumanization of people in an industrialized society that posits the absence of thought over forms of contemplative and critical introspection. The names borne by the buttons point to individual human beings among the work force

who had undergone a metamorphosis into the shiny inanimate objects. Furthermore, the name of the person transposed into a button encompasses all those bearing the same name. The mutates have been dispersed as buttons throughout the world and it is impossible to gather them once into one meaningful personality (AU 11-73).

Murder and Self-Resuscitation in Ingeborg Bachmann's *Malina*

Margaret McCarthy

In the mid-1980s Sigrid Weigel wrote two extended articles documenting the literary texts by German women which emerged on the heels of the women's movement in Germany a decade earlier.[1] As in the 1970s, issues of language, identity, and the body continued to predominate in the texts Weigel examines, although she paints a landscape in which all the contours have shifted entirely. First and foremost, Weigel emphasizes that the first phase of German women's literature spawned a subsequent "diffusion and plethora of very diverse *literatures*" by women in the 1980s (Part 1, 55). In fact, she identifies such diversity among women's texts already published during the 1970s, although she faults German feminists for their failure to recognize the significance of several key texts, including Ingeborg Bachmann's *Malina* (1971; *Malina: A Novel*, 1990).[2] Characterized by dense, elliptical prose and chaotic, fragmented structure,[3] *Malina* initially perplexed critics, male and female alike. Not until the 1980s, when discourses of psychoanalysis and poststructuralism began reconceiving femininity in its abstract and textual form, did Bachmann's novel receive a wealth of nuanced, critical attention. And what emerged in texts like *Malina* and those produced during the 1980s was something Weigel calls "radical subjectivity."

Unlike the literary texts of the 1970s, which Weigel faults for remaining trapped within a bourgeois private sphere, socially sanctioned forms, and false solutions, the 1980s texts thematize the very construction of the self through language. The female authors of these texts are less concerned with representing undocumented female experiences and attempting to overturn external causes than with articulating the larger forces shaping subjectivity. As Weigel defines it, "radical subjectivity" emerges from the circumscription of external structures, revealing the "aggressive elimination of the consciously logical subject and the formation of its nonuniformity in textual coherence" (Part 2, 9). The textual selves created, Weigel argues, flouted demands for narrative coherence, revealing instead gaps, losses, and non-identity.[4] Their words "record the present relations of power and aggression by means of all five senses and investigate the patriarchal imprints on women's bodies and psyches as well" (Part 1, 17). The body, Weigel argues, exposes the violence of symbolic inscription via actual physical injuries or psychic conflicts taken literally and materialized by the body.[5] In both cases, the body appears to "speak"— to reveal the conditions that produced it—and, according to Weigel, to counter the silences otherwise imposed on women in patriarchal cultures.

Weigel's account of radical subjectivity, however, leaves little space for agency within the forcefield of social, cultural, and historical conditions. Recourse to both poststructuralist and psychoanalytic theory sheds light on the *process* by which subjectivity is formed and individuals are placed upon particular paths of socialization. At the same time, however, recent autobiographical criticism examines the process by which subjects pursue circuitous routes, byways and detours along predetermined paths. As Sidonie Smith argues, autobiographers are not merely actors following ideological scripts, but agents who embody such scripts in various ways.[6] Despite the body's embeddedness in larger cultural forces, the autobiographical or first-person singular "I" may, in fact, create its own, alternative narratives around a socially inscribed body otherwise beyond its control. Autobiographical texts often become spaces in which textual selves contest culturally inscribed identities, creating instead counter-narratives full of ambiguity and contradiction.[7] As the body speaks the violence of cultural inscription, the "I," in her textual rendition of herself and her body, may assert a narrative agency that produces alternative meanings around an otherwise "docile" body—one which, according to Foucault, is habituated to the particular forms of femininity (or masculinity) at a given historical moment. Thus, meaning is not merely produced by culture and passively received by the body; the subject participates in the making of that meaning. In understanding a text like *Malina*, it is crucial to look beyond the violence and murderous forms which characterize the nameless protagonist's life; more compelling are the resistant moments which surface in the way she experiences and *articulates* the effects of such violence.

Psychoanalytic and poststructuralist theory may explicate the basic conditions of the protagonist's unhappy life, but they cannot account for the manner in which she not only manages to survive, but also constructs her own unique and singular voice, one of the traditional aims of autobiography. Originally rejected as a confused and bitter auto-biography, Bachmann's text documents the emergence of this unique voice through, rather than over and above, the various forces—cultural, symbolic, linguistic—that shape the protagonist's identity. This voice emerges in her manner of embodying—both metaphorically and liter-ally—these same forces. On one level, she performs what Luce Irigaray would call a form of "mimicry" that enables her to create new meanings from the circumscribed roles she is forced to assume. On another, she literally brings her own body into the act of signification, in so far as she experiences and articulates the pull of what Kristeva calls the "semiotic," which, in turn, enables her to articulate a living, breathing, libidinally-based language.

Such narrative agency, however, flies in the face of the novel's overall tone—its representation of the untenable conditions of female subjectivity as it is lived in patriarchal cultures. These conditions have their very foundation in language, in the impossibility of an identity untouched by deficient, if not violent, cultural and linguistic forms. Throughout the novel the protagonist is simply designated as "Ich" ("I") and, therefore, manifests the instability of an identity resting on a linguistic "shifter" or arbitrary word that acquires meaning only within a locutionary act. The sparse information which initially describes her—very general data about her physical appearance, her date and place of birth—appears to have been lifted from her passport and hardly provides the foundation for a firm identity. This unstable information—her occupation and address have each been crossed out numerous times—serves not to anchor her in language but instead provides an obviously deficient representation. Language, as the very foundation of subjectivity, at best offers the protagonist a fragmented, incomplete, and culturally mediated sense of self. Many of her locutionary acts, as articulated in inchoate letters or phone calls full of non sequiturs, signal the deficiency of the linguistic forms through which she knows herself.

In many ways, das Ich[8] typifies the alienated Lacanian subject; throughout the novel, she suffers the alienation that arises when exter-nal cultural forms determine identity.[9] Das Ich maintains extremely ambivalent relations with external forms; while they provide an otherwise divided, chaotic self with firm linguistic boundaries, they also pose a destructive threat. In *Malina* these forms are both metaphorically and literally dead. Generally speaking, language mediates the protagonist's identity with static—hence lifeless—representations of femininity that have persisted over centuries. In Lacanian terms, language partitions das Ich from her very being, from her originally unmediated contact with the world. Worse still, language in *Malina* threatens to sever all contact with the libidinal flow, which, according to Julia Kristeva, serves as its foundation. To be "spoken" by its forms thus instigates a variety of "Todesarten" (ways of dying). In this sense the protagonist's ambivalence towards language extends beyond the alienation associated with finding identity in external forms; language becomes the site where she literally struggles for her life.

Treading the path of the Lacanian subject,[10] das Ich must first escape her childhood memories of Klagenfurt, a city built on a swamp, a location that accounts for her persistent fear throughout the novel of water and drowning. To move beyond that originary "oceanic" state of non-differentiation, das Ich must enter the symbolic realm, with all the loss that this progression entails.[11] The greatest loss, according to the Lacanian narrative of subjectivity, is that of the mythical, originary "whole" that constitutes the self, a loss which inspires a lifelong desire to recover a missing complement, to amend all subsequent forms of lack. Das Ich not only dreams of merging with her lover, Ivan, and creating a "neues Geschlecht" (new gender), but also writes urgent letters to the fictional "Herr Ganz" (Mr. Whole). As subjects progress through Lacan's Mirror Stage, they discover in their reflection a "Gestalt" (form, aesthetics) that provides the illusion of unity and "complete subjectivity." By internalizing this reflection, subjects undergo a "primary identification" which initiates a lifelong process of pursuing identity in external forms,—i.e., objects, people, or language that all compensate for the loss of an originary whole.

Both Ivan and the protagonist's enigmatic roommate, Malina, assist her entry into the symbolic order by participating in two different kinds of mirror scenes with her. In a scene in their shared apartment, Malina mediates the way das Ich perceives her own mirror reflection:

> Malina doesn't answer, he leads me into the bathroom, takes a washcloth and runs warm water over it, then he uses it to wipe my face and says kindly: Just look at yourself, what's the matter this time? Malina is smearing mascara all over my face, I push him away and hunt for a remover pad, go to the mirror, the smears disappear, the black marks, the reddish-brown traces of cream. Malina looks at me. (36)[12]

By washing her face and proclaiming, "Just look at yourself!," Malina mirrors the protagonist's face and inspires her sense that she is seen, that the basis of her identity resides in the perceptions of others or in forces outside of herself. Malina's action drives her to the mirror, armed with the self-awareness that he instilled, to confront her own reflection, that image of external coherence that confers identity. She confronts an image already marked by Malina's perception of her, or by patriarchally defined conventions of femininity. By ineptly attempting to wash off her smeared make-up and thereby improving her appearance, Malina affirms the terms that constitute feminine beauty.

At the protagonist's initial meeting with Ivan, another kind of mirror scene transpires, one which strongly determines the path she will later traverse. While walking in her neighborhood, das Ich pauses before a flower-shop window to gaze at a bouquet that she describes in extraordinary terms: "...on the Landstrasser Hauptstrasse in front of a florist whose name I have yet to discover,...there was a bouquet of Turk's-cap lilies in the window, red and seven times redder than red, never seen before..." (12). Unlike the mythical moment before the mirror, das Ich engages in an imaginary transaction with the bouquet, rather than with her own reflection. This moment ends abruptly as she spots Ivan reflected in the window, upon whom she then displaces her identification. Soon after, she quickly departs with him: "And in front of the window stood Ivan, I don't know what else was there, since I left with him immediately..." (12). She departs with him for the post office, and in doing so decides to inhabit "das Haus Ivan" (the house Ivan), rather than to opt for the sensual experience of the bouquet. By deflecting her identification away from the flowers to his own image, Ivan installs himself within the imaginary transactions that constitute her identity, an intervention with profound consequences. Her altered trajectory here foreshadows the moment in the dream sequence when a murderous father figure tramples the flowers the protagonist's mother gives her, an action which also reroutes her path towards an entirely different destination. The flowers, like the blooming magnolia tree in the Stadtpark,[13] signify intense sensory experiences connected with a barely recoverable past, and, as I will argue, the possibility of another form of signification. Such experiences are sacrificed as she enters a symbolic realm where lifeless rather than sensual forms constitute the means through which her identity is constructed.

While Malina directed das Ich to a mediated image of herself, Ivan displaced her imaginary identification onto his own form. Rather than enable das Ich to "complete" herself with her own mirror reflection, Ivan symbolically embodies all the external forms that confer identity. His name, not the man himself, becomes the sign in which she imagines her ultimate victory: "I will triumph in this sign." With Ivan's arrival, she chooses to abandon the past and inhabit the present and the future that he signifies to her, finding much of her identity in Ivan and all the external forms that bear his name. Das Ich imagines herself triumphing over all the threats and potential dangers of the external world with the help of Ivan's name, a fantasy which reduces Ivan to a mere linguistic form with which das Ich could do battle to stake her place in the world.

As a man who represents external, symbolic forms, Ivan has much to offer das Ich. Not only does he offer das Ich a bodily image of himself in a flower-shop window, but also the possibility of a "convergence" that creates a "whole" new gender: "A good, easy basis, whatever falls on my ground thrives, I propagate myself with words and also propagate Ivan, I beget a new lineage, my union with Ivan brings that which is willed by God into the world" (65). Unlike the swampy region of her past in which nothing flourished, this ground provides the basis for das Ich to reproduce or "propagate" herself with words, and she imagines herself flourishing within the forms of language. Whether life with Ivan will enable her to realize this form of signification remains, however, unlikely. Ivan not only completely identifies with his name ("...since it is completely natural to him"), but he also "enters into" and by extension "dies" within his name ("Ivan goes into his name completely") (86). (The German verb in the original—"eingehen"—could be translated as both "to go into" and "to die.") By abandoning the bouquet and following Ivan to the post office, das Ich finds herself in a land where language is parceled out into small packets of words or "Satzgruppen." Her ability to communicate with Ivan via such "Satzgruppen" is highly doubtful, as the following phone conversation reveals:

> Hello. Hello?
> It's me, who'd you think?
> Oh right, of course, sorry
> How I am? And you?
> I don't know. This evening?

> I can barely understand you
> Barely? What? So you can
> I can't hear you very well, can you
> What? Is something?
> ...(19)

Such words are stripped of all the life das Ich envisioned in the previous passage. Later she admits that none of their "Satzgruppen," which Ivan controls, include sentences about feelings. The protagonist's efforts to master such forms resemble a child's; she speaks of "conquering" the first sentences, which she and Ivan practice again and again. Such efforts are most visible during their chess games, which Ivan simply refers to as "das Spiel" (the game). Das Ich associates her participation in "das Spiel" with the acquisition of language, as she attempts not only to master the rules of chess but also the Hungarian words that Ivan often exclaims.[14] In this arbitrary game of words that Ivan nevertheless controls, comprehension is less important than simple repetition. The overall effect of her "mimicry" of his words, however, seems to counter the protagonist's dream of reproducing herself and flourishing within the forms of language. Instead she more firmly anchors herself within Ivan's identity, a process with potentially deadly implications.

While linguistic forms may provide das Ich with a solidity that counters the threat of "drowning" in that pre-oedipal space of non-differentiation and unmediated libido, they also confine her within highly restrictive boundaries. Life within the symbolic brings the threat of a metaphorical death at the hands of narrowly defined cultural forms. Such dangers are most forcefully played out during the dream sequence. Here a murderous father figure forces das Ich to assume murderous roles again and again, roles which support the father's ascendant position and the protagonist's lack of any position. In the scenes that unfold during the dream sequence, he assumes the role of her jailer, an opera singer, a film director, and an interior decorator, among others. An extremely mobile figure, the father serves as a kind of impresario, insofar as he devises myriad ways to torment das Ich, who must continually transform herself to accommodate him. While only some of the vignettes that constitute the dream sequence actually take place on stage, the dream has a highly visual, theatrical quality which demands closer analysis.

As with Ivan, das Ich appears to assume the linguistic and

symbolic forms the father thrusts upon her. However, in the overblown theatrical quality with which she assumes these forms, a unique, resistant voice emerges in the process of mediation that informs the gendered roles both father and daughter assume. If the murderer-father embodies a dominant power that subordinates women to its own forms of representation, then the dream also reveals that his position is not natural, but itself merely a pose.[15] The dream also demonstrates that dominant power structures rest on a process of mediation, where subjects take up certain arbitrary, but culturally coded positions that reflect an agreed upon, but not "naturally" given ideology. In the dream sequence, das Ich often manifests her awareness of the mediated, arbitrary nature of this process. Forced into a badly fitting costume and tormented with straight pins during alterations, das Ich protests her ignorance of the ways of opera singers ("It is not my role"), even as her father forces her to perform a role for which she lacks a libretto. But even though she has learned, thanks to Malina, Ivan, and the father, to inhabit patriarchally inscribed forms, das Ich may, in fact, inhabit them with a difference. A closer look is needed at her manner of appropriating the patriarchal forms and to what extent she mediates new meanings, or constructs a unique and singular voice through them. Her turn as an opera diva during the dream sequence serves as a striking example.

When das Ich steps on stage at her father's behest, she assumes the role of an opera diva with manic fervor. After she has been forced into her costume and on stage, an unknown text is thrust upon her. As she attempts to sing a duet with the young man beside her, the music drowns out her own voice so that only his is heard. After a while das Ich simply forgets her lack of training and "sings for her life," choosing, however, a piece from another opera. Eventually the audience disappears and she sings alone on stage: "All is dead, all is dead." Finally das Ich falls from the stage and lies among scattered chairs and music stands, her neck broken. According to Susan McClary, prima donnas ideally embody a "male constructed" fantasy image and must accede to the public's demands and "conform to…ideals of femininity, temperament, sexual behavior, beauty, and weight."[16] At the same time, convention not only demands a metaphorical death at the hands of highly circumscribed, static conventions governing opera divas, but also a literal death or submission on stage for the sake of narrative closure.[17] Catherine Clément emphasizes the spectacular visual quality of such dying prima donnas: "With their voices they flap their wings, their arms writhe, and then there they are, dead, on the ground."[18] Certain operatic roles, like Lulu, Carmen, or Lucia di Lammermoor, however, may submit to such deadly conventions, yet they also provide a highly excessive, ostentatious view of femininity. Such roles, particularly when performed in the overblown, highly theatrical style which characterizes das Ich in her death throes, make it possible to witness the process of mediation that necessitates these deaths in the first place.

Das Ich becomes what Luce Irigaray would call a "bad copy" of an already excessive form of femininity by dying in a manner even more excessive and spectacular than her stage directions would warrant. Such "mimicry" necessitates "assum[ing] the feminine role deliberately," which "convert[s] a form of subordination into an affirmation, and thus...begin[s] to thwart it."[19] These paradoxical gestures of affirming but also thwarting feminine roles describe how women willingly assume the roles assigned to them, but thwart these roles by exposing the production process that generates them. Such exposure also reveals the ideology, itself a provisional, culturally produced form, that underlies the assumed role. Women may call attention to the very mechanics of role-playing by playing roles with a vengeance, instead of disappearing into and naturalizing them.

Das Ich not only performs a metaphorical and literal death at the hands of fixed conventions that have persisted over centuries, but she also challenges such conventions with her own forms of excess. Refusing to be contained within the space on stage, das Ich chooses to throw herself from the stage and break her neck. Given the wrong text to sing from, she "sings for her life," rather than hide her lack of the correct libretto and the proper training. By singing even after her audience has disappeared, das Ich performs a "feminine" ending, an ending where the final sonority is postponed beyond the downbeat. As Susan McClary writes, such endings, traditionally coded as "weak," also signal an excess, or an ending that "refuses the hegemonic control of the barline."[20] By singing from the wrong opera, das Ich also challenges the authority of the composer whose text was thrust on her, an act which also signals her unwillingness to merely enact his creative genius.[21] In this sense, she appropriates certain roles with a vengeance, but exceeds them as well.

Das Ich resists not only a metaphorical death at the hands of such conventional forms, but also a literal one. Another form of "excess" within language and symbolic forms often manifests itself in the novel, an excess which has its basis in libidinal flow, which, according to Kristeva, erupts in language in the form of tonality, rhythm, and intonation to challenge the boundaries of linguistic practices. Libidinal flow figures prominently in Kristeva's account of the subject's entry into the symbolic. Unlike Lacan, who traces a movement from the imaginary to the symbolic realm, Kristeva describes these two phases as processes—the semiotic and the symbolic—whose interaction constitutes the signifying process. The semiotic operates in the pre-oedipal phase, with all the pulsations of the primary processes that function there. These pulsations form the space of the "chora," which "precedes and underlies figuration and thus specularization, and is analogous only to vocal and kinetic rhythm."[22] The dialectical commingling of the semiotic and the symbolic form the basis of the signifying process, as the semiotic perpetually threatens to erupt within and challenge the boundaries of the symbolic. More specifically, the vital, libidinal forces within the speaking subject continually challenge these boundaries by remaining apart from or in excess of them. As such, Kristeva's speaking subject is not entirely caught up within and can never be restricted to the boundaries of the symbolic.

The protagonist's intense pleasure in the intonations, rhythms, and tones of both music and colors extends beyond what these forms might signify and manifests the breakthrough of semiotic forces. She infuses otherwise dead forms and conventions with libidinal flow, which makes it possible for her to experience and embody visual and aural forms in pleasurable ways.[23] Such pleasures manifest themselves in the frequent moments of song in the novel, as well as the oft-invoked Venice motif. In an early passage, das Ich describes a sensual experience while watching Mann's "Death in Venice" at a theater on the Kärntnerring:

> ...the cinema where I first saw Venice, for two hours in extravagant colors and a lot of darkness, the oars beating the water, a melody accompanied by lights passed through the water as well, and its da-dim da-dam carried me along, all the way inside the figures, the coupled figures and their dancing. In this way I arrived in a Venice I would never see, on a clanking, windy winter day in Vienna. (11)

Music literally draws das Ich into the figures on the screen and elicits a bodily pleasure not entirely inspired by her imaginary identification with the forms she views on the screen. This music, with its rhythmic "da-dim, da-dam," enables her to become one with these figures, to "embody" them in pleasurable ways. Music and colors appear with a third element here—water, which, as I have argued, signals the fluidity of the earliest phases of life, with its libidinal base. By viewing and listening to the representational forms of a film, das Ich experiences effects that literally transport her body to a more sensual realm and that recall an earlier phase of life. Injecting empty, two-dimensional forms with her own libidinal flow, das Ich experiences these forms in ways that exceed their function as forms that signify Venice.

This living, breathing linguistic practice can be traced back to the protagonist's mother, who appears briefly in the dream sequence, and her legacy of blooming flowers. The novel, in turn, links these flowers with the tonality of human voices:

> My mother is holding three flowers, the flowers for my life, they aren't red, or blue, or white, but they must be for me, and she throws the first one in front of my father, before he can approach us. I know she's right, she has to throw him the flowers, but now I also know that she knows everything, incest, it was incest, but I'd still like to ask her for the other flowers, and I watch my father in deadly fear as he tears the other flowers from my mother's hand, to take his revenge against her as well, he tramples them, he stomps on all three flowers...(118)

The mother remains passive in the face of the father's rage: "My mother stays silent and doesn't move," actions which das Ich soon imitates. Das Ich also notices that, because of her father's actions, she has lost her voice:

> I notice that...from the beginning my own voice has been without sound...he's taken away my voice as well, I can't pronounce the word I want to scream at him, and with my mouth dry, open, as I am straining it comes once more, I know I'm going crazy...but there's no saliva left, hardly a breath from my mouth reaches him. (118)

This scene links flowers, which appeared earlier in the form of the blooming magnolia tree and the small bouquet, with the tones in the human voice. As the flowers wither, the protagonist's voice too dries up and grows silent. This process of desiccation dries up the fluids necessary to articulate words, a fluidity that could also be linked metaphorically to the libidinal basis of language and the fluid, pulsational rhythms of the semiotic chora. Language needs this libidinal base, just as water is necessary to sustain life. The flowers here and earlier in the text could thus represent words planted in the firm soil of the symbolic, which also flourish thanks to the fluidity of a libidinal foundation. By extension, they also represent a signifying practice linked to the semiotic, one in which the subject literally breathes life into otherwise dead forms via the semiotic forces that erupt within language. If correctly nurtured, words can breathe life by bearing the traces of libidinal forces and bodily drives within the speaking subject. Yet in the dream sequence, a murderous father figure destroys the mother's legacy of a living, breathing signifying practice. This act then provides the basis for an entirely different signifying practice consisting of representational forms that support the father's ascendant position and the protagonist's lack thereof.

Ultimately, das Ich cannot escape the murderous effects of such signifying practices. The novel concludes as she disappears into a crack in the wall, an image which reveals the cost of residing fully within the external cultural forms through which identity is constructed. In the end das Ich literally disappears within their confining boundaries. The possibility of a living, breathing form of signification, one that lacks a patriarchal imprint, resides only in the brief utopian moments set apart in the text. It is only here that she can envision wholeness and the dream of the unified subject. Yet, for the present, there is no escaping the lack, fragmentation, and disintegration of life in the symbolic order. Through the novel, a unique voice emerges in the cracks around the roles and forms she encounters. More specifically, these roles crack as das Ich assumes, embodies, and exceeds them—both performatively and libidinally. If her excess is ultimately excised, it nevertheless forms the basis for a unique voice whose singularity emerges through, and in spite of, the forces that eventually murder das Ich.

Davidson College

Notes

1. Sigrid Weigel, "'Woman Begins Relating to Herself': Contemporary Women's Literature," Part One, *New German Critique* 31 (1984): 53-94; "Overcoming Absence: Contemporary Women's Literature," Part Two, *New German Critique* 32 (1984): 3-22. Subsequent references to these two articles will be cited by Part and page number.
2. Weigel points out that women involved in literary production and political activity initially spoke very different languages, and thus two movements existed side by side but were not united. Ingeborg Bachmann, *Malina* (Frankfurt: Suhrkamp, 1971).
3. For instance, Marcel Reich-Ranicki referred to *Malina* as Bachmann's "late, incidentally weak and confused novel." Quoted in Sara Lennox, "In the Cemetery of the Murdered Daughters: Ingeborg Bachmann's *Malina*," *Studies in Twentieth Century Literature* 5.1 (1980): 76.
4. Such a description has particular resonance for the genre of autobiography as well as for the structure of *Malina*, a text with many autobiographical traces. Benstock writes that women autobiographers in particular have often resisted narrative structures that render the "I" organic, coherent and fully conscious. Instead, many admit internal cracks and disjunctures, rifts and ruptures, without attempting to cover over gaps in memory or dislocations in time. *Malina* reveals everywhere the impossibility of constructing a unified, cohesive self, one of the traditional aims of autobiography; Shari Benstock, ed. *The Private Self: Theory and Practice of Women's Autobiographical Writings* (Chapel Hill: University of North Carolina Press, 1988).
5. Weigel writes, "The language contained in chronicles of illness is frequently a secondary means of expression for women, preceded by the primary language of the body. It is the woman's body, the representational locus of femininity, that records and acts out her disillusionment." Part 1, 83-84.
6. Sidonie Smith, *Subjectivity, Identity, and the Body: Women's Autobiographical Practices in the Twentieth Century* (Bloomington, Indiana: Indiana University Press, 1993).

7. As Leigh Gilmore writes, gender identity is frequently contested by autobiographers. For such authors, "even when the non-textual possibilites for changing normative heterosexuality, racism, and classism—whether in relationships, communities, or professions—may not exist, the imaginative grounds for such praxis may be constructed in autobiography." *Autobiographics: A Feminist Theory of Women's Self-Representation* (Ithaca: Cornell University Press, 1994), xii

8. How to refer to a character who lacks a proper name poses a problem. Critics refer to her in various ways: the Ich (Sara Lennox), ICH (Robert Pichl), die Ich Erzählerin (Angelika Rauch), the narrator (Karin Achberger), and das Erzähl-Ich (Birgit Vanderbeke). I have designated her "das Ich" because in Bachmann's Frankfurt Lecture entitled "Das schreibende Ich" ("The Writing I"), she writes about a variety of "I's," referred to as "das Ich," "das Tagebuch-Ich," and "das Brief-Ich;" Bachmann, *Frankfurter Vorlesungen* (Munich : R. Piper & Co., 1982).

9. When she looks into the mirror, for instance, she finds space where it is "always Sunday," a space which demands her adherence to respectable appearances, to rituals of self-improvement religiously performed.

10. Sara Lennox's seminal article "In the Cemetery of the Murdered Daughters" sets the stage for a host of psychoanalytically-based readings of the novel and very well may have initiated the boom of critical response to the novel that was lacking during the 1970s.

11. Significantly, the process of entry into the symbolic begins on a bridge suspended above water. As das Ich stands on the Glanbrücke, two young boys approach her with the words: "you, you over there, come here, I'll give you something!" What they give her is a slap in the face. Das Ich associates this incident with a loss of innocence, stating that for the first time she had "fallen among men." In fact, she has "fallen" into the patriarchal domain of the symbolic, hailed by a young boy whom she approaches with the unsteady steps of a child. Her brutalization at the hands of this young boy signals a movement from watery origins into the symbolic.

12. All translations of block quotes are from Philip Boehm's translation of *Malina* (New York: Holmes and Meier, 1990).

Shorter translations are my own. Subsequent references to this text will be marked by the page number.

13. In her descriptions of the Stadtpark (Vienna's city park), das Ich emphasizes the figure of a chalk-white Pierrot who sings "Oh old scent of fairy-tale times" and a blooming magnolia tree. The Stadtpark is also a place of hardly distinguishable forms, of shadows and dark figures, and a place that threatens das Ich with its nearness. Escaping the park's attraction is like rising above water for her. Like far-off Klagenfurt, the Stadtpark suggests, as Sara Lennox writes, the pull of non-differentiation, and its highly charged sensory forms—its sights, sounds, and scents—can be linked with the earliest phase of life. The significance of such sensory forms, however, remains unclear until much later in the novel.

14. The only Hungarian words das Ich masters, however, are "jaj" and "je," a combination which, like the fort/da game Freud observed his grandson playing, recalls the originary difference upon which language is based. Meaning, in other words, derives from oppositions among words, rather than from a direct link between words and what they signify.

15. At one point in the dream das Ich proclaims, "my father went to the theater. God is an imagination, a performance." This statement not only affirms the dream's theatrical qualities, but also reveals that authoritarian forms may, in fact, be nothing more than straw men. Through the protagonist's eyes, the father, with his evil laugh, also becomes a mere "Vorstellung," or a bad copy of an authoritarian figure. According to Lacan's semiotic model of subjectivity, the patriarchal position rests on a signifier, variously called the "name-of-the-father" or the "symbolic father," which signals power, authority, potency. Real human agents merely occupy this position but can lay no natural claim to it. Through the protagonist's eyes, it becomes clear that the father merely occupies a symbolic position, playing a variety of roles that accord him a power he does not naturally possess. Das Ich even proclaims, "It is not my father. It is my murder." He simply acts out the epic proportions of the symbolic father.

16. Susan McClary, Foreword, *Opera, or the Undoing of Women,* by Catherine Clément, trans. Betsy Wing (Minneapolis: University of Minnesota Press, 1988), xvi.

17. Ibid.
18. Clément, 5. In fact, the myriad ways in which opera divas die onstage constitutes a whole subset of "Todesarten" for women. Clément writes: "Dead women, dead so often. There are those who die disemboweled...there are those who die for having embodied too well the false identity of a marionette-woman or for having simply affirmed that they are not there where the men are looking for them...Those who die of nothing...of fear, or fight or sadness, or anxiety. Those who die poisoned, gently; those who are choked, those who fold in on themselves peacefully. Violent deaths, lyrical deaths, gentle deaths, talkative or silent deaths...You could easily draw up a list of them. In other times, in serious structuralist conclaves—in days now known as bygone—you would have been entitled to a clean blackboard, just to classify them all, these dead women, according to the instrument of their death or the guilty party." Catherine Clément, *Opera, or the Undoing of Women*, 47.
19. Luce Irigaray, *This Sex Which Is Not One*, translation by Catherine Porter (Ithaca: Cornell University Press, 1985), 76.
20. Susan McClary, *Feminine Endings: Music, Gender, and Sexuality* (Minneapolis: University of Minnesota Press, 1991), 11.
21. As McClary writes in *Feminine Endings*, the excesses of operatic madwomen often serve as "a pretext for [the composer's] compositional misbehavior," 102. Arnold Schönberg, for instance, challenged the limits of tonal certainty with elements of dissonance, chromaticism, and excess, all of which had traditionally been aligned with the feminine. While excess needs containment when associated with women—operatic madwomen are often framed and surrounded by male singers on stage—it signals the revolutionary genius of male composers.
22. Julia Kristeva, "Revolution in Poetic Language," *The Kristeva Reader*, ed. Toril Moi, trans. Leon S. Roudiez, et al. (New York: Columbia University Press, 1986), 93-94.
23. Music plays an important part in Kristeva's notion of "poetic language." In Julia Kristeva, *Desire in Language,* ed. Leon S. Roudiez, trans. Thomas Gora, et al. (New York: Columbia University Press, 1980), she examines the music inscribed in Philippe Soller's novel *H*, emphasizing that the basic structure of sentences acts as the lower, not the upper limits of

enunciation. But "through and in conjunction with these limits," Kristeva argues that the primary processes, which are dominated by intonation and rhythm, may break through. This "musicating" and its disruptive forces intervene in language at the moment when symbolic structures appear to "kill" what they rely upon, i.e., the libidinal basis of language. Such musicating allows symbolic structures to "sing." Kristeva also emphasizes how the breath and intonations of human voices also constitute a "dismembered score," a model which appears to describe a living, breathing, signifying practice.

Mayröcker's Fictional Autobiography

Beth Bjorklund

The provocative book title *Who Comes after the Subject?*[1] pre-supposes the disappearance of the subject and simply proceeds to the next question (with an editorial discourse on whether the personal interrogative should [not] be replaced by the impersonal "what"). That collection of essays is simply one among many regarding the "decentering of the subject," which is an important topic in current literature, philosophy, and psychoanalysis. As recent thinkers have demonstrated, it is impossible to go straight to the matter of the subject; the goal is rather "to detect how we have objectified ourselves into these forms that are simultaneously the forms that shape us."[2]

This essay attempts to explore the works of Friederike Mayröcker in light of some of the work on the theory of the subject. Specifically, I would like to suggest that Mayröcker's works constitute an autobiography, albeit not in any traditional sense of the term. Her works are admittedly highly nonconventional, and Schmidt-Dengler writes as follows: "I find the skepticism and reserve with which literary critics regard the works of Mayröcker understandable and warranted. Her texts resist all attempts at analysis in terms of the traditional categories of literary scholarship."[3] Given that as a starting point, let us look at some ways in which her oeuvre may—or may not—be regarded as autobiographical. We shall here focus primarily on Mayröcker's recent major prose works, which form a type of "series" that comprise ten books written between 1973 and 1994.[4] They represent some of the most highly acclaimed books among the more than sixty titles that Mayröcker has published within the past fifty years.

Some of the arguments for autobiography include the fact that many of the texts are narrated in the first person with the "I" (ich) functioning as the central consciousness. The works often include references to empirical places and living persons, most prominently parents, partners, and friends, occasionally referred to by name. *Je ein umwölkter gipfel* (One of Each of the Cloud-Covered Mountain Tops) incorporates a real-life photo of the author as a young person (112), and she often writes about her childhood in Deinzendorf.[5] Even the authorial disavowal places the work in close proximity to autobiography: "No autobiography, nonetheless authentic" (HD 64). Or, as a question: "What happens actually in the conception of writing reality and first person?" (SL 54).

Mayröcker commented as follows in a statement about her work: "The texts stand in contrast to the absence of biography as a way of life. My own past proliferates recklessly in the texts."[6] In an interview she said: "All of my prose figures are basically shadings of myself or of people near to me."[7] Another interviewer posed the question directly: "There are two opposing views on your way of working: the one maintains that your entire work is autobiographical and to be understood only in that context; the other claims that your work is completely nonautobiographical and operates only with language." The author responded as follows: "In any case, I think that the autobiographical element is very important in the period from 1972 to the present; at the same time it is however mixed with linguistic aspects."[8]

Arguments against autobiography include Friederike Mayröcker's well-known opposition to narration—of the self or anything else. Her rejection of narration appears frequently as a topic in the texts: "Having a narrative form? But what narrative form can be relied upon, what narrative form is still defensible, we don't want to have a story told to us anymore, we don't want to have to tell a story anymore" (RN 105). "Absolutely no story!, in no case permit a story!, at most a narrative course, like a life course, thus no history, no life story" (HD 121). Or, as affirmative query: "Does a nonfigurative literature, a nonfigurative narrating exist?" (L 33).

That stance requires investigation, and Schmidt addresses the question: "Why cannot and will Friederike Mayröcker not narrate?"[9] Skepticism regarding the possibility or desirability of "storytelling" can be regarded as an outgrowth of the Austrian tradition of language skepticism, which culminated in the so-called "experimental literature" of the postwar era. At stake is the issue of whether language is an adequate medium for rendering experience; or whether reality instead is not being insidiously distorted by the linguistic means used to evoke it. Conventional linguistic usage imposes causal connections, hierarchic order, and psychological coherence that are often absent in reality. Lived experience thereby escapes verbal formulation and thus remains ineffable. That predicament has led many contemporary writers to eschew traditional forms and to experiment instead with innovative techniques such as multiple perspectives, the collapsing of temporal and spatial categories, and the simultaneous presentation of linear developments. Mayröcker shares in that development with other writers, such as Ernst Jandl, Thomas Bernhard, and Peter Handke.

Memory, which on some level is mediated by language, is also called into question, for our "memory" is always only a present-day interpretation foisted upon a past-time event. In recognition of the impossibility of recapturing the past, of "remembering" in any true sense of the term, Mayröcker renounces the attempt, as the narrator emphatically asserts: "I forget everything, to tell the truth I have become a person without memories, I have literally forgotten everything that was ever important to me in my life, here and there it may still flash up in my mind, and I see the past go by in front of me, but I have forgotten most of it, actually everything" (RN 28). Or, "so that it will some day come to the point of having to live entirely without a past, thus completely without personal history and prehistory" (HD 136).

A past time is nonetheless narrated without, however, any pretense of mimetic recall, a situation that clearly requires the renegotiation of the border between nostalgia and critique. Fragments from experience and memory, dream and fantasy, perceptions, reflections, associations, and heterogeneous elements of thought and feeling are brought together in an atemporal amalgam. Time, that is, life, is seen as a process in which nothing, least of all identity, remains fixed; rather, everything is caught up in the movement of change. Levels of recent and remote pasts are superimposed on present, future, and future perfect possibilities of consciousness, as if time were an empty screen on which we project our specific interests and discrete illusions.

That obviously entails a rupture of realistic conventions, and the intent is to challenge the epistemology behind the "given" structures. Reality is presented in the texts as discontinuous, nonlinear, fragmentary, and ambivalent; and it is precisely this open-endedness that is more central and significant than anything which can be objectively established. The works can be regarded as an intense exploration of the preverbal, in part subconscious, perhaps unconscious experience, a flow chart of the energies pulsating through the body of an as yet unconstituted subject. If the medium is nonetheless language, it is because a writer is bound—and liberated—by language, just as a painter is by paint or a musician by sound. The medium's emancipation from the expectation of representing the external world frees language to express an internal reality. It could be said that literature of this type is more "realistic" than are externally mimetic forms in the sense of being true to experience, as a quick examination of the contents of one's own consciousness will demonstrate.

Although Mayröcker's polemics against "storytelling" and "memory" are embedded in fictional texts, the statements must be taken at face value, for the fictional texts contain their own nonfictional theory. For example, the interlocutor in a fictive dialogue speaks as follows: "If you are against a story, as you always maintain, then you must necessarily declare yourself for a non-story and back it up with theory; otherwise nothing will work" (HD 142-143). Another interlocutor, who is perhaps modeled on Samuel Beckett, voices similar opinions: "In the FRAGMENTS of Schlegel, Samuel said, there is a lot that one could apply to your books, Samuel said, the self-reflection of the book in the book...thus a book that narrates nothing" (SL 174). Such passages can be regarded as meta-poetic commentary on the creative process, and the resulting poetry contains its own theory of poetry.

As Schafroth notes: "What Friederike Mayröcker has to say about poetics she usually says as a poetic work; occasionally even—disguised and covered over—in the poetic work."[10] Schmidt-Dengler is even more explicit: "Poetry is for Friederike Mayröcker at the same time also poetics. The separation of two discourses is suspended: poetic practice absorbs theory and also the reverse: poetics is poetry. Expressed another way: the work itself is the work about the work."[11] Indeed, the partial suspension of the distinction between theory and literature, between author and narrator is what makes the issue of autobiography, in the final analysis, indeterminate.[12]

"Writing" itself is the most persistent motif of writing, for "writing comes into being only from writing" (HZN 113). The focus on the writing process invites inquiry into its nature and function. "I exist I write" (HZN 33), or "I write that I write" (SL 73), or "something within me writes" (SL 59). Writing subsumes all modes of thought, emotion, memory, and imagination. What results is "an anti-novel" (HZN 119) or "dialogically expanding consciousness-prose" (SL 100). Writing becomes the means for examining the structure of human perception and the process by which the mind confronts and imposes an "order" on the world. There are numerous references in the texts to writing, which is the central activity portrayed—and, recursively, the activity that produced these very texts. The grammatical object of writing, the "self," is constituted in the process, although obviously also presupposed as the agency of writing: an Odysseus (or Penelope) who becomes his (her) own Homer.

To take the self as the topic of poetry, indeed, presupposes a strong sense of self. "To take oneself as the center of the world, at least for several hours, is one of the presuppositions for fruitful work" (SL 55). Who among us can so trust his or her impulses? Would it not be easier to define the self with reference to the outside world, or at least to project a desired image? What, finally, is the point? "Writing: not to understand others, but to be able to understand one's self—IS THAT IT?" (HD 66). "My writing—the sole piece of evidence, constantly repeating itself, for myself" (SL 148). Assuming the self as subject and taking that self as the object of writing means that personal identity is connected to poetic inspiration, which has far-reaching consequences.

The self that is thus constituted by the process of writing may be a construct; but, it is presented as authentic and as valid for its duration. The self is seen as alternating between extremes of withdrawal and involvement with the world, distance and nearness to other persons, dominance and submissiveness, and dependence and independence. Psychology becomes an embarrassment in art, for all that emerges from the deep dark depths is an uninterrupted flow of words: "A linguistic perpetuum" (L 147); and to break through repression would be to destroy one's mythology. Contradictions and mutually exclusive view-points exist simultaneously, for there is no privileged position in a decentered mode such as this. Since paradox and ambiguity cannot be stated without self-contradiction, they are instead established in the presentation, and form becomes content as any perspective established is again called into question.

The tension in a text that has no plot is textural rather than temporal. It is structured by images that operate incrementally to form chains of allusions, resulting in rich cross-references. A motif may be initiated seemingly unobtrusively, and it then recurs in various contexts, each time with accrued implications. After having amassed a chain of associations it, at some point, goes spiraling to a climax: "Something that...intensifies at particular points to a spark-emitting spherical ball" (RN 101). The narrative breaks off, and the motif reverts to dormancy. It may, however, spark off other motifs, or it may itself be reactivated and participate further in some larger complex.

The bottom line for any and all of us is death, and there are numerous references in the texts to death—of a parent, of friends, and of one's own approaching death. "That BASTARD DEATH actually manages to pull it off, and thus we are torn out of all connections, everything is finished for us, done and gone" (RN 59). Therein we see the purpose of writing: "Above all, I write to ward off death, thus I write against my own death" (L 96-97). "Who would not become cynical under such conditions of life, Samuel said. God is with the insane, I reply, the most important morality concerns resistance, dream" (SL 194).

Speaking or writing so as not to die is undoubtedly as old as language itself. The fictive speech that borders death is also poised against it; and, to stop the death that would stop it, language turns back upon itself, doubling itself to become its own mirror. Writing refers then not to the outside, but to language itself; it divides itself to tell its own story in an infinite series of duplications. The language of repetition gives up the power of signification that would subordinate language to thought and stresses instead its metalingual potential.

The repetition could continue indefinitely, perhaps in a murmuring reminiscent of a Beckett novel. The Beckett-figure speaks: "We want the new style, Samuel says. We do not want fullness anymore, we want emptiness" (SL 9). "A preoccupation with death presupposes a renunciation of life (in view of its finiteness). One lives in NOTHINGNESS, one lives toward NOTHINGNESS, toward NON-BEING" (SL 29). If art aspires to be the single, brief, comprehensive cry of a person caught at the moment of death; and if all expression that is not this piercing summation is too trivial to bother with; there is a kind of prolonged discourse that can be derived from apologies for the failure of expression. The postironic evasion of the obligation to express bears witness to the significance of what it evades.

Awareness of the imminent finality leads to a positive evaluation of the time one has, and at the center of each work stands the experience of what it means to be alive in the present. The question then becomes: "How to live, how to live here, how to stand up to the world?" (RN 125). "Most things in life are double and multiple. It is good to get used to seeing things from various, often contradictory sides" (SL 12). Or, "how do you stake out your extremes?" (HD 21).

Just as there is no transcendence, there are no ethical-moral imperatives, for there is no omniscient point of view that would resolve the relativity of all cognitive and emotive categories. There is, however, the experiencing self, and the authenticity of its mode of being guarantees the validity of the experience. The power is in the concretion, and any abstraction would be false, for it is truly a phenomenally experienced world: "To see and hear with all eyes and ears" (RN 128). The obligation is to the self or to life itself: "Daily duty: not to by-pass life or let life be by-passed, rather to imagine it in every particular refraction" (HD 34); that is, to live life to the fullest in the present. "I still want to extort the remaining time, press and entice everything out of it" (RN 122). "Important is only to be happy and to create life in abundance, thus not only for oneself but for anyone who happens to pass by" (HD 164).

That, as we all know, is more easily said than done, and the texts contain long passages of regret and remorse, faulting the world but primarily the self. Inscrutable fragments of experience contain both urgent signals and obscure menaces, and the central consciousness functions both as nucleus and as generator of the forces that seem designed to break it apart. The despair reaches a nadir at distinct points in each text. For example: "Everything done wrong, everything wrong, it's all only lies, I call, everything a lie! it's fake the way people talk and look at each other and act, it's all only lies, everything a lie, one's entire past as well, everything wrong, it's all a fraud, a sham, oh if only I could do it over again!" (RN 41). Such passages alternate with those of joy, renewed energy, and creativity, as the self thrills in response to the beauty of the world: "Perceiving the world so lively and fine with such rested nerves in the morning, I say, that everything seems connected to everything else, everything suggests an association with everything else, every network of thoughts immediately wants to be spun out further and other high-flying landscapes" (RN 100). These "associations" are a large part of what the text is about. "One must play with real cards, I say, but one must try to establish superreal connections, actually VISIONS. The more real the material, the more transparent, spiritual the results" (L 42). Clearly, it is a subjective, irrational realm, and any imposition of external order would constitute falsification. "Sometimes I think that all order is hypocrisy" (HD 118). Rationality is seen as paralysis: "Feelings of hard rationality and numbness, in which condition nothing is imaginable anymore" (L 60). "The realm of the unconscious is your actual realm of life, Mario says. New life comes to you from that realm" (L 59).

Metaphors for this life of imagination and creation abound, drawn from memory and many other sources. On the one hand, the loss of memory is seen as virtually synonymous with the loss of life, and approaching our "goal," the past becomes decreasingly accessible: "Until we all will finally have reached our destination, namely, will have become masters of memorylessness" (RN 136). On the other hand are very vivid memories, particularly of childhood. "While writing, my attention is momentarily suspended again and again; against my will it smuggles in complete and precise visual memories" (SL 52). And, all visual memories, I say, transform themselves into language. That is the answer to all questions, is it not, everything concrete, fed by actual experience" (L 218).

Not only memory, but also dream and vision are an important source of poetic inspiration: "Reality and dream-situations congruent" (SL 18). "The production of visions and delusions has now become the main content of my life" (SL 51). "Your notes are the translation of signs, perceptions, and feelings into a language that does not exist" (L 43). Thus arises literature: "One picks up a thread, spins it further, it is joined by another one, and slowly it weaves itself into the fine fabric of a new work of fiction" (SL 71).

Eroticism is also an important trampoline (SL 58), i.e., source of poetic inspiration. It often takes the form of a "ménage à trois," comprising one male and two female figures (LL, FF, A, HD, HZN) or one female and two male figures (RN). The doubling can be seen as the speaker's projection of an alter ego, presenting two sides of the same figure; and, the same basic constellation is reusable because it serves merely as a skeleton for thoughts, feelings, and dreams: "We carry out the actions with all sexual partners" (HZN 133). There are also many crossovers, and androgyny is an important theme: "Very androgynous, a masculine and a feminine peak" (HZN 43). The partners in dialogue are often identified specifically as male and female, and it is tempting to link the ideas presented to gender-roles, as Schafroth suggests.[13] The question must remain open for further investigation, for the variability of positions precludes an easy identification.

The texts are nonetheless "gendered" but less by virtue of content than by form. The linear "masterplot" of traditional narration is a male mode of activity in that it builds up to a climax followed by rapid resolution. In contrast, the rhythms and dynamics of female sexual— and textual—experience are different. The varying manifestations of male/female sensibilities can be sought in areas such as incipience, association, repetition, inclusion, accretion, recurrence, and closure—or absence of such, since closure is not sought and assiduously avoided.

The distinction between fact and fiction, finally, proves to be immaterial, since "our human life has a strong fictional feature" (HD 21). There is, of course, the empirical person and who the author is for the outside world. That aspect comes up for consideration in the numerous references to the reader and the reception of Mayröcker's literature. But who the narrator is for the self remains a matter of daily accomplishment: "Am I separated from myself. It is hell, as always, when I cannot work. I believe to have lost myself" (HD 78). To "find" or to "be" oneself—i.e., to create the self ever anew—that is the task, "presumably the sole tactic for survival into the twenty-first century" (L 107).

Creating the self entails many requirements. "The most important thing is to maintain an autonomous inwardness" (SL 151). In identification with the figure Chopin, Mayröcker writes: "In regard to theory / dedicated to death: / it is less a question of being inspired than of maintaining a nonsuspendable vulnerability to the world" (HA 17). The muse of modern art is revealed, not as an external power transmitting inspiration from on high, but as a personal, internal capacity—cognitive, emotive, volitional—to live and to experience life to the fullest. Art is part of life, and artistic creation ultimately has its source in what it means to be most human.

What emerges is a portrait of an artist, that is, a view of the creative process itself. In that her oeuvre takes the self as the subject, it may be regarded as a type of "autobiography"; but, the centrality of the writing process leads one to view it as creating the self it portrays, for this type of literature is as formative as it is reproductive. Autobiographical elements are included but are so transformed that the recovery of the self's own history becomes a fictional documentation of the creative process as a series of imaginative possibilities. The ontology of the self is subjected to a process view, which is presented as engulfing all of life; and the creative process produces an artist and individual, at once fictional and real-life, demonstrating that creativity is what it means to be alive.

University of Virginia

Notes

1. *Who Comes after the Subject?*, eds. Eduardo Cadava, Peter Connor and Jean-Luc Nancy (New York/London: Routledge, 1991).
2. Martin Schwab, Foreword, *What is Neostructuralism?*, by Manfred Frank, trans. Sabine Wilke and Richard Gray (Minneapolis: University of Minnesota Press, 1984), xxix.
3. Wendelin Schmidt-Dengler, "'ich lebe ich schreibe': Friederike Mayröckers *mein Herz mein Zimmer mein Name*," *The German Quarterly* 63 (1990): 421.
4. What I have termed a "series" comprises the ten books listed below, all published by Suhrkamp in Frankfurt a.M. (with the exception of the first book). Given, in each case, is the date of publication and, preceding the title, the abbreviation used in this essay. UG *je ein umwölkter gipfel* (Darmstadt: Luchterhand, 1973), LL *Das Licht in der Landschaft* (1975), FF *Fast ein Frühling des Markus M.* (1976), HA *Heiligenanstalt* (1978), A *Die Abschiede* (1980), RN *Reise durch die Nacht* (1984), HD *Das Herzzereißende der Dinge* (1985), HZN *mein Herz mein Zimmer mein Name* (1988), SL *Stilleben* (1991), L *Lection* (1994). All texts from these sources were translated by me.
5. While references to her childhood home are scattered throughout the Mayröcker oeuvre, they are collected in two recent works: *Blumenwerk. ländliches Journal/ Deinzendorf* and *Gang durchs Dorf: Fingerzeig*, with photographs by Bodo Hell (both at Weitra: publication PN°1, Bibliothek der Provinz, 1992).
6. "Weshalb man immer hartnäckiger wird. Dankesworte anläßlich der Verleihung des Großen Österreichischen Staatspreises am 3. Juni 1982," *protokolle* IV (1982): 67.
7. "Ich lebe unter ganz wenigen Figuren: Senta Ziegler interviewte Friederike Mayröcker," *Literatur und Kritik* 181/182 (1984): 79.
8. Siegfried J. Schmidt, "'Es schießt zusammen': Gespräch mit Friederike Mayröcker (März 1983)," *Friederike Mayröcker*, ed. Siegfried J. Schmidt (Frankfurt: Suhrkamp, 1984 [Suhrkamp Materialien 2043]), 261.
9. Siegfried J. Schmidt, *Fuszstapfen des Kopfes: Friederike Mayröckers Prosa aus konstruktivistischer Sicht* (Münster: Kleinheinrich, 1989), 75.

10. Heinz F. Schafroth, "Mut zur Autorisierung subjektivistischer Weltsicht," *Friederike Mayröcker, TEXT+KRITIK*, ed. Heinz Ludwig Arnold, 84 (1984): 55.
11. Schmidt-Dengler, 422.
12. The relative possibilities of determinacy not only of literary genre, but also of real-life truth value represent a complex issue. The following essay presents an interesting theoretical discussion of the parameters of (in-)determinacy: Rolf Tarot, "Mimesis und Imitatio. Grundlagen einer neuen Gattungspoetik," *Euphorion* 64 (1970): 125-142.
13. Schafroth, 59-61.

Doris Mühringer at Seventy-Five: "Reisen wir"

Maria Luise Caputo-Mayr

"Full of astonishment / how it is possible / that I live" (R 159)

Doris Mühringer, born on September 18, 1920, in Graz, Styria, presently lives in Vienna, in an early twentieth century building in a middle-class district near Belvedere castle, only two blocks away from the birthplace of musician Clemens Kraus. Circumstances brought her to Vienna early in life when the whole family moved there in 1931; stepping into her apartment with the inherited period furniture, one moves back in time. Petite and agile, she moved about her drawing room during a recent visit, among massive pieces of dark wood furniture, facing a red tapestry on a wind screen with embroidered regal white roosters (which appear in her poetry and on the cover of her last collection of poetry). There is an enormous chandelier in the room; it seems as if she has hardly changed anything in her apartment since her mother died in 1971. This is where she lives today as a free-lance writer, respected for the quality of her work, a member of the Pen Club; she also belongs to the group of writers associated with the literary periodicals *Podium* and *Konfigurationen*.

Mühringer has remained the quiet voice among better known contemporary Austrian women poets; although her life has been withdrawn and intensely private, her lyrical voice has gained growing attention ever since she received the third prize in the poetry competition of the prestigious German literary journal *Neue Deutsche Hefte* (with Gottfried Benn as one of the jurors), after Christine Busta and Christine Lavant, in 1956. Other prizes and official recognitions followed, culminating in the *Silbermedaille der Stadt Wien* (1981), the *Große Literaturpreis des Landes Steiermark* (1985) and the professional honorary title "Professor" from the Austrian Government (1991). Her lyrical oeuvre is small, perhaps two hundred poems at most, which, in their disciplined reduction to an essential form and meaning, provide her very private vision of the world in our time. In an unmistakable voice that transcends male/female categorization, she comments on themes such as loneliness, the relation of human beings with each other, with the animal world, and with nature; she writes on love, death and the meaning of life, the goal of our human journey, the mysteries of faith and communion, and the metaphysical aspects of our existence.

Modest and unobtrusive, Mühringer spoke in retrospect during an interview this summer about her conviction that a poetic mission had been entrusted to her: "...that I am a poet is a mission imposed on me; I never made any compromises, I am learning something new with every poem, I widen my range of tools [and]...basically we are not creators, but sieves and tools."[1]

Mühringer's early influences were fairy tales, folk songs and the poetry by Hölderlin, Rilke and Trakl. Perhaps her personal and artistic life could be understood as a process of listening and waiting for her inspiration, a humble journey of learning and finding her place, her conviction of her artistic role and the obligation to refine her craft. Yet she does not consider her writing to be autobiographical. Although Doris Mühringer views the modern literary mass media frenzy with suspicion, she recognizes seminal external events that have shaped her work, such as an early severe illness as a child in Graz, her family's move to Vienna in 1931, her own flight from there to Salzburg in 1945 and her decision to leave her secretarial job in 1950. After her return to Vienna in 1953, she encountered Eastern philosophy and became involved with a Buddhist community (1960-1966). Reading tours to Poland, the former German Democratic Republic, Yugoslavia, Romania and the USA (1969 and 1990) followed. During her reading tour through the USA in 1969, she finally realized that she was indeed a poet and that her voice could reach others. This newly won trust in herself never left her, not even after her mother's death in 1971—the time she refers to as finally becoming an independent person.

Doris Mühringer is celebrating her seventy-fifth birthday and mentions that her most recent volume of poetry, *Reisen wir. Ausgewählte Gedichte* (Let's Travel. Selected Poems),[2] although not purposely prepared for this occasion, fulfills her desire at this time to see in print once more poems spanning her entire life. *Reisen wir* is drawn from her four poetry collections, which are all out of print[3]: *Gedichte* (1957; Poems); *Gedichte II* (1969; Poems II); *Staub öffnet das Auge. Gedichte III* (1976; Dust Opens the Eye. Poems III); and *Vögel, die ohne Schlaf sind* (1984; Birds Who are without Sleep).[4] In addition to numerous contributions of poetry to periodicals and anthologies, she also has written children's books, *Wald und Wiese und Dorf und Stadt* (1960; Woods and Meadows and Village and City), *Das Märchen von den Sandmännlein* (1961; The Story of the Sandman) and *Ein Schwan auf dem See* (1983; A Swan on the Lake); she has collaborated with H. Valencak in a poetry/photo memory volume, *Mein Tag—Mein Jahr* (1983; My Day—My Year), and published a collection of short rhythmical prose pieces, written over the preceding fifteen years, in *Tanzen unter dem Netz* (1985; Dancing under the Net). Recently she published a collection of comical poems, *Das hatten die Ratten vom Schatten* (1989; a second, revised edition 1992; That's What the Rats got from the Shadow) which is based on impressions of everyday life, on the train, on the street, and written or construed in a grotesque, critical and comical vein. Besides writing poems and publishing essays, she also works as a translator and did editorial work for publishers such as Ullstein and Zsolnay Press. Currently, she has a manuscript ready for a new poetry collection with the working title "Neuer Gedichtband" (New Volume of Poems), and she is busy working on a volume of commentaries and interviews about her as yet unpublished juvenilia, originating mostly between her fourteenth year of life and the appearance of her first volume in 1957.

At the beginning of her poetic self-discovery lies a near-mystical experience as a child in Graz when, after a serious illness, she came across a volume of fairy tales by the brothers Grimm printed in old German script with illustrations. She points in particular to the story of the "Machandel-boom" (actually a juniper tree) which appeared much later in the poem "Der Vogel im Mandelbaum" (The Bird in the Almond Tree) (R 29). Mühringer recalls the magic of language imbuing her and mentions that the archetypal elements of fairy tales have reappeared in her works, where they are interwoven with her own life experiences. She still owns this fairy tale book which she took along on her escape to Salzburg in 1945.

Motifs from fairy tales occur in her work, such as the stranger asking for shelter in the evening, the greedy all-devouring yellow moon, the brown snake, the birds singing in a bush, the raven, crane and cormorant, and hunter and hunted, or as direct quotations (e.g., "If your mother knew that / Her heart would break in her body," R 21; or "As white as snow as red as blood as black as / Ebony," R 61). In addition, Mühringer uses fairy tale symbols, especially those that she deems connected with her concept of archetypal rituals of eating and partaking of the other, of earthly beings, demons, and spirits ("Ein Herz" (A Heart), R 120-121). Mühringer can express through these motifs and symbols what otherwise cannot be expressed by words—this is what she calls the ultimate mystery of a poem. There is nothing romantic or playful about her use of fairy tale elements; they signify archetypal human experiences and secrets of life on the same level as the religious and philosophical components from many traditions which inspire her work.

Vienna has been her home ever since Hans Weigel, after reading her poems, invited her to return from Salzburg, where she had lived for eight difficult years from 1945 to 1953. She commented ironically, "my return to Vienna on April 1, 1953 was an April Fool's joke" (Int). As a child, her first approach to Vienna had been a "forced transplantation of a human being from an open space with heaven, trees, clouds and brooks into an abyss of houses" (Int), a move caused by economic circumstances. The sensitive, eleven-year-old defended herself from this trauma by shutting Vienna out of her life; at night sitting on the windowsill of her parents' apartment, she often prayed to the moon. These memories resurfaced in a much later poem:

> When I was a child / And learned to walk / And walked / and walked to school / And went to life's school / As they say / I was forbidden to ever play in the park again / Or in other fantasy-lands / Then I walked out at night / Under the full moon / Onto the windowsill in the city / And walked full of moon /.../ Floating like a spirit / And thus avoided / As they say / The school of life. (R 70)

The poem appeared only in her second volume of poetry in 1969. Generally her method of writing poetry is the following: letting images, thoughts, experiences, and memories mature in her being until one day the poem erupts: "I can't *do* anything, for me it must explode. Then, I throw a lot out and I am very self-critical. That is the artist in me" (Int). This "long process of gestation"[5] enriches, as Mühringer says, a "fund of materials," until a poem is mature and wants to be born, usually finding its own form, when it is ready. Consequently, she does not write much, but has been steadily productive—her poems are polished gems, small masterpieces, perfected in form and content, intense and lapidary, condensed often to one word in a line. She spoke about the form of her poetry, insisting that:

Intuition comes in form of a line or two, at the beginning, I feel what type of form the poem wants to have, rhymed or not rhymed; but what is important is the music, the rhythm, the free rhythm; the idea brings along the form; the poem appears also in my ears. If I know the form already, I can finish the poem and feel then that it is fine. I leave it lying there for another two weeks to gain distance and may correct it. Occasionally there are donated poems in rhymed or unrhymed rhythms which I can so-to-say copy, they write themselves and I don't have to change them at all. (Int)[6]

Although she had been writing for a long time—actually since her childhood in Graz, during her literary studies at the University of Vienna, and later in Salzburg—she did not realize until later that she was to become a full-time poet. Working at an office job in Salzburg ("it was hell," Int) and writing simultaneously, with the total concentration typical of her, she developed another serious illness in 1950. As a result, her health deteriorated so much that she decided to give up the security of a monthly salary in order to follow the dictates of her inspiration. In Vienna, she joined the prestigious circle of poets around Hans Weigel and finally found congenial company. Her poems were published in the well-known anthologies *Stimmen der Gegenwart* (Voices of the Present). Her first book publication, *Gedichte* (1957), contains traditional verse, in respect to historical reference and rhyme, with regular rhythm. Next to these there are already very personal creations which would later be termed "confessional poetry" in the sense of "a quest of an individual to find meaning and authenticity in life."[7] This collection contained the poetry of alienation from her Salzburg years in the forties and fifties, which was represented with the prevalent motif of the stranger who searches in vain for a house. This is illustrated in verses such as: "Where it is leading me? / I don't know / I don't know the wave / On which I'm carried away / One thing I know / It doesn't lead me into a house / I will forever sleep outside / With the moonshine and the animals in my open eyes" (R 17).

Mühringer, at that stage, had already lost her illusions about life and, thus, her poems describe the negative reactions to the stranger's quest; echoes from Rilke and Trakl are discernible and the main themes, death and sacrifice, are linked with fairy-tale elements, the sacrificial rituals of eating, and the yearning for communion and friendship

("Sehet ein Mensch" (See, a Human Being), R 22; "Das Mahl" (The Meal), R 24). Delicate love poems alternate with death poems, expressing longing for gentle peace and disintegration (*Das wiederge-fundene Paradies* (The Rediscovered Paradise), R 37).

In the late fifties Mühringer became interested in Eastern religions and philosophies. Her involvement with a Buddhist community led her through years of total withdrawal from the world and into an existential crisis from 1960 to 1966. Today she characterizes this time as one of the most destructive of her life, undermining her independence and creativity, reducing her again to the frightened child who confronted her father's negative judgment that she is "incapable of doing anything and becoming anything" (Int). She was able to liberate herself, but her crisis led to depression and thoughts of suicide, "I was only a piece of matter." With her mother's help she recovered and the relationship between them deepened, even though her mother lacked understanding for her art. Many years later this existential experience turned up in her poem, "Les Enfants du Paradis" (The Children of Paradise) (R 73), that reveals the deceit perpetrated upon her in the name of religion. The cruelty of the verses indicate perhaps the nadir in her search for the metaphysical at that stage, but, as she recently confirmed, not her nihilism:

> Then the angels came / Enchanting and colorful / Birds / And they let me in / To join them / And they sang: / Fly with us / Sister of ours / Fly / And we flew / And so they sang on / In the sleepy heavens above / But /.../ Above / They stopped singing /.../ And fell upon me / And devoured / les enfants du paradis / My name / The sockets of my eyes / The root of my tongue / So I stopped screaming / And into cavities of my head / They built their nests.

After physically recovering from her illness, Mühringer felt forgotten as a poet because a new way of writing, which she did not follow, had become fashionable with the Wiener Gruppe. In 1969 she published her second poetry collection, *Gedichte II*. Here she explored the new possibilities of rhythm in favor of rhyme and concentrated more intensely on the themes of solitude and death; love poems such as "Vis-à-Vis du rien" (Across from Nothing) (R 49), "Sag nicht ich lieb dich!" (Do Not Say I Love You) (R 50), and "Die Absage" (The

Cancellation) (R 51) present the precariousness of tender feelings and relationships; death becomes a determining and consoling factor: "Whatever you do— / always, the silvermoon sails westward. / Do not be afraid! / Isn't death for certain?" (R 65). Again the reader finds fairy tale motifs and childhood memories present in Mühringer's work.

The final break with the years of crisis occurred during a lecture tour through the USA in 1969, namely because of her extraordinary positive experience with the audience: "There I felt that the people enjoyed listening to me and that they could take something with them—something that is good for them, beautiful and worthy of reflection" (Int). The newly-regained self-confidence also liberated her from guilt feelings of not having a "practical" career. She remembered that even her style of reading and expression had changed as a consequence to the positive and welcoming reception in the USA. Nevertheless, she declined an invitation from an American university to stay on because she felt that her aging mother needed her. The bond between mother and daughter had deepened during these years, although Mühringer feels today that she sacrificed many professional possibilities in order to be with her mother. Finally, the experience of the mother/child role reversal, "my mother became my child" (Int), heightened her insight into the complexity of the other personality, as a separate entity with an inner organization that should not be disturbed.

This respectful shyness towards another person might also explain the delicate reservation expressed in her love poems. After her mother's death in 1971, the spiritual bond remained so strong that she had for a long time the sensation of her mother's physical presence and a feeling of protection from beyond. This sensation, decisive in restoring Doris Mühringer's belief in the continuation of a spiritual life after death, is received as a final gift to her by her mother. It was also during this time that she studied a Tibetan death book which influenced several poems of her last collection. Mühringer recalls ten years of such phenomena and how they became linked once again with the memory of a fairy tale in which a queen mother returns after death to visit her child and her pet deer a number of times repeating magic sentences, e.g., "...now, I'll come one more time, but afterwards never again..." During these ten years, she turned her attention, to a greater extent, to her professional writing concerns, "...only then did I create my own world" (Int).

Participating in a cultural exchange program with Romania in 1973, Mühringer experienced a period of great creativity—contrary to her usual slower working pace—during which a powerful cycle of poems, "Gespräche mit rumänischen Göttern" (Talks with Romanian Gods), came into existence under the influence of the primordial nature of that country. The poems are included in her third volume of poetry, *Staub öffnet das Auge*. This collection is characterized by poems with highly abbreviated and condensed lines, a writing style that sometimes approaches speechlessness and entails a greater tendency towards hermeticism; although, with Mühringer's poems, the message always remains clearly discernible. We witness the dissolution of conventional syntax and a new focus on the aura of single words, separated by intervals, which intensify the meaning, while simultaneously heightening the tension within the poem.[8] A poem like "Warten" (Waiting) exemplifies her new style:

Waiting

Wind
Changes
Storm
Opens the eye
The
Curtain
Trembles
Waiting
Ashes
Could fall
On the dress
Ashes could
Fall
On the Shroud

Waiting

Dust opens the Eye. (R 76)

Each of these words and expressions now evoke complex layers of experiences and associations. Variations on the topic of death appear in poems as those in memory of Ingeborg Bachmann's death in Rome and Paul Celan's suicide (R 79, R 80-81), as well as her own mother's passing away ("Zwischen Orgel und Karo-As") (Between the Organ and the Ace of Diamonds) (R 84-85). Does she draw a self-portrait in "Die alte Dame spricht" (The Old Lady is Speaking) (R 104-105) which ends with the telling lines: "Darkness is good / Darkness / Is light enough?" Mühringer's fourth volume of poems, *Vögel die ohne Schlaf sind*, continues the tendency towards compression, but conveys a more conciliatory mood, again encompassing all her personal topics, from love to death, in an unstable world; memory, fairy tale motifs, and wisdom are sometimes expressed in poetic forms that remind the reader of Japanese haikus. Extreme simplicity and a sovereign sense of form, based on her masterful craft, show that she is still perfecting her art: "I am learning something new with every poem, I perfect my tools," (Int). It seems as though the contrasting aspects of her search for a meaning and a goal in life are reconciled and harmonized on the aesthetic and formal level of her poems.

While her work has not yet found wide critical treatment, the bibliography shows regular attention to her published works in the Austrian and European press. Christian Loidl, probably the best connoisseur of her art, believes that in spite of her private questions and her general and timeless themes, her poetry shows connections with historical developments over the past decades, such as the existentialism of the fifties and the "psychocosmic expeditions of the hippie-decade."[9]

Mühringer took a long time to face her own (and our) threatening world on her terms, and her attempts to find a place for man/woman characterized by darkness, night and instability, can be gleaned from the rich variety of often contrasting movements, religions, cultures, and philosophies that influenced her life and her poetry.

These days she goes out even less, does not attend the theater, and still works at night, as she has always done. Her preferred author remains Stifter, whom she calls her "Body and Soul author" (see the poem "Beim Lesen von Adalbert Stifter" (While Reading Adalbert Stifter) when she says: "I don't read Stifter / I'm being read by him: / Examined / Weighed / Pulled / Dominated / Shaken up / Torn to shreds / Sometimes Accepted / And Never / Abandoned," R 158). However, she also enjoys books like J.R.R. Tolkien's *The Lord of the Rings,* "because they go beyond daily occurrences" (Int). Among her preferred contemporary poets are Erich Fried, Christine Lavant ("diese Verzauberin"; The Magician), Ingeborg Bachmann, Heinz Janisch, and the early poems of Friederike Mayröcker. Aging has enriched her, she confesses, it makes her happy when young people ask her for advice and help. Today Mühringer radiates a great sense of peace: "Let's travel / But where to / I ask / Homeward / But where is that / I ask / Within you / The voice says" (R 133).

Temple University

Notes

1. My interview with Doris Mühringer in Vienna on August 12, 1995, to appear in its entirety in *Österreich im amerikanischer Sicht 9* (Austrian Institute, 1996), is referred to in the text with "Int." In this article the following biographical sources were consulted: "Doris Mühringer: Bio- und Bibliographisches," 1995, compiled by the poet; Beth Bjorklund, "The Face behind the Face: Interview with Doris Mühringer," *Literary Review* 25 (1982): 201-205, and "Doris Mühringer" *An Encyclopedia of Continental Women Writers,* vol. 2, L-Z (New York/London: Garland, 1991), 882-884. The interview as well as all texts from these sources were translated by me.

2. Doris Mühringer, *Reisen wir. Ausgewählte Gedichte* (Graz/Vienna/Cologne: Styria, 1995).

3. A comprehensive bibliography of Mühringer's primary and secondary literature has been compiled by Jorun B. Johns, "Doris Mühringer: Eine Bibliographie," *Modern Austrian Literature* 25.1 (1992): 109-122.

4. Poems mentioned in this article will be quoted from *Reisen wir,* the selections from Mühringer's four out-of-print poetry volumes, and referred to by "R" and corresponding page numbers.

5. Beth Bjorklund, "Reading Doris Mühringer: Some Questions about Craft and Composition," 2, (unpubl. manuscript, 13 pp).

6. Ibid., for treatment of style and form of Mühringer's poetry; also Beth Bjorklund, "The Face behind the Face"; Jürgen Koppensteiner and Beth Bjorklund, "'Dunkel ist Licht genug': Zur Lyrik von Doris Mühringer," *Modern Austrian Literature* 12.3/4 (1979): 192-207.

7. Bjorklund, "unpubl. manuscript," 3.

8. Cf. Christian Loidl, Nachwort, *Reisen wir*, by Mühringer, 173; Loidl's doctoral dissertation on Mühringer's work, "Wege im Dunkeln. Möglichkeiten zur Analyse von Doris Mühringers poetischem Werk," University of Vienna, Austria, 1983, seems to be the most in-depth treatment of her work so far. Mühringer is collaborating with him presently on the "Kommentarband," on her early unpublished poems, and has designated him as her literary executor.

9. Loidl, Nachwort, 168-170.

Ruth Klüger's *weiter leben: eine Jugend*:
A Jewish Woman's "Letter to Her Mother"

Jennifer Taylor

Ruth Klüger's 1992 Holocaust memoir, *weiter leben* (To Continue to Live: A Childhood) is a rich and highly constructed work, situating the reader simultaneously in the present and in the past and focusing on the difficulties Klüger faced and still faces, first as a young Jewish girl growing up in the anti-Semitic Austria of the thirties and, later, as an inmate of Theresienstadt and the Auschwitz-Birkenau concentration camps. At the same time, the text reflects upon the contradictions she faces while integrating her identities as a Jewish Austrian woman, a professor of German in the United States and, perhaps most important, as the daughter of a Jewish survivor-mother and as a mother herself.

The work of an Austrian-born author, *weiter leben* does not immediately strike the reader as an Austrian book. In spite of the fact that the book's first part is titled "Wien" (Vienna), it appears to be more a German or even an American work than an Austrian one. Published in the town of Göttingen in German, *weiter leben* is specifically dedicated by its survivor-author to "Den Göttinger Freunden" (the friends from Göttingen), to the Germans themselves instead of to the international community at large as are so many of the Holocaust memoirs. Furthermore, Klüger, though born and raised in Vienna before the Shoah, moved to the United States after 1945 and now lives and works in California. Certainly, there is little sense here that the author has the Austrians in mind as a friendly readership.

Nevertheless, I find *weiter leben* to be one of the most important Austrian works written in the postwar period, precisely because Ruth Klüger remains outside of its geographical borders in order to assert her claim to the Austrian, and specifically to the Jewish Austrian, cultural inheritance that was denied her from early childhood on, primarily by the Nazis, but also by her patriarchal family. Physical distance to her place of birth (and to her dead family members murdered by the Nazis) allows Klüger to examine both the Austria and the family in which she spent the first years of her life—which no longer exist—in a highly critical and provocative way. The Austria of her childhood becomes in this book what Klüger calls a *Zeitschaft*, a place in time to which one cannot ever physically return. Here her return to that imagined Austria is a literary journey taken from the relative safety and "neutrality" of California and Germany.

weiter leben is in many ways attempting to do some of the things we see in texts of other Jewish German writers such as Edgar Hilsenrath and Jurek Becker, namely, to reclaim the German (here I use the term *German* to mean the entire literary canon of the German-speaking peoples) literary and cultural past for the Jewish Germans. As I will show later, Klüger elicits the memory of the works of Austrian Jewish literati such as Paul Celan and Franz Kafka in reclaiming a Jewish German literary voice. This act of reclaiming is complicated, however, by the fact that the author is a Jewish Austrian *woman*, while the literary and cultural heritage is largely composed of texts by men. Klüger's book is specifically about Jewish Austrian women, or about the way in which gender has affected the author's own experience as a Jewish Austrian child and later as a Holocaust survivor. Thus while Hilsenrath and Becker might be able to see themselves as literally reclaiming a voice which Jewish men once had in German culture, Klüger is faced, both as a *Jewish* woman and as an *Austrian* woman, with the task of carving out an original voice. Ironically, she does this by taking up the literary and cultural past and rewriting it to a large degree as I will describe below.

The Jewish Woman's Voice

One of the most striking characteristics of this book is its focus on silence as the marker of a Jewish woman's identity. Ruth Klüger depicts herself, in all of her identities, as a daughter, a granddaughter, and even as a mother, as defined primarily by muteness: her experience is consistently denied throughout the text by those who, like her children's friends in California, cannot imagine a woman in the role of survivor. Writing the book breaks the silence while at the same time memorializing it.

The autobiographic text, *weiter leben*, can then be understood as a mapping out and simultaneous undermining of the image of the Jewish woman as mute on the many levels Klüger herself experienced. First, the text is a protest voiced against the Austrians and Germans themselves for silencing her both during the Third Reich as well as afterwards. Second, it is a voice raised to contradict the strict rules of her childhood Jewish religion for not allowing a woman an official role in the rituals. Furthermore, this is a book which asserts a voice in her own family, but especially in regard to her mother; *weiter leben* is, like Franz Kafka's *Brief an den Vater* (1975; *Letter to His Father*, 1966), written, published, and yet meant (perhaps) never to be read by the addressee. The work might very well be read as a modern "Brief an die Mutter," written to her own mother[1] who silenced her for being a girl, for being a child and for being a daughter. *weiter leben* simultaneously recalls the Austrian cultural inheritance of Kafka while rewriting it in the voice of the Jewish daughter.

Engpässe: Women's Voices as Jewish Survivors

Ruth Klüger writes that she and German friends were at a dinner party exchanging stories when the subject of tight places or claustrophobic experiences ("Engpässe") came up (the word *eng* draws the reader back to Celan's "da liegt man nicht eng" as well as to Klüger's use of *weiter*, lending more resonance to the title). Her friends, all of them of her generation, were talking of elevators that had been stuck, of closets that were locked or of tunnels that seemed endless. Suddenly she found herself in an *Engpaß* of a different sort: her own experience, she realized, was not *salonfähig* (proper), for her *Engpaß* was the suffocating train ride that took her and her mother to Auschwitz. She describes this moment at the dinner table:

> I could offer my trip in the cattle wagon and thought about it incessantly, but how should I add that to the discussion? This story would have so dampened the discussion, would have broken the rules so completely that only I would have still been speaking. The others, more or less affected, dejected, would have been silent, struck mouth dead by my experience.[2]

In fact, then, her *Engpaß* was not narrow enough; it was too broad for the discussion at the table. Her story about the train would have crossed an unstated line and, would not, as she said, have been *salonfähig*. Better, she thinks, that she remain *mundtot* (silent) than that they become so after hearing such a story. After all, she is used to being *mundtot*, her life has been spent *mundtot*. And so, at this dinner, Klüger tells another story in place of the train story, namely a story about a schoolteacher in Munich whose classroom was bombed by the Allies in World War II. She says she can tell her German friends the stories of the Jewish *people*, but not her own: "My childhood falls into the black hole of this discrepancy" (WL 109). *German* stories about the war are about being bombed or being hungry. *Jewish* stories are about deportations and concentration camps. And yet, as Ruth Klüger's story points out, all of these people were (are) Germans (or in her case, Austrians), had been neighbors, would have been fellow citizens but for the Nazi years. That the Jewish stories are, by definition, foreign, in spite of the fact that they stem from a native Austrian of the same generation, underscores the irony of being both Jewish and German/ Austrian after the Shoah.

And yet, of course, Klüger does not remain *mundtot*; she writes the story of the transport in a book dedicated to "Den Göttinger Freunden," reflecting before she begins about the need to build bridges from one set of memories to another, not to replace one with the other. "But if there is no bridge between my memories and yours, why then am I writing this here anyway?" (WL 110). Writing the book breaks the silence; her voice, no longer *mundtot*, allows for those other voices to stay alive, to be connected to hers with a bridge. In light of the recent debates among the historians in Germany about writing history, Klüger's assertion that we build bridges without making each other *mundtot* sounds hopeful if not reconciliatory.

Reclaiming the German Fairy Tale

Giving a voice to the Jewish woman's survival story is just one part of Klüger's mission, however. The book also attempts to go back further in time before the Holocaust and to reclaim the German literary tradition for Jewish women. Like Jurek Becker, Edgar Hilsenrath, Bruno Bettelheim and other concentration camp survivor-authors, Klüger relies greatly on the fairy tale as a vehicle for telling some of her survival stories. Jurek Becker (*Bronsteins Kinder*; *Bronstein's Children*), Hilsenrath (*Der Nazi und der Friseur*; 1977; *The Nazi Who Lived As a Jew*; 1977) and, to some degree, Bruno Bettelheim (*The Informed Heart*, 1986) construct texts in which there are thematic as well as structural elements from German fairy tales such as *Hänsel and Gretel*, which thematize the struggle for survival against terrible odds. Fairy tales are rich sources for literary depictions of the Shoah experience for many reasons. Their very structured form, from the formulaic language of "if they are still alive..." to their rigid narrative patterns, makes their *literariness* or "constructedness" transparent, thus underlining the author's awareness of the difficulty of using language to describe the indescribable.

Furthermore, that fairy tales have a perceived double status, both as a part of high (written) and low (oral) culture within the German literary canon, adds to their usefulness in telling the Shoah story. The survivor-author can both locate her or himself within a high German cultural context and identify her or himself as a "mainstream" German by re-telling the famous Grimm tales, which have their beginnings as literary texts during the first German nationalist movements before 1848. These writers, then, can use these particular literary texts to call attention to their own identity as members of high German culture. Such an act of assertion becomes necessary for Jewish survivors, who had been told that they were not members of the dominant group in German culture and that their language was false, their discourse *degenerate*. Thus, in rewriting and undermining the fairy tale, these authors are claiming an intimacy with German culture that is not allowed to an outsider. They are staking a familial claim by treating the cultural history in a critical though familiar way.

The main fairy tale in *weiter leben*, though, is not *Hänsel und Gretel*, as we see in the men's texts, but *Schneewittchen* (Snow White), the story of a princess driven into a dark forest by a malicious witchlike stepmother. In Klüger's complex text, the voice of the child, which is differentiated from that of the adult narrator, often paints the mother as evil and at fault for the entire camp experience, just as Snow White's stepmother had forced her into the forest. Several of Klüger's experiences underline the reasons a child might have for painting such a picture of a mother. When Ruth Klüger and her mother arrived in Birkenau in the summer of 1944, her mother suggested that they throw themselves onto the electric fence in the yard so that they might be spared watching each other suffer. She was horrified that her mother could suggest her death (WL 113-114). Klüger was twelve when they arrived in the camp, an age in which *children* are supposed to be taking risks, endangering their lives, while the parents should be cautious and conservative, worried about the safety of their children. Her life in the concentration camp turned the world upside down for Klüger. Thus, it is not hard to imagine why the child protagonist likens her mother to the fairy tale witch and herself to Snow White, the innocent victim.

Fairy tales are associated with a fixed past, a former way of working through trauma (according to Bruno Bettelheim),[3] but the function has clearly been disrupted for Klüger, a child survivor. Nothing in the fairy tale can serve to minimize the real experience or even to help inform the reader of reality. The child is trapped. Lawrence Langer writes of the function of fairy tales in Holocaust fiction:

> The fairy tale allusion produces extraordinary reverberations, since in many respects it epitomizes the continuity in experience which characterized the imagination's attitude toward life before the advent of *l'univers concentrationaire.* "Once upon a time," the traditional refuge for children, always ended "and they lived happily ever after," assuring an uninterrupted adventure from past to future—what the narrative voice calls a "readiness to live."[4]

For Ruth Klüger, the rewriting and breaking down of the fairy tale is to some degree a reckoning with her own destroyed or broken childhood. This connection sets into motion a whole process explored in her text of rewriting and reunderstanding the past, as the many voices of her own persona take turns telling her story. Klüger's retelling of *Schneewittchen,* as a literary representation of the Shoah, allows both the author and the reader to indulge in certain (perhaps therapeutic) fantasies about survival. The fairy tale realm becomes a world in which the former child-survivor plays out fantasies of guilt at having survived or anger at having almost died; the narrator can align herself with one or with all of the figures taking part in the fairy tale power struggle (in this case the struggle was with the mother), and thus relive her own power struggle as a child-victim of the Nazis, in which she had absolutely no control.

Ultimately, although the child's voice and the fairy tale narrative structure is essential to the intricate texture of *weiter leben,* it is the voice of the adult Klüger which has the final say. The book is, above all else, an act of forgiveness of her mother. For as a mother herself, and as a mature adult, Ruth Klüger is now able to understand the dilemma faced by her own mother who had asked her to throw herself onto the electric fence. In her book, the author states: "Only when I had children did I understand that it is justifiable to kill your own children in Auschwitz rather than to wait" (WL 113-114).

Kaddish: Reclaiming the Woman's Voice in the Jewish Community

As a child and as a girl, but even now as a woman, Klüger claims she felt stripped of the ability to count, to say *kaddish* for the dead, to be a source of memory. She writes that she has always been suspicious of rituals because they did not include her. Women in the Jewish community were excluded from the important rituals. According to Klüger:

> Before his daughters he talked this way to a dog, and my mother told me about it uncritically. She just took the put-down the way a Jewish daughter should. It was meant to be funny. Were things different and I might be able to, as they say, *officially* say Kaddish...for my father, then I might be able to make friends with this religion...(WL 23)

To some degree, then, the title *weiter leben* also implies a learning to come to terms with her past frustration at the Jewish religion, a frustration and anger which is marked in this story as highly ambiguous: Her anger at her mother for not contradicting the grandfather, whose story is clearly marked as harmless and comical, is conflated here with the anger at her mother for not having stopped the camp experience. Klüger has lost everything—family, language, status, father, mother, identity—and in trying to piece together a viable post-Shoah identity, she finds that she must "make friends" with the past, with the Jewish religion itself. Thus, the text becomes a mapping out of her identity as a writer, as a scholar, and as a literary voice.

Ironically, it is only through taking on the traditional role of the man in the Jewish mourning ceremony, by "writing the book" and, in so doing, saying *kaddish* for the dead, that she is able to take that step and begin the process of making friends with Judaism again. The book becomes the *kaddish* she never said for her father, for her grandfather, and for her lost brother, for even as she complains bitterly about not having been allowed to say the prayer, she begins to remember her father, to recount his life, and to mourn for him.

This work of mourning is colored, however, by the guilt she feels at having no way of bringing together her everyday memories of him, some bad, some good, with his death which is too terrible to imagine. And this guilt, in turn, produces in her narrative a tone of aggressive anger at a man for dying a death after which she cannot express the normal anger a child might have felt toward a parent ever again. His death, which she imagines, is indeed horrible. She sees him naked in a gas chamber, attempting to scratch his way to the top of the pile, and she tries to imagine whether he, like many men, was stronger than the others and thus able to crawl up over the children, children who were perhaps her own age. Such a vision, planted into her head by the stories she had heard after the war, haunts her as she attempts to remember him not only as a victim, but as a father. This *kaddish* is an attempt to rescue his memory—to exercise such visions by writing them down.

History and Living On: *weiter leben*

The title of the work itself, which translates into English literally as "Going on with life" or, more interestingly, as "living more widely, with more room," conjures up several images which generate questions for the reader. On one level, the title describes what she has herself done; she has lived on and this is her story. At the same time, though, the words "weiter leben" can be construed as a rough order or a strong admonition for other survivors and, especially, for her younger German audience to live on. This is quite literally a book for the Germans of younger generations who will read her story and live on.

On another level, the title refers to Klüger's life in America, especially in California, where all is spatially wider ("weiter") and, (at least apparently), more open. She writes that, after her years of being boxed in both in the camps and in New York City which caused her to experience a "Käfig-gefühl" (a feeling of living in a cage) (WL 237), the openness of the California freeways and wide landscapes came as a shock:

> My university lies between two interstate highways…When I first came to Orange County and got lost every few days on the highways, I imagined that hell must be like this, that everyone would have to travel these highways, alone in their own tin jails, separate from all the others and yet visible for everyone…(WL 280)

The wideness of California was not just terrifying, however; Southern California's desert landscape offers what appears at first to be a break with the past for all who have endured too much history. Ultimately, though, Klüger comes to like California in spite of its unfulfillable promise of new beginnings; California is still home:

> Meanwhile I am at home again in Southern California, in
> Orange County. This is a county whose history consists of the
> fact that its inhabitants fled here to escape history, European,
> Asian and finally even American history, in as far as it took
> place further eastward...I like living here. This sea and desert
> landscape, threatened by earthquakes, blessed by the sun,
> plagued by drought, this landscape has taken on the foolish and
> tragic mission of getting rid of the past by denying it, by
> replacing the present with another present before the first one
> can get old. This is impossible and that's why it is foolish.
> (WL 280-282)

Is California comforting because so many like her who tried
unsuccessfully to escape history live there? Here, one is not alone with
the past, but one lives every day in the vain hope that history might be
replaceable. Like Becker's characters in *Bronsteins Kinder*, Californians
are seeking to recreate themselves by running away from the past, and
all are doomed to failure. Klüger sees a difference, though, between
Germany and California, the ultimate last frontier of the frontier-land,
America. The Germans, in order to recreate themselves, must deny that
history affects them. The Californians, expecting their histories to catch
up with them any day, know they are running from something which
does affect them.

The word "weiter" in the title has more than a spatial meaning,
however; "weiter" also calls to mind the lines of Paul Celan's complex
poem to the dead, *Todesfuge*, and thus links Klüger's work closely to
the Jewish-German literary past. Celan writes in his poem of the smoke
of the burning, murdered Jewish victims rising up into the air where "da
liegt man nicht eng."[5] Klüger's title, one can almost imagine, echoes
the *eng* with *weiter*, and, as we shall see, Celan's *liegen* (lie) with *leben*
(live). The association between the two works is by no means
inconsequential; it is highly fitting that Klüger, in this highly
constructed and yet emotionally laden memoir, pays tribute to Celan,
the great Jewish German poet of the former Austro-Hungarian empire.

The two works of mourning can be read against each other in
interesting ways. Klüger's ambiguous word "weiter," directed both to
the living and the dead, seems to be a response to Celan's poem to the

dead, itself full of contradictory imagery and rhythms. While Celan's dead do not lie (*liegen*) narrowly, Klüger's figures are exhorted to live (*leben*) widely. His is a negative statement (da liegt man nicht eng), hers is positive (weiter leben). His lie, hers live—two German words which are similar in rhythm and sound and yet vastly different in this context. Her title and the book itself is an ambiguous exhortation to both the living and the dead to live on, if only in memory, while Celan's vision in his poem is directed only toward the past, the dead. Like Celan's, Klüger's dead will live on only in the book itself, not *eng*, but *weiter*, but her living will also live *weiter*, perhaps even in the open spaces of California. Klüger's text functions then on many levels simultaneously: it is a prayer for the living to live on, and it is, like Celan's, a *kaddish*, the Jewish prayer of mourning for the dead, for those who will not live on except in memory. In the end, *weiter leben* becomes a tribute to the Jewish German literary past, a *kaddish* written, very appropriately, as a German literary text.

Bridging Two Worlds

The publication of *weiter leben*, as well as her ongoing work and teaching in both California and Germany (she takes exchange students from Irvine to Göttingen regularly), make it necessary that Klüger travel back and forth between Germany and California—as a survivor, she belongs to both of them equally. *weiter leben*, with its associations with the literary past, has returned to her her lost status as a member of the German-speaking community from which she was violently removed, while her "home" in the United States has literally meant life and a chance to begin again. It is hard to imagine ever being able to reconcile the new world, in which everyone is running from history, with the old, in which all are embracing the past in some sort of masochistic ritual that brings no relief. And yet, this is, to a large degree, one of the primary functions of this text, to bridge these two worlds that are so much a part of the survivor's identity. To what degree Austria plays a role in the bridge between the two worlds remains to be seen. Austria appears to be a place left behind, a *Zeitschaft* full of painful memories and yet the focus of so much of the book's energy, both positive and negative.

College of William and Mary

Notes

1. At the time of publication (1992), Ruth Klüger's mother lived in a nursing home and had not yet read the book. In the meantime, the mother read it and is reportedly "furious."
2. Klüger, *weiter leben: eine Jugend* (Göttingen: Wallstein, 1992), 109. All texts from this source were translated by me. Further references to this text will be cited with WL and the page number throughout the text.
3. See Bruno Bettelheim, *The Uses of Enchantment and the Informed Heart* (New York: Vintage Books, 1977).
4. Lawrence Langer, *The Holocaust and the Literay Imagination* (New Haven and London: Yale University Press, 1975), 158.
5. Paul Celan, *Todesfuge*, in: *Deutsche Gedichte*, eds. Theodor Echtermeyer and Benno von Wiese, 17th ed. (Düsseldorf: August Bagel, 1986), 664-665.

History from a Woman's Perspective:
Renate Welsh's *Lufthaus*

Beth Bjorklund

'Tis strange,—but true; for truth is always strange; Stranger than fiction: if it could be told, How much would novels gain by the exchange! (Lord Byron, *Don Juan*, XIV. ci)

Renate Welsh is well known as an author of literature for young people. Born in Vienna in 1937, Welsh has published more than fifty books for children and adolescents, which have won numerous prizes and have been translated into many languages.[1] Perhaps less well known is the fact that Welsh also writes for adults. Her best-selling fictional biography, *Constanze Mozart*,[2] speaks in the narrative voice of Mozart's widow, fifty years after the composer's death. The relationship between children's literature and literature for adults is well explicated in Renate Welsh's *Poetikvorlesungen* (Lectures on Poetry).[3] The aesthetic criteria and sociopolitical stance of that poetics help to elucidate Welsh's most recent book for adults, which is the focus of the present discussion.

Welsh's new book, *Das Lufthaus* (The House in the Air),[4] has received wide acclaim; and rightfully so, for it is an amazing work. The story it tells is "true," thus confirming Byron's insight, which has since become an adage, that truth is stranger than fiction. Book dealers would probably classify it as a "historical novel," which is not so much wrong as it is an oversimplification. If the traditional form of that genre is situated between historiography and fiction, modern innovations entail a "subjectivization of history."[5] Welsh's book comprises many different levels, including historical documentation and literary fiction, also biography and even autobiography. The artfulness inheres in the amalgam of diverse elements and the juggling of different perspectives. Before exploring those issues, I would like to comment briefly on its unusual origins.

The male protagonist is an *Urgroßvater* (great-grandfather) of the author, five generations back; and the documentary materials came into the author's hands through family channels. Those documents consist of letters, diaries, memoirs, portraits, and other materials, which are in part reproduced in the text in italics. They give evidence of a family for whom writing and letter-writing was clearly important, a family eager to preserve its memory for posterity. Welsh comments in the text in regard to the *Urgroßvater:* "It was obviously important to him how he would be judged by his son and by following generations" (28). As if to preserve the memory, "as if the careful recording of his ancestors could secure his own survival." (23), the family carried the documents with them in their many moves around Europe, to the United States, and back to Europe.

Around those documents the author has woven a tale, interpreting the materials, commenting on them and extrapolating from them, and thus creating a context. The book is autobiographical to the extent that it is narrated in the first person, from the perspective of the present-day author. It considers the difficulties of interpretation—a classical problem of hermeneutics. A critic writes of postmodernist fiction as follows: "The hermeneutic interest has superimposed an additional level upon the conventional model of historical fiction, with the result that the search for the past as it continues in the present is represented alongside with a segment of the past itself."[6] That "search for the past" includes assessment of the level of consciousness of the writers and the degree of self-stylization and its possible intent. Welsh writes: "Sometimes it almost seems to me as if they [the letters] were directed less to the individuals than to the descendents" (148). There are also inevitable gaps. In some cases, the author consciously chose to preserve the empty spaces, for what is *not* said is itself revelatory. In other cases, particularly in regard to the historical period, the author did a great deal of research. Although the erudition is not apparent on the surface, the work presents an accurate picture of the times, the mid-nineteenth century.

If the narrative "I" (*ich*) is the voice of the author, the work is addressed to a second person, the female protagonist. The "you" (*du*) is Pauline Marx, a young Jewish woman who married into a Christian family. The book is Pauline's biography, one might say, and the author moves easily between second-person and third-person pronouns. Pauline is a willing and/or unwilling accomplice in her husband's political causes, economic exploits, and travel adventures. That took her from her home in Karlsruhe to Steyr and Vienna, also to Leipzig, further to Paris and London, and on to "Amerika." Women's lives, however, were not well documented; and thus the author had to extrapolate from the historical materials to arrive at a woman's perspective.[7]

The figure identified above as a male protagonist, the *Urgroßvater* of the author, is Pauline's father-in-law, Maximilian Joseph Gritzner. The entire book, indeed the entire life of the family, stands under his all-pervasive influence, and it is his memoirs that comprise the majority of the documentary materials. He is a strong figure, in both a negative and a positive sense, and the author finds herself having to resist the tendency of letting him take over the narrative: "I would very much enjoy quoting Gritzner's ship-diary...But that is your story, Pauline, even if he plays a larger-than-life role in it" (132). Pauline's husband, who bears the same name as his father and who is called "Max," is shown with divided loyalties, vacillating between wife and father. Addressing Pauline, the author poses rhetorical questions: "Did you experience father and son as a unit and you as a dividing link between them? Was their relationship as frightening to you as it was to me sometimes in reading?" (70).

Although there are many flashbacks to an earlier time, the plot effectively begins in 1848, when Pauline, at age twenty-three, marries into the family. Eighteen hundred forty-eight was, of course, a fateful year in Austrian and German history, and that is an important aspect to which we shall return. The biography necessarily ends seven years later, in 1855, when Pauline, at the age of thirty, becomes insane. Now if the book were a work of fiction, one might suspect the author of attempting to manipulate the reader's emotions. But as a historically documented fact, the strong ending forces the reader—as it did the author—to consider seriously the events leading up to the end of this short life. After the incipience of insanity, the author briefly narrates Pauline's terminal institutionalization and the family's return to Europe. The book ends in 1872, when father Gritzner dies, and the family, left without a center, disperses.

Eighteen hundred forty-eight was indeed an impotent epoch in European history, and father Gritzner and his son Max were liberal revolutionaries. The tension between public, political life, on the one hand, and private, domestic life, on the other, opens the book and remains operative throughout. Gritzner was active in politics; he served as a representative at the Paul's Church in Frankfurt. His son Max, age twenty-four in 1848, gave up his budding career in engineering to participate in the revolution as editor of the radical newspaper *Constitution*.[8]

Enter Pauline; but actually, entry was not that easy. Pauline and Max had met four years earlier while he was a student in her hometown of Karlsruhe. Her close-knit family was strong in its Orthodox Judaism, and her father vehemently refused to allow his daughter to marry outside the faith. The young people, however, decided to follow their dreams; and with the aid of Max's father, Pauline joined the Gritzner family in Steyr. Is it a love story? It has all the trappings thereof, but there was little time for love.

Pauline lived under the surveillance of Max's mother and sister while Max and his father stormed the barricades. Pauline sees the "Women's Battalion" from a distance and questions "Why can't I do anything?" (65). Women did participate in the revolution, as is well documented,[9] and 1848 saw the beginnings of a women's movement. Women of the bourgeois class, such as the Gritzners, however, stayed at home. As the author writes, addressing the protagonist: "You had to obey the rules of this family all the more because you had broken those of your own family" (30). Pauline is portrayed as making forays into the fray with the servant women, but she was excluded from political action.

With the collapse of the revolution, Max and his father had to flee. They remained in flight, in a sense, for the rest of their lives. Their path took them first to Breslau, then to Leipzig, where Pauline joined them and married Max. A prerequisite for marriage was baptism in the Christian church, which entailed renunciation of her Jewish religion and heritage, and thus also of her family. With so many changes, Pauline comes to question her identity: "Who am I anyway?" (89). The question recurs, as she is forced to adapt to ever-changing situations. The pain at the loss of her family was initially overcome through her love for her husband; but only in retrospect do the participants realize that the elastic was stretched beyond its limit.

Hearing that France offered exile to failed revolutionaries, they moved to Paris, where they lived in a refugee colony. In dire financial straits, Max sought work, as Pauline gave birth to their first child, a boy. But there was no safe haven in Europe from the secret police, and thus they decided to emigrate to the New World. The image of America in the minds of Europeans at the time was one of liberty and opportunity; and they thus hoped for the freedom for which they had fought in vain in Austria. Father Gritzner had left already in 1849; and a year later, after a stay in London, the young couple joined him.

They arrived in New York in 1850 and moved on to Virginia. At that time, within a decade of the Civil War, we hear the rumblings of slavery in the background. It was also the time of the Gold Rush in California; and father Gritzner, true to his adventurous self, made two trips—via Cuba, Mexico, and Panama (the second time, Nicaragua)—to California and the Wild West. Max found work as a coast surveyor in the Florida region and later at the State Department in Washington.

That left Pauline mostly alone at home, where a woman's work was, for the most part, undocumented drudgery. A second child, also a boy, was born in 1852. Pauline played the typical female role of providing her husband a haven from the tribulations of the world and saving the proud or despairing man from himself. The "heroine" struggled, on the one hand, with the great demands placed upon her and, on the other hand, with the isolation and lack of opportunities for communication. The author presents a very sympathetic portrait of Pauline, reminiscent of Christa Wolf's narrative stance in *Nachdenken über Christa T.* (1969; *The Quest for Christa T.*, 1971). Yet Welsh is careful not to allow her reflections to go beyond the limits of documented evidence. "Did she even have a right to think beyond the demands of the day?" (152).

In 1855, after seven years of marriage, five of which were in the United States, Pauline became insane. The reader can sense it coming on; but the men in Pauline's life (i.e., her husband and her father-in-law) were essentially clueless. The author, after having done as much investigation as the data will allow, presents her own hypothesis:

> As long as your love was large and entirely intact, it justified your leaving father and mother and religion to follow that golden ball wherever it rolled. But when the large love changed into the small currency of everyday life and the golden ball was no longer round and whole, then you could not be whole either, and you disintegrated into parts. You were endangered precisely because you tried so hard to please everyone else, because you had so little self-esteem to set against the demands of others. (303)

The remainder of the book, about twenty percent, is devoted to Pauline's illness and her path through a series of institutions. The author skillfully portrays the dimensions of Pauline's insanity, as based on reports by her husband, her father-in-law, and various caregivers, as well as her own nonsensical writings. It is necessarily sketchy, since the protagonist is essentially "gone"; but those sketches are very sensitive. Welsh writes:

> Part of me would like to fill the gaps in your story and give you a well-rounded biography, as if anything could be made good by it. That seems, however, almost as if I were neatly to stuff the empty spaces in a lace work or weave a spider's web into a firm fabric. Precisely where something is missing, I believe I sense you. (334)

The family eventually returned to Europe where the children went through school. A reunion of sorts took place with Pauline's mother and siblings, but her father had died in the meantime. In fact, his death coincided with the onset of her insanity. Although the causal connection remains a mystery, Pauline's internalized sense of patriarchal authority seems to have precipitated her collapse when the possibility of reconciliation was gone forever. Pauline's husband was subsequently successful in business in Paris, which the boys later took over. But "his sons remained strangers to him" (379). They never married or had children, and the family line continued through Max's sister.

There are many levels on which the book could be read, for example, liberal ideology in Europe or immigrant experience in the US. If the author had wanted to focus on those aspects, however, she could have chosen a male protagonist, since the public sphere is traditionally a male domain. Instead, the author chose a female protagonist, and that shifts the focus to the private sphere, where the issues are those of personal interaction. There the men failed miserably; or perhaps everyone failed. The author wisely refrains from assigning blame, and thus the book does not fall into the disparaged category of "victim literature." But the thrust is clear, as in the following scene near the end: "'Collapsed,'" Pauline repeated, but Max still did not understand. He kissed her, the boys kissed her, the father kissed her, and then they filed out the door in a row; three generations of Gritzners, handsome, intelligent people who did not understand a thing, nothing at all" (373).

A prime suspect in the tragedy is the authoritarian father Gritzner, who was also a person of remarkable vitality. He was already fifty-five years old when he first went to America, and many of the adventure-tales of life in the New World and the Wild West are taken from his memoirs. Decades later he was still going, and at the age of seventy-six he traveled to Italy, Greece, Egypt, and Turkey—under travel conditions that were primitive even for that time.

However heroic his exploits, in personal relations Gritzner was distinctly unsuccessful. His unusually intense relationship with his son manifested itself already in the boy's adolescence in ambivalent attraction-repulsion patterns, which the father described as a "magnetic affinity" (50). The homoerotic undertones of the father's stance were apparently never resolved but rather sublimated. Father and son were united in their political ideals and their fight for a more liberal, democratic society in Austria in 1848. But even in regard to that time, the author speculates on Pauline's possible skepticism of the allegedly idealistic stance: "A sentence must have sounded hollow to you at some time or another; at some point it must have become clear to you how widely their talk and their life diverged from each other" (107).

Those energies were transferred in the New World to countless projects, such as machines, inventions, engineering feats, real estate ventures, and financial exploits. As Max's sister wrote of her father: "He will concoct a thousand plans, begin them all and follow through with none of them" (163). Father Gritzner's own marriage had failed, and he had been estranged from his wife, Max's mother, ever since Max was a small child. Welsh relates an incident from that time, humorous in retrospect, in which Gritzner's wife attempted to take revenge on her husband. The author writes in conclusion: "In any case I now know that an 'immoral lifestyle' was a possibility for middle-class women to avenge themselves on their husbands" (26).

Their son, Max, stood constantly under the influence of the father, which drew Pauline into the orbit as well; or rather, Pauline was largely excluded from the orbit. Max, perhaps unconsciously, imitated his father's behavior in many respects, including effectively ignoring his wife. Gritzner called Max his "alter ego" (268); and indeed, the two men were nearly inseparable, in thought if not in deed. That created an imbalance of power; and even if power relations were never seriously questioned, the father seemed to regard his daughter-in-law as a rival for his son's attentions. In that his accounts are the primary source of the written history, "he had the opportunity to write down his view of things" (27). In contrast, "one sees by your handwriting, Pauline, that writing was not nearly such a matter of course for you" (147). Welsh, speaking for Pauline, shows another perspective, which diverges greatly from the male version. Wesseling's view of contemporary writing is relevant here:

> Postmodernist alternate histories all focus on the problematic exclusion of minorities and other subordinate groups from the historical records...Postmodernist writers articulate the idea that the privileging of a certain textual tradition enforces a specific version of (historical) reality at the expense of rival versions...Postmodernist alternate histories expose the power play by means of which the textual tradition is brought into being in the first place.[10]

A recurring theme in Pauline's life is "the loneliness" (115, 192) and "the emptiness" (98, 192, 251). Alone at home with two children and little money, she had no opportunity for self-realization. The book documents her attempts to learn English, but there was little time or occasion to talk to anyone other than the immediate family. "You are my everything" (204) she would write to her husband; and "without you, I don't even know who I am" (278). When he was not there, all she could do was wait (besides, of course, the housework and child care). "Benign neglect," one might call it; but Max did not seem to realize that no personal neglect is "benign." Welsh portrays it well in a fictive scene:

> I'm so empty, Pauline thought. This emptiness within me eats me up. She perceived her father-in-law's letters as threatening, as directed against her. 'But that doesn't have anything to do with you,' Max said. He did not understand that that was precisely the problem. It did not have anything to do with her. (170)

The title *Das Lufthaus* can be interpreted as an extended metaphor of this loneliness and emptiness. Max affectionately called Pauline his "house," with all the empirical, emotional, and sexual connotations of that image: "'You are my house,' he said yesterday, 'my real house and my home'" (98). Pauline was indeed a stabilizing factor for her husband in his search for a place to live and a way of life. But the great price that this role cost her, only she knew: "You say that I am your house.

A house without ground to stand on. A house in the air" (242). The image itself suggests the unreality of the enterprise, a "house of cards." Pauline was ever-mindful of her "house"—her Judaic heritage and family, from which she felt estranged.

Societal conditions in the nineteenth century led to a split allegiance and to an irresolvable conflict. The theme of Judaism-versus-Christianity is reflected through Pauline's Christian marriage that took her away from her Jewish family. The title *Das Lufthaus* can thus be understood as a sinister foreshadowing of the fate of the Jews at the hands of the Nazis less than a century after Pauline's time. The association is as anachronistic as it is unavoidable, since the genre of the historical novel was changed forever by "the irreducible hiatus of the Third Reich."[11] The discontinuity between past and present is consciously built into the texture of the work. Thinking of her own century, the author writes: "I must not furnish you with ideas, Pauline, that presuppose a knowledge which you could not have had" (123).

The rationality of Pauline's stance is not open to question, since such factors obviously have an emotional basis. The author understands that well because, as she writes in another context, she is convinced, "that every thought was once a feeling, arose out of a feeling—or, perhaps more precisely, out of an idea that was rooted in feeling."[12] Welsh wonders about the level of consciousness on which Pauline confronted these issues, without however, coming to a conclusion, since one cannot get back behind the written documents. "Did you have to place Max so high above you and make yourself so small to be allowed to love him? Or did you have to protect that terrible love from yourself?" (212).

Sexuality is a prominent topic, and the marriage was initially happy. "The bed was the raft on which they save themselves after every disappointed hope" (100). Max demonstrated more sensitivity toward women than did his father; but Max was too weak a figure to achieve independence from the father's dominating ego, and both of them were too restless to give much attention to human relations. The men did not understand Pauline's illness at all, and their reports indicate a greater interest in her menstrual periods than in her person. Welsh writes: "It almost sounds as if they suspected the locus of your illness to be in your womb" (318). Max seemed helpless to deal with the situation and largely withdrew, leaving the field open for the dominant influence of the father. Welsh speculates about his authoritarian stance in a passage addressed to Pauline: "Sometimes I think I to detect a gloating behind the regret, but maybe that is unfair to him. It is certain however that he recoiled in horror at your sexuality" (346). The author offers a summarizing comment:

> Of course he was right, had always been right, cannot be anything other than right. The longer I work on your story, the more often I feel like interrupting your father-in-law. I become increasingly annoyed at his self-righteousness and his know-it-all manner, and that while definitely maintaining respect for his qualities. (348)

Gritzner's patriarchal stance stands in marked contrast to the democratic ideals for which he was allegedly fighting, and throughout we see the contradiction between the public and the private sphere:

> A man went out to reform the world, to make a home for reason and with it for his understanding of humanity. After the failure of all his big plans, he wanted to build an ark for his own family in which his values could be salvaged for a better time. But insanity was now not merely external and controllable; it held his daughter-in-law in its claws and thus waited in ambush for his son too. With all of his education, his versatility, his intellectualism, his sportliness, and his daring, he stood there and realized that his hands were empty. What good is an ark when there is nothing left to be saved? (349)

One is reminded of Bachmann's *Malina,* where the woman, situated between two men, virtually disappears. "It was murder," concludes Bachmann.[13] A similar conclusion presents itself in Welsh's book, which is almost more appalling in that it is presented in the context of everyday life.

The book is not a critique of nineteenth-century liberalism, for I am sure the author would concur with the progressive ideals that set the family clock in motion. The failure of those ideals in Austrian and German society had indeed fateful consequences that determined the course of history for the subsequent century. But the author also shows that it is not enough to be revolutionary in public life if those ideals are not extended to private life as well. In politics the Gritzner men were fighting against the very same authoritarian structures that they established and maintained at home.

It was more than a century later, after generations of consciousness-raising, that the women's movement in the United States and elsewhere coined the slogan, "the personal is the political."[14] If a nineteenth-century woman did not fully see the contradictions, or even if she did see them, she would see no way out of them except "to flee into insanity" (345). Insanity as the only alternative to unbearable empirical conditions has only recently begun to come under investigation. Showalter writes as follows: "There have always been those who argued that women's high rate of mental disorder is a product of their social situation, both their confining roles as daughters, wives, and mothers and their mistreatment by a male-dominated and possibly misogynistic psychiatric profession." Recent theory takes that one step further: "Feminist philosophers, literary critics, and social theorists...have shown how women, within our dualistic systems of language and representation, are typically situated on the side of irrationality, silence, nature, and body, while men are situated on the side of reason, discourse, culture, and mind."[15] The implications for the writing of history are clear. History, as written by men, tells mainly about the victories and defeats of political causes, obviously male. If "the path to historical consciousness runs through the self,"[16] that "self," in most cases, is male. Women have largely been written out of history, and the cost in human life on either side of an ideological power struggle is probably equally great.

It was a surprise to find a newspaper review of the book that emphasized the financial success of Max and his sons after their return to Europe: "They were successful entrepreneurs," writes the reviewer.[17] Perhaps it is natural to outgrow youthful idealism to arrive at a more pragmatic stance. But no matter how great the material accomplishment, in what way can it be regarded as successful if the participants sacrifice their women in the process? That is not so much a biblical admonition about gaining the world and losing one's soul as it is a question of human values.

The characters in the novel are forever pursuing "happiness," believing to see it just around the next bend. "We'll be happy, his father wrote to Max, Max wrote to his father. We'll be happy. Like a defiant refrain. 'We shall be damned happy,' said Max" (168). If happiness is indeed the goal that we all pursue, it must include personal, immaterial values, as well as political ideology and material gain. As an inquiry into the nature of values, among other things, Welsh's book is extremely important and eminently successful.

University of Virginia

Notes

1. For a complete bibliography see "Renate Welsh," *1000 & 1 Buch* (Bundesministerium für Unterricht, Kunst und Sport) 3 (1992): 9-10. See also Beth Bjorklund, "Realistic Idealism: Welsh for All Ages," *Österreich in amerikanischer Sicht* 8 (Austrian Institute, 1995), 1-20.
2. Renate Welsh, *Constanze Mozart. Eine unbedeutende Frau* (Vienna: Jugend und Volk, 1990). *Constanze Mozart. An Unimportant Woman* (Riverside: Ariadne, 1997).
3. *Poetikvorlesungen*, delivered at the University of Innsbruck (1993). Published as *Geschichten hinter den Geschichten, Innsbrucker Beiträge zur Kulturwissenschaft. Germanistische Reihe* (Innsbruck: Obelisk 1995).
4. *Das Lufthaus* (Graz: Styria, 1994). Page numbers in the text refer to this edition. All quotes were translated by me.
5. Elisabeth Wesseling, *Writing History as a Prophet: Post-modernist Innovations of the Historical Novel* (Amsterdam: John Benjamins Publishing Company, 1991), 75. See also Richard Humphrey, *The Historical Novel as Philosophy of History. Three German Contributions: Alexis, Fontane, Döblin* (London: Institute of Germanic Studies, 1986).
6. Wesseling, 193.
7. For an analogous account from a traditional male perspective see Josephine Goldmark, *Pilgrims of '48: One Man's Part in the Austrian Revolution of 1848 and a Family Migration to America* (New Haven: Yale University Press, 1930).
8. The Library of Congress catalogue lists several titles under his name. Maximilian C. Gritzner, *An Wien. Der politische Himmel ist düster, die Luft ist drückend schwül*; and *Gritzner! auch deine Stunde schlägt!*, are both political broadsides from 1848. The latter title is from a right-wing political poster of the time

to which Welsh refers in *Das Lufthaus*, 80. See also Gritzner's later book: *Flüchtlingsleben* (Zürich: Schabelitz, 1867).

9. Gabriella Hauch, *Frau Biedermeier auf den Barrikaden: Frauenleben in der Wiener Revolution 1848* (Vienna: Verlag für Gesellschaftskritik, 1990).

10. Wesseling, 193-194.

11. David Roberts and Philip Thomson, eds. *The Modern German Historical Novel: Paradigms, Problems, Perspectives* (New York: Berg, 1991), 53.

12. *Poetikvorlesungen* (manuscript), 4.

13. Ingeborg Bachmann, *Werke*, ed. Christine Koschel, Inge von Weidenbaum, and Clemens Münster, vol. 3 (Munich: Piper, 1978), 337.

14. For a summary of the discussion, see the entry "The Personal Is the Political," in Cheris Kramarae and Paula A. Treichler, *A Feminist Dictionary* (Boston: Pandora Press, 1985), 333-334.

15. Elaine Showalter, *The Female Malady: Women, Madness, and English Culture, 1830-1980* (New York: Pantheon Books, 1985), 3. See also Phyllis Chesler, *Women and Madness* (Garden City: Doubleday, 1972).

16. Roberts and Thomson, 174.

17. *Die Zeit im Buch* (January 1995): 4.

Barbara Frischmuth's Use of Mythology in Her "Demeter Trilogy"

Pamela S. Saur

Barbara Frischmuth, born in 1941, has produced a spate of children's books, television dramas, and diverse lyrical and narrative works since publishing her popular first novel, *Die Klosterschule (The Convent School*, 1993), in 1968. Although she has shown resistance to the label "feminist," many of her books have focused on women's experiences, choices, and constraints, and some contain specific and pointed protests against oppression of women.

In the late 1970s, Frischmuth published an ambitious and sweeping trilogy of novels, peopled with a gallery of diverse characters and incorporating mythology and fantasy, both original and borrowed, interwoven with stark contemporary realism.[1] The trilogy's contemporary stories were made not only more fanciful and intriguing but more serious and authoritative by the underlying mythology. The trilogy contributed to the literary tradition at that time a validation of women's authentic lives, particularly in the roles of artist and mother. Approximately a decade later, Frischmuth published a second trilogy of novels, also centered on women's lives, which she refers to as her "Demeter trilogy." This trio of books, unlike the earlier one, remains in the world of scientific causality, eschewing fancies such as cloud-travel, spirit and fairy characters, and metamorphosis of souls. Like the first, however, the second trilogy combines a surface realism and contemporaneity with a significant mythological foundation.

An early Homeric hymn tells us the story of Demeter, Goddess of the Corn, who brought barrenness to the earth when her only daughter, Persephone, maiden of spring, disappeared. Finally, the sun told the grieving mother that her daughter had been taken by Hades, king of the underworld, to be his queen. Zeus, Persephone's father and king of gods, tried unsuccessfully to persuade Demeter to return fertility to earth, so he intervened. In the end, Persephone became queen of the underworld, but returned temporarily, and the cycle of her leaving and returning became the cycle of the seasons. Demeter came to be worshiped at Eleusis and the worship is called the Eleusian Mysteries.[2]

Even in this brief sketch, one can appreciate the multivalence and contemporary feminist relevance of the Demeter story. It can serve, in fact, beautifully as a paradigm of female lives, a paradigm anchored and dignified by its association with the fascinating notion of the Eleusian Mysteries which evoke thoughts of female culture, female ceremonies, mysteries, secret property, female religions and deities that elevate women's real and literary lives to a serious, powerful, or even holy level. If Oedipus is the model for the life span of a man, then Demeter functions as the model for a modern woman. Unlike the beautiful Helen or the faithful Penelope, both passive and traditional role models, Demeter has superhuman powers, successfully defies her husband, and is not only active and determined, but aggressive and vengeful. Moreover, her story has two heroines: the daughter and mother, representatives of two generations, who give the story a relationship and a bond. Together the pair represent the youth and maturity of women, and at the same time the cyclical rhythm of the seasons, of life, growth and death that relates to Demeter's power over fertility and sterility.

Like the Oedipus saga, Demeter's story also represents a family drama and triangular rivalry. Its plot represents the movement toward the resolution of the tension created when the daughter breaks away from the mother to join her partner in mature life and form her own family, and is accompanied by temporary conflict between Persephone's mother and father. It is problematic, of course, for modern readers to accept the prototypical founding of the daughter's marriage as a rape or abduction, but as the myths are constantly rewritten, it is perfectly justifiable to assume that she went willingly. Furthermore, a daughter moving away from her mother could choose goals other than marriage; Hades could represent, for example, a lesbian partner; the underworld is any realm other than the parental home. While *any* story of a daughter's maturation and independence fits the Demeter structure, for Frischmuth the myth signifies primarily fertility and control over fertility and sterility, as well as the mother/daughter relationship, separation, and reconciliation under new terms. Frischmuth has drawn a parallel between Oedipus and Demeter, stating, "Quite the opposite of the story of Oedipus, whose status, particularly in the literary realm, has been greatly inflated ever since Freud, the story of Demeter retains its literary freshness and innocence."[3]

Frischmuth's first trilogy centered around Amy and Sophie, a two-person or double protagonist: two women representing two different generations and at the same time different phases of every woman's life.

The interwoven stories of the two women, augmented by a host of varied secondary female characters, serve to suspend time, to counter our society's tendency to devalue and discount older women, and to establish a bond of sisterhood that entails a symbolic if not a literal mother/daughter relationship. In her second trilogy, too, Frischmuth mixes points of view, generations, levels of time, and uses the technique of doubling characters and having them share the status of protagonist.

Often in both trilogies, the female characters' thoughts reveal a desire to find a level of understanding of themselves and of reality that goes beyond the surface of daily life. This tendency is seen in the first sentence of *Herrin der Tiere* (1986; Mistress of Animals), the first volume of the Demeter trilogy: "No one knows what is really true."[4] The protagonist, a stable hand who longs to become a horse trainer, does not dwell in the realm of the analytical and bookish, a realm Frischmuth frequently shies away from, but rather in the rhythmic, fertile, sometimes disgusting or cruel world of animals and crops. Her aspirations and her inner life of dreams and fantasies involve horses. The issues of plant, animal, and human fertility and sterility, as well as alimentation and elimination, are frequently mentioned creating a strong sense of the rhythms of life, procreation, and death that is evocative of the Demeter myth. A superstitious male concern for virility is seen when two men eat the castrated testicles of a horse: "And Bodo and Philipp still believe in the transfer of potency."[5] Frischmuth has linked the protagonist's affinity with horses, which sometimes bears a sexual tinge, with the myth that Demeter took the form of a mare to escape being raped by Poseidon, god of the sea. However, as Paul M. Lützeler points out in an essay on this trilogy, "Not Poseidon the rapist, but a genuine lover appeared then in the form of the agronomist victor."[6] In addition to this romantic sexual encounter in a barn, striking events in the book include another character's suicide attempt. Suicide, like abortion, which is mentioned several times in both trilogies, recalls Demeter's harsh decision to make the earth infertile.

Frischmuth's books show her love of storytelling, fantasy, and adventure, and her characters' enjoyment of the beauties and pleasures of life. At times she seems to be admonishing critics to appreciate her fiction, and perhaps even life itself. After all, her 1991 book of essays on literature, *Traum der Literatur* (Dream of Literature), opens thus, "Where to begin? Maybe with the idea of pleasure..."[7] Nevertheless, *Herrin der Tiere* does present feminist issues. A salient message in the slender book is the harsh fact that the protagonist, however traditionally feminine her affinity for nature's creatures may be, is thwarted in her ambition to become a horse trainer because of her lack of capital and the fact that her chosen career is exclusively male dominated. She makes an individualistic and self-liberating decision to leave her traditional clerical job, even with scant prospects of advancing past stable chores. Resisting her mother's wishes, she later confronts another advocate of conformity to society and expected sex roles: Her boss's sister Else expresses disapproval of her choice of equine society over her chance at her own family. Else warns her, "One day you'll wake up and not be able to bear how ugly you've become...How long do you think you can stand this—living day and night in horse stalls, with no husband, no children, only horses?"[8] The novel, thus, emphasizes unequal opportunities for women. It presents the problem of women facing conflicts between their natures and societal pressures, yet it ends without presenting any real solutions. While the emphasis on inequality in the first volume might seem to set a feminist tone for the trilogy, the overall content of the three books can be read as emphasizing the potential breadth, enjoyment and glory of women's lives.

In writing both trilogies, Frischmuth clearly enjoyed the clever and occasionally startling juxtaposition of realism and mythology/fantasy. In a comment about *Herrin der Tiere*, she points to the divergent impulses she attempted to unite "I cannot remember which stimulus to write came first: the image of a young woman who trades office drudgery for a career with horses, or the image of a contemporary Demeter with the head of a horse..."[9] Frischmuth comments: "Above all, I wanted to keep a thread running through the novel connecting it with Demeter and her daughter Kore, who became Persephone, the Goddess of the Underworld, because this myth lies at the core of this whole novel. However, I didn't want to be too obvious."[10]

The main characters of the second volume, *Über die Verhältnisse* (1987; About Relationships), clearly show parallels to the Demeter myth. Like the ancient story, the novel centers on an archetypal family drama of a triangular relationship: mother-daughter-daughter's suitor. The mother, Mela, is shocked when her twenty-year-old daughter Fro suddenly elopes to Turkey, and believes herself called to retrieve Fro from this strange other world. Also present in Frischmuth's text is a modern Zeus figure, not the king of heaven, but the Austrian head of state. Mela's Hungarian friend Borisch is reminiscent of the mythical figure Botond. Borisch, who accompanies Mela to find her daughter, tries to persuade Mela to derive some enjoyment from their sudden and unexpected journey to Istanbul. The novel is introduced by an epigram, a quotation from Homer, which brings forth the two-sided, and in a sense contradictory nature of ancient Demeter as a modern feminine archetype: she is both traditional in her fervent devotion to her maternal role, and at the same time unfeminine in her rebellion and determination: "But no one could dampen her resentment; she persisted in her anger and scorned every suggestion. Never, she said, would she enter sweet-smelling, high Olympus; never would she allow crops to grow, until she saw her dear daughter again."[11]

Mela, the Demeter figure, like several other women characters in the trilogy, is attuned to nature. She grows up on a farm and studies biology, but dislikes its academic manifestation: "She loved direct contact with ANIMALS and PLANTS more than an academic field from which she couldn't expect anything more than creating and transmitting knowledge, knowledge that might cause trouble in future generations."[12]

The novel traces the relationship of mother and daughter, Mela and Fro. The two women are close and affectionate, although both display a reluctance to discuss their sexuality. Mela's silence about the identity of Fro's father complicates their relationship, yet it allows Fro to fantasize about her origins. In fact, the truth reminds us of a fairy tale since her father is Austria's head of state—a modern-day ruler. When Fro is equally silent about her love affair and marriage, Mela, like Demeter, assumes that her daughter has been abducted by a man or maybe enchanted by a lover and feels that she needs to save her. Just as Demeter must turn to Zeus, Persephone's father, to have her returned from the underworld, Mela demands and receives help from Fro's father in searching for their daughter. In the end, mother and daughter are reconciled. The mother must accept her daughter's marriage and relinquish control of her, just as Demeter modifies the terms of Persephone's marriage to Hades and allows her only temporarily to spend time away from her new home in the underworld. Mela's journey functions as a psychological one, namely to mark and help bring about the mother's release of her daughter and recognition that she is a separate being, not an extension of herself.

Mela is a contemporary woman who has chosen an unconventional but rewarding lifestyle: she chooses to live as a single mother and successfully supports herself and Fro as a restaurant owner. This setting provides her with social relationships that function as a kind of family. She has several lovers over the years, but remains single and independent. Her lifestyle suggests, perhaps, another possibility for successful patterns of life for single women which Frischmuth explored in *Kai und die Liebe zu den Modellen* (1979; Kai and the Love of Models), the third book of her Sophie Silber trilogy. Mela is successful in her role until Fro reaches maturity. Then, her daughter, whom she regards at times as a second self, not only quits the university to opt for marriage, but chooses marriage in a patriarchal society.

Frischmuth invests the Demeter myth with a general psychological meaning. Fro reveals that she regards her journey to Turkey, away from her mother and toward her chosen husband, as representing maturation and independence, movement away from her mother's dominance and toward her own authentic identity. She states, "I will live DIFFERENTLY than SHE does...I am SOMEONE ELSE."[13] Such an identity can be seen, in feminist terms, as a regression from Mela's modern, liberated Western European lifestyle to the role of a wife accommodating herself to a traditional Eastern society. The book indicates, however, that Fro is genuinely in love with her husband, that he is admirable and extremely sensitive, and that her new role in his family has developed her respect and sensitivity for her elders, specifically her husband's grandmother; apparently the reader is to conclude that her decision is right for her. The story can be said to pose a challenge to easy answers feminism might provide. It seems to suggest that feminism cannot establish an ideal of feminine freedom that ignores marriage, the rights of women who choose traditional roles, or the reality of the entrenched customs of all unmodernized, patriarchal cultures.

The third book of Frischmuth's Demeter trilogy, *Einander Kind* (1990; Children to One Another), weaves the stories of several characters together in alternate passages, a technique which effectively evokes the reader's interest and sympathy, enables the reader to see characters from each other's points of view, suspends and blends levels of time, and simultaneously portrays characters at different ages. The novel presents several generations of people whose fates are intertwined with Austrian history, including the history of the Third Reich and its aftermath. Its central concern is less mythological than historical and generational, but, like *Über die Verhältnisse*, it continues to emphasize the issues of human connections to nature, fertility, and sterility, and phases of the female life span.

The novel opens by introducing us to Trude Schwarz, a charmingly hedonistic publisher's bookkeeper near retirement who has created a private Eden by cultivating an urban roof garden. We learn that she was active in the Austrian resistance movement against the Nazis, and her thoughts of her youth comprise one of many points in the book at which time is suspended. She thinks, "Nothing ever comes to a complete stop. She knew it with her whole being. In real life, nothing at all could come to an absolute end."[14] Her efforts at recycling and connection to the plant world are augmented by her associations with death and infertility as well: her witnessing a child dying from a fall, her recollections of losing her husband to World War II and an abortion she underwent fifty years earlier. The decision to have an abortion, which Amy Stern decisively rejected in Frischmuth's earlier trilogy, raises a contemporary women's issue that can also represent Demeter's purposeful embracement of infertility.

A pair of characters of grandmotherly age, Sigune Pröbstl and Vevi Schwarz, the latter Trude's niece, also functions like Demeter and her daughter. They are each other's doubles, in that Sigune works for Vevi, an actor, and is helping produce her autobiography, parts of which come to life within the book. Vevi's recollections are blended with Sigune's recollection of her own youth and the genesis and disintegration of her marriage to a Hungarian refugee of the 1956 revolution, who is now in prison for murdering a woman. Both women struggle to find a sense of identity: Sigune recalls that her mother, rather like Else in *Herrin der Tiere*, admonished her, "You really have a nice face...And a good figure...You need to take full advantage of it."[15] Vevi says of her life story, "My goal was not to glorify myself with this book...But I need to find out who I am."[16] Just as she did more directly in her first trilogy, in which the main characters lived a fairy tale preexistence, Frischmuth again makes use of a mythological foundation to portray her protagonists' struggles with identity and lifestyle choices as serious and not trivial. In literary history, the fates of male characters have always been taken seriously, if not viewed, even without reference to the Oedipus story, as representing the "universally human." Even today, women's fates and lives are easily trivialized. Such trivialization can be countered by reference to powerful mythological females like Demeter.

Discussing her own literary use of mythology in an essay in *Traum der Literatur*, Frischmuth, in 1991, makes this sobering comment, "The word *myth* is dangerous enough: its misuse by the Nazis still makes it suspect even today."[17] In *Einander Kind*, however, Frischmuth (true to her name) dares not only this dangerous practice, but another: she relates her characters' experiences and losses during the Third Reich in a way that humanizes some Nazi characters and evokes sympathy for their wartime losses. For example, she gently satirizes a woman mourning the loss of several sons while putting eggs in a carton. She professes allegiance to the Nazi establishment of "Order," but adds naively, "Order—why does order have to be paid for with so much bloodshed?"[18] Despite the Nazis' own use of mythology for their political, racist and military goals, in the context of *Einander Kind* the Nazi era is a matter of realism. It is in Frischmuth's own autobiography and her generation that the Nazi era and the mother-daughter bond are connected, as she writes in *Traum der Literatur*: "Above all, my generation hasn't wanted to be like our parents, with our soldier fathers and our silent or silently consenting mothers, whether or not they were guilty of anything. But in the end...we aren't so different as those who came before us."[19] In the novel, memories of war and Nazi rule play a major role, and such ineradicable memories are a major impetus for the book's emphasis on the ever-present past.

The creation of motherhood, the fertility of the planet, the processes of life and death, and the cycle of one generation giving way to another are fundamental to human existence, and in a sense this fundament underlies not only this trilogy but all of our human lives and stories. Such a message is one level of significance of the Demeter myth to the Demeter trilogy. A second central message, however, can be found in the title of Frischmuth's third volume, *Einander Kind*. This message adds an intellectual and moral dimension, which goes beyond our roles as archetypal biological agents. Late in the book, Pröbstl decides to ask her husband if he really loved her. She explains: "I want to know if he thinks that he loved me, truly loved me. Or if both of us just stumbled into this marriage, with the expectation that we would be able to act as each other's parents."[20] She goes on to associate the general concept of motherliness with the story of Demeter and Kore, emphasizing their interchangeability, just as the roles of mother and child in the sense of nurturer and nurtured are interchangeable between husband and wife or any caring pair of individuals.

These two messages are prominent in the trilogy, although accompanying complications and contradictions bar a simple, didactic interpretation. The same can be said of the endlessly rich, variegated and often contradictory tapestry of classical mythology. Despite its hoary authority and potential conservative use, it has and has always had an advantageous flexibility, as Frischmuth has pointed out: "The wonderful thing about working with a myth is that myths have no definitive version, no canonized original text. Myths were always around, and whatever version we listen to or consider original, the next mythographer will tell the story differently, or link it with different traditions..."[21] The conflicting authority and flexibility of myth is also emphasized by Paul M. Lützeler, who comments, "Nothing is more at odds with the self-reflexive, self-critical, skeptical, ironic-parodying literature of the postmodern era, than to work on creating new myths or on relegitimizing the old ones."[22] However, he explains Frischmuth's motivation thus, "contemporary interest in myths focuses on reworking old mythologies in new ways, not on validating myths as closed religious systems."[23] Furthermore, the ideas we might extract from the trilogy resist closure, for they are themselves flexible and dynamic. This can be said about the trilogy's messages about cyclical processes of life, about Mela's and Fro's differing lifestyles, and about the notion that everyone acts sometimes as a child and other times as a caretaker. The composite view of human life and relationships that emerges is based on neither hierarchical roles nor absolute moral principles.

To the word "flexible" may be added the word "inclusive" to describe both trilogies, which present two panoramic, sweeping visions of women's lives. Problematic for feminists is the fact that this broad inclusiveness incorporates conservative as well as progressive views. Just as Mela and Demeter accept their daughters' traditional marriages, it seems, most feminists apply a nurturing, accepting "Einander Kind" principle in their interactions with their more traditional foremothers, mothers, sisters and daughters.

Lamar University

Notes

1. Barbara Frischmuth, *Die Mystifikation der Sophie Silber* (Salzburg: Residenz, 1976) (trans. The Mystification of Sophie Silber); *Amy oder die Metamorphose* (Salzburg/Vienna:

Residenz, 1978) (trans. Amy or the Metamorphosis); *Kai und die Liebe zu den Modellen* (Salzburg/Vienna: Residenz, 1979). An interpretation by the present author is Pamela S. Saur, "A Feminist Reading of Barbara Frischmuth's Trilogy," *Modern Austrian Literature* 23. 3/4 (1990): 167-178.

2. This sketch is based on material in Edith Hamilton, *Mythology. Timeless Tales of Gods and Heroes* (New York: Penguin, 1969) and Pierre Grimal, *The Penguin Dictionary of Classical Mythology* (New York: Penguin, 1990).

3. Ibid., 65.

4. Frischmuth, *Herrin der Tiere* (Munich: Deutscher Taschenbuch Verlag, 1990; Salzburg/Vienna: Residenz, 1986), 5. All texts from the Demeter-Trilogy were translated by me.

5. Ibid., 79.

6. Paul Michael Lützeler, "Barbara Frischmuths Demeter-Trilogie: Mythologische Finde-Spiel in der post-modernen Literatur" in *Barbara Frischmuth*, ed. Kurt Bartsch, *Buchreihe über österreichische Autoren*, vol. 4 (Graz/Vienna: Droschl, 1990), 82.

7. Frischmuth, *Traum*, 5.

8. Frischmuth, *Herrin*, 81.

9. Frischmuth, *Traum*, 68.

10. Frischmuth, *Traum*, 25.

11. Frischmuth, *Über die Verhältnisse* (Salzburg/Vienna: Residenz, 1987), epigram, no page number.

12. Frischmuth, *Verhältnisse*, 12-13.

13. Ibid., 223.

14. Frischmuth, *Einander Kind* (Salzburg/Vienna: Residenz, 1990), 15.

15. Ibid., 26.

16. Ibid., 32.

17. Frischmuth, *Traum*, 53.

18. Frischmuth, *Einander*, 60.

19. Frischmuth, *Traum*, 70-71.

20. Frischmuth, *Einander*, 212.

21. Frischmuth, *Traum*, 65.

22. Lützeler, "Finde-Spiel," 76.

23. Ibid., 77.

Anna Mitgutsch's Portrayal of Women: Not Only a Feminist Issue

Gerd K. Schneider

Waltraud Anna Mitgutsch, or Anna Mitgutsch, as she calls herself now, writes about women and their fates. This has led feminists to claim her as one of their own, but Mitgutsch rejects this categorization: "I resist the term women's literature which to me means ghetto-ization...also in the sense...that my women do not follow the ideological guidelines of feminism."[1] Mitgutsch states in the same interview that women have been oppressed for a long time and that the time has come for them to attain their self-identity. This process, however, is only possible through the effort of many generations:

> One cannot change, crush, alter anything in a short time, one can only continue to proceed towards a goal, and all of my heroines are on their way, and they are on their way up, not down. But I just deny them the sparkling results, the sparkling attainment of a goal. And most of the time I let my women stand in the rain at the end.[2]

Changes do not occur fast; one has to work continuously at them. The coming of a new liberated woman means first that attitudes have to change, perspectives which have prevailed for generations. This applies not only to feminist issues but also to other ideological concerns as well. Mitgutsch's work explores how women are on their way to gain their self-identity and how the value system of society changes, especially political credos. These individual and societal processes are analyzed diachronically, extending from the present back into the Hitler era and the pre-Hitler epoch. Nineteen forty-five is not a zero hour to her. The present emerges from the past and if we do not reflect on the past, the same or similar attitudes will continue to hold sway. The link between present and past can be seen in almost every novel Anna Mitgutsch has written.

Mitgutsch's first novel, published in 1985 entitled *Die Züchtigung* (*Three Daughters*, 1987),[3] begins with the following question:

> "Was your mother like you?" my twelve-year-old daughter
> asks, leaning against the bathroom door and watching me
> comb my hair. The question jumps at me out of many years of
> silence. I let my parted hair fall over my eyes. "No," I say,
> "no, your grandmother was completely different." "Different in
> what way?" "Think of the opposite." She hesitates, looks at
> me quizzically. How can she imagine the opposite, when I am
> a mystery to her? A mystery and yet something she takes for
> granted. Like my mother to me, even now. (Z 1-2)

Just how different the girl's grandmother was becomes apparent in this
family saga which spans three generations: grandmother, mother, and
daughter. The grandmother, born and raised at the turn of the century in
Austria, close to the Czechoslovakian border, lived in a patriarchal
society, in which she was considered a "thing" by a father who hardly
spoke to her for years and by her husband to whom she was primarily a
sex object. Within eight years she gave birth to seven children. Marie
was one of the offspring of this unhappy relationship. Her wish to
become a teacher ran counter to the demand of her father who considered
the fourteen-year-old as cheap labor. What is worse is that she had no
hope for a better future:

> Milking, mowing grass, having cream soup with pieces of
> bread in it for breakfast, turning hay, cleaning out the manure,
> taking it to the manure pile, having cooked pork with
> dumplings and carrots for lunch, feeding the livestock, carrying
> wood, pitching hay into the wagon and unloading it in the hot,
> sticky barn, milking, separating the milk and lugging the pails
> to the village stand, having bacon, cottage cheese, and bread
> with cream soup for supper—this was to be her life, day after
> day, from now on until a man would take her away to another
> farm and the same thing would start all over under the thumb
> of her mother-in-law. She didn't want to marry; she was
> repelled by men, repelled by what the adults did secretly in the
> haylofts, between the rows of potatoes, and in bed, and she
> didn't want to know about it or ever have anything to do with
> it. (Z 21)

Marie, however, could not escape her fate: She married a day-laborer named Friedel, who was too weak to give her a life of "wealth and recognition." She loathed sex but accepted her husband's cohabitations dutifully. Pregnant against her wish, she hoped that the child would be a son:

> Her child would help her escape from the misery of marriage, of her whole life. Her child, a son, would not only be her comfort and support and give her the love she had hungered for for twenty-five years; he would also take her out of her present life into a life of wealth and recognition. He would achieve things she couldn't achieve even in her dreams; she would harness all her strength for this; she would sacrifice her own life for him and he would reward her royally. Through him she would make it after all. (Z 65)

However, she gave birth not to a son, but "only" to a daughter who, nevertheless, was burdened with her mother's unfulfilled dreams. Vera, as this unwanted child was called, had to excel at any cost, at anything she undertook at school and at home. She was subjected to daily heavy beating, primarily by her mother, and the instrument of torture was a carpet-beater, "a fat, curved rubber sausage, wound around with an iron spiral, an instrument of torture" (Z 4). Reasons for this severe punishment were manifold: "[A]nswering a command with *no* or *why*, coming home from school half an hour late, giggling with other kids in church, writing below the line in penmanship and mixing up 'f' and 'k,' getting a reprimand from a teacher or a C grade" (Z 5). The result is, as Vera later on recorded, that she became the most well-behaved child in the family. This daily disciplinary castigation was invisible to the outside world; among the neighbors the mother was considered a respectable member of the community who sacrificed her whole life for the upbringing of her child.

Although Vera's physical punishment stopped when she reached fourteen, the psychological damage was irreversible. Vera has no self-identity; she is at every moment the person people expect her to be, as is evident later on in her many love affairs:

> Who do you want me to be, I ask my lovers and disappear into the roles they like best. I am Ophelia, Desdemona, or Lulu, according to their wishes. I extinguish myself in my battle for

love, and desperate, step out of my role, get stuck, can't go on, am chased off the stage, a bad actress. No matter how willing, how obedient I am, I always lose the battle, because behind the roles I am starving and want applause for myself, not for Lulu, Desdemona, or Ophelia. (Z 156)

She focuses on self-destruction and feels unworthy of love, undeserving of attention: "Self-destruction was the title of my research project; suicide in literature, through literature; regression, loss of self; overstepping and avoiding the boundaries of the self" (Z 156). Vera is used to being put down and tells her psychiatrist:

No, Dr. Shrink, I am not a masochist, I really don't enjoy being tortured, but I know I have to be punished because I am a bad person and unworthy of love. When you beat me, I know there is order in the world: no one can be trusted and I can stop suffering the pains of love; I can kick you in the teeth because your evident pleasure in torturing me incriminates you. Therefore I change mothers and lovers like shirts, and in the end they all have the same face in my disappointments from which I rise laughing with pain because I never expected anything else. (Z 99-100)

This oppression seems to continue in Vera's relationship with her own daughter, the same daughter who had asked about her grandmother at the beginning of this novel. After her divorce, Vera brings up her daughter by herself and, although she has refrained from beating her, the wish to do so is still there:

No, I have never beaten her, but I presented her with an unrestrained show of pain and rage and tears, of banging my head against the wall of fate, and I realized much too late that I was destroying her capacity for happiness...I never beat you, child, but the day I shook you in front of the stone wall, mute in my fury, there was such a little space between you and the wall. I knew then that I was capable of pushing your head against that wall and, horrified, I let go...I did not succeed in breaking the chain. Here, too, I have remained my mother's daughter. (Z 136)

These individual psychographs of the grandmother, mother, and daughter form the surface of this generational novel, *Die Züchtigung*. Mitgutsch has created a novel about women who set out to seek their own self-identity, but who go through painful psychological degradation before they free themselves of the demands and expectations society casts on them. In addition, Mitgutsch shows clearly what happens when these children, socialized through physical punishment, reach maturity. Brought up not to ask questions and trained to obey authority, the youngsters raised in such an educational system become true believers in a society which expects blind obedience, as was the case during the Hitler era and the pre-Hitler epoch.

This is where Mitgutsch's social and political criticism is centered. The men in this agrarian community are too weak and fearful to resist the change from the Republic to the *Anschluß*, or the annexation of Austria by Germany in 1938. Only the priest and the professor dare to oppose, and after their arrest by the SS, everyone was relieved, including Marie, "since for once it wasn't her head on the block. This time it was someone else's turn, perhaps everyone's turn would come, but if you crawled into the woodwork and attracted no attention, other people's turns would come first for a change" (Z 28). Marie agrees with everything, because she is raised in the belief that politics is a subject for men only. Neither she nor anyone else inquired about the fate of the two "village idiots" who were "put away" by the SS after the *Anschluß*. No one raised objections when the first letters arrived, drafting young men. Soon letters followed informing families that their sons or fathers had died on the battlefield. Everyone was silent, because questioning authority had not been a part of their upbringing. After Stalingrad, when everyone knew that the war was lost, everyone kept quiet: "'Shut up or you'll end up in a concentration camp': this fear had reached into the villages, too. And you cupped your hands in front of your mouth when you mentioned the Gestapo and the fact that they had been picking up people in the middle of the night again" (Z 37). After the war, when the inmates from the concentration camps came to the village and informed the people of the atrocities that had been committed there, invisible to the outside world, the villagers were surprised. But even these revelations did not lead to reflection: "But none of them was really affected by the war, neither my mother, who did not wish to remember her joyless girlhood, nor Aunt Rosi, who could not understand how the concentration camp inmates could suddenly be running around free" (Z 43). Even later they still did not understand what happened and why it happened or even their own role in these events. The eyes of those being asked about this turned away and the recurring reply was: "We did not know what took place." Here Mitgutsch's unmitigated criticism of her fellow Austrians is unveiled. When Vera began to ask about the past, "their mouths hardened and they looked away: 'we didn't know anything, we didn't do anything, we couldn't stop them, we only followed orders, because we weren't dreamers like you, idealists, ideologues, we were just plain flesh-and-blood human beings'" (Z 47). This denial of having been involved occurs frequently in this novel, as for instance in the following passage:

> Didn't you say, Shut up or you'll end up in a concentration camp when someone said that the war was lost; didn't you live in constant fear of being denounced? People who weren't there shouldn't talk about it, you say, giving us a stern, disapproving look. But I've seen photographs of the Hitler Youth girls; I recognized my aunts in them—photographs, you understand, evidence. The three-cornered neckerchiefs, the figures in formation, the raised right hand, the evening meeting at which they sang patriotic German songs—there are pictures of that, too. (Z 44)

The "raised right hand" in the above context indicates an approval of the Nazi ideology, even if some, undoubtedly, joined in the salute out of fear for their own life.

Mitgutsch is especially critical of the role that women played. Until recently, the question was heard: "And what was your part in the war?" with the *you* referring strictly to men. Here this question is asked, too, but equally important is the new question: "And what did you do *before* the war?," and this inquiry is primarily directed to the women whose task it was to raise the children. The mentality which led to the Third Reich did not evolve overnight; it was prepared through many generations and women lent a helping hand—holding a whip. The result was, as Mitgutsch repeatedly states, that people only followed orders, even if these orders violated everything that was humanly decent. Mitgutsch attributes the responsibility for the catastrophe of the Hitler era not only to the political activists, but also to the ones who stood passively by and let things happen because they were taught not to question authority. The devastating aspect of using physical brutality to raise a child is that, after a while, one can stop inflicting physical punishment but the power of assertion of the developing child has been destroyed. As Mitgutsch clearly shows at the end of her novel, the "self" of Vera is not herself but the "self" of her mother:

> She is everything that is outside, night and the sun, sleep and the rain, love and hate and every person who crosses and darkens my life, and most of all myself. She has transformed herself into me; she created me and slipped inside me; when I died sixteen years ago, when she beat me to death thirty years ago, she took my body, appropriated my ideas, usurped my feelings. She rules and I serve her, and when I gather all my courage and offer resistance she always wins, in the name of obedience, reason, and fear. (Z 216)

At the end of the novel, Vera seems to be able to free herself because she takes time to reflect. She realizes what happened and she asks questions, raising the hope that this authoritarian method of child raising, honored by past societies, will end. Although attitudes are hard to change, Mitgutsch leaves us with the hope that the following generations will educate their children more democratically, preparing them to be politically more responsible adults.

Hope for a new beginning is also the subject of Mitgutsch's second novel, *Das andere Gesicht* (1986; The Other Face).[4] There are two protagonists, Jana and Sonja, who are attracted to each other because of their differences: Jana comes from Eastern Europe, suffers from depression, leans toward reflection and meditation, has difficulty communicating with others, and lives in a dream world into which others can hardly follow her; she is a stranger and is considered abnormal. Sonja, on the other hand, is guided by reason, apparently knows exactly what she is doing, is well-liked, and lives in the real world. Both women narrate their own stories, sometimes referring to the same situation, but from different perspectives. After an unhappy marriage, the loss of her only child in Indonesia, and a suicide attempt, Jana finds refuge with Leah, an empathetic tourist. At the end, Sonja intends to visit her, and Mitgutsch leaves the reader with the slim hope that Jana has found a home where she can be happy.

The central theme of this novel is the feeling of estrangement. Jana is a foreigner on Austrian soil whose looks show that she is not born there: her exotic features and her long black hair give her the appearance of a "rare animal." Jana feels unwanted, unappreciated and misunderstood in this rural community, and the only friend she has is Sonja who protects her and with whom she shares her longing to visit far away places. But no place is tempting enough to make Jana want to stay there; when once asked by Sonja "of which place would you say, here I am at home" (G 173). Strangeness also characterizes the relationship between these two different women, or as Sonja remarks: "We remained strangers even then when I had believed to be very close to her" (G 173). Jana seems to be incapable of integrating with her surroundings; she does not have a feeling of belonging, no matter where she is:

> Once upon a time there was someone who was condemned to see something which she never found. This is the way my story began. But what actually was it that she was seeking? A conception of home, maybe the place of her early childhood or security, the sense of safety and belonging to a group. She apparently did not enjoy always remaining apart and looking on, although it was she herself who excluded herself...Why had she been on a flight from country to country for ten years with, literally speaking, a restlessness that was wearing her down? Did she want unequivocally to make visible the condition of her strangeness which surrounded her in the familiar and excluded her, did she finally look for a reason of her strangeness? Or did she believe that she would find the place somewhere, to stumble by accident upon the place where she felt safe? (G 312-313)

This novel can be interpreted on the psycho-pathological plane as the story of a young woman who feels insecure, and who does not fit into society. She is depressed and panics when left alone. She wants contact with others but because of her differences is ostracized. This also affects her ability to communicate verbally:

> The more I retreated, the further away were the others, the more incomprehensible became their language to me, the more absurd was every word which they directed toward me. Beyond the border, in my realm, one spoke another language, that

which was absolute truth for others had no value here, and nobody found out about my laws. Here I wanted to stay, forever. But I had to make daily trips across the border, and it became more dangerous every time because I often could not recall the password. I had become a stateless person because in my country no passports were issued, and on the other side over there one did not like strangers. (G 73-74)

Jana experiences again and again the extent to which strangers are barred from the community held together by their *Heimatgefühl*, or common bond of belonging to the land: "I had proof, the school bag in the garbage pail, the stinging nettle on my naked upper thigh, the trampled down flute, the cuss words ringing in my ears even in my dreams" (G 74). It also does not help that she, contrary to her sister, looks foreign: "My face they defined by the landscape from which I came, and they said that my aversions and preferences had to do with my ancestors" (G 76). To others she is *Das andere Gesicht* or the other face, a face that does not belong here and will not be accepted.

Interpreted on the psycho-mythical plane, the story points to the conclusion that Jana and Sonja are two sides of one existence. There is a mutual feeling of attraction, since Jana feels alone without Sonja and Sonja without Jana. Sonja, at the end, visits her alter ego:

> I am journeying to her in the hope that it is possible to annul the strangeness, to comprehend her life which has touched me always, even though I could not understand it. I hope to change the separating silence into another silence if it has to be, into a silence that is inclusive and communicative. Sometimes it appears to me that she and I had by mistake received only one life and never learned to share with each other. If one was happy, the other one got nothing, and while one had something, the other one felt cheated. It always seemed advisable to separate, but even then we did not win anything. (G 5-6)

At the end, Sonja has the vision of merging with Jana. In a dream she looks into an old mirror. She cleans away the patina of centuries "and my face appeared, dark, mysterious, and at the same time Jana's although we are hardly similar. I recoiled. I approached again, disbelieving, but indeed, it was my own reflection. When I woke up, I was very happy" (G 331). This new person is made up of Jana and Sonja, a unity also indicated in their names: *Jana-Sonja.* Sonja now accepts her other strange half which she had suppressed in her earlier life because it had interfered with her plans and lifestyle, but Mitgutsch leaves open how well she is able to live with her alter ego.

The topic of being a stranger in a close-knit society is continued in Mitgutsch's third novel *Ausgrenzung* (1989; *Jakob*, 1991).[5] A better English title would have been *Ostracism*, because this is exactly what happens to the boy and his mother in this novel. Jakob is a child with autistic symptoms which interfere with his ability to function normally in society. Jakob's mother, Marta, is married to Felix, a rich upstart, whose egotism and mental brutality makes married life hell for Marta and her son. After a separation from Felix, Marta tries to normalize her life by taking a job as well as by dedicating her life to the upbringing of her son.

First she has to overcome the feeling of guilt which is put on her by the psychologists and members of her husband's family. It is she who is held responsible for her son's ailment and everyone tries very hard to convince her of this. When Marta visits a psychiatrist looking for help and affirmation that her son is not autistic she again is expected to assume her guilt:

> She would do anything to help her child, she would find connections where there were none, find answers even if they made no sense to her…Again and again, in more therapists' offices than she could count, in the hospitals and clinics to which she had taken her son—taken him with renewed anguish and renewed hope—they had pointed to her own childhood, argued her blame, until she was ready to accept that blame, the guilt for things she had never done. (J 1-2)

She is not helped in these trying times by her husband, who is primarily interested in his studies and a subsequent career change. He refuses to assist her at home, and as justification for his behavior he tells the story of a friend of his:

> This friend went to Felix's school and was burdened by a wife and a small child. Suddenly the wife took it into her head to

become a feminist, went out to meetings every evening, and left him stuck at home with the baby. The wife went out more and more often, on account of all this women's liberation nonsense, until finally the husband failed his exams and flunked out. The lesson Felix intended by the parable was clear. No one needed to put it into words. (J 13)

Later on, when Jakob turned four and the hope that he would ever become normal dwindled, the two spouses grew more estranged:

In the first weeks following the diagnosis, Felix spoke to Marta only in short commands, as if every word he addressed to her was an effort. He kicked at her at night, often driving her out of bed. Every animal can give its young what they need to survive, he stormed, but not you! She was an idiot, stupid. So unbelievably stupid, it hurt to watch her, he would say in disgust, as she sat on the floor with Jakob trying to get him to play, or at least take some notice of her...Bitch,[6] he would say, jostling Marta as he passed. He never called her by name anymore, just bitch. (J 44-45)

Felix had been raised in the old-fashioned tradition that the place of a wife is at home, and her primary task is to raise her children. Marta does not fit the mold; she has a degree in biology and is set on a career which would give her not only economic independence but also psychological satisfaction. Her husband's family considers her an intellectual and the hatred against intellectuals is evident even before her marriage: "One cousin, seated diagonally across the dinner table, kept dwelling on intellectuals and told one anecdote after another about various scandals for which an egghead was always to blame. And now they were addressing her as doctor and bowing sarcastically" (J 20). Felix's mother advises Marta to employ a baby nurse prior to the birth, but by no means an intellectual: "Not a brain like you, she said, a simple woman with strong maternal instincts" (J 25). Intellectuals do not, so these people believe, possess heart, feeling, or compassion. These stereotypes, reminiscent of the Jewish stereotypes in the Third Reich, are also shared by the physicians she consults. One female physician concludes her report with "[t]he mother is emotionally impoverished and overly intellectual" (J 50). Here the coordinating conjunction *and* seems to be used in the meaning of the causal conjunction *because*, since "[m]others of autistic children, the professional literature said, often were highly intelligent sociopaths" (J 50). This proves, according to medical opinion, that Marta is indirectly guilty of her son's autism. She has to go through therapy because autism is a "severe disturbance in the relationship between mother and child..." (J 98).

As the relationship between Marta and her son improves, her son's relationship to his peers grows worse. The children do not want to play with Jakob, and they also are forbidden by their parents to do so. Jakob tries everything in his power to be part of their group:

> He was so willing. His face, his whole body a cry of longing. Marta stood at the window hardly able to bear the sight, she wanted to run out and promise the children anything if only they would include Jakob. "Play with the children," cried Jakob, stepping in front of an oncoming bicycle. The boy on the bike managed to brake in time and shouted, "Jakob, don't run into me like that, you jerk!" (J 109)

Passive ostracism soon turns into active aggression. The children begin to mistreat Jakob; "[t]hey were hiding behind an evergreen hedge and throwing horse chestnuts and acorns at him. Jakob saw the flying pellets, they hit his body, his head, but he couldn't find the children. Weeping with anger, Marta went out and brought him inside. And Jakob had understood" (J 110); he had understood that he was not wanted, not by the children and also not by their parents. Statements like the following are indicative of the attitudes behind the actions: "If we had known there was a handicapped child in the neighborhood, we wouldn't have moved here, one mother told her curtly" (J 110). The only advice Marta gets from the parents is to beat Jakob: "As the boy grew bigger, people paused more often to shake their heads in disgust and, ignoring the mother's embarrassment, would threaten the squalling child or turn on Marta. 'What's the matter with him, what he needs is a good spanking'" (J 46). Beating inculcates discipline, Marta was told, and in order to bring up a child one has to resort to physical punishment, which Marta loathes and which Mitgutsch claims can lead to political consequences, as *Die Züchtigung* showed.

The social criticism of this novel is primarily directed against all those who hold attitudes not allowing the integration of children like Jakob, or anyone who does not conform to the norm. This includes, as Mitgutsch shows, euthanasia, as practiced in the Third Reich, the treatment of Jews and the appropriation of their property. It seems that the nightmarish experiences of the past repeat themselves again since Marta receives threatening telephone calls, the tires of her car are slashed and the telephone line is cut. At the end, Marta succeeds in becoming independent but the price she has to pay for this is social isolation for herself and her son. The attitude of not accepting strangers in a close-knit community is hard to change; learning to accept others for themselves will probably take generations.

In Mitgutsch's fourth novel, *In fremden Städten* (1992; *In Foreign Cities*, 1995),[7] the Boston-born protagonist Lillian goes to Austria as an exchange student, where she meets her future husband, Josef. She spends fifteen years with him in Innsbruck. Her two children are integrated in Austrian society but her husband's family continues to consider her an outsider, a stranger, and a foreigner. After an affair with an American singer whom she meets in Innsbruck, she decides to leave her family and return home to Boston. She visits her sister and then her father on Cape Cod, who had hopes of becoming a writer but now turns out advertising slogans instead. Lillian sees his hopelessness and in a moment of mental breakdown sets fire to her father's house. It is not quite clear if he finds death in the flames and whether she commits suicide or surrenders to the police.

It would be too easy to explain Lillian's behavior as psychotic. Lillian is a person who does not feel at home, either in Innsbruck or in the United States. She expects too much and is always disappointed because reality can never reach the perfection of her fantasy. She is restless and travels from one foreign land to another, as one critic remarked.[8] She is a romantic being who stands between places and is unable to grow roots.

In addition, her problems become more acute because of the language barrier. Words for Lillian are more than entries in dictionaries. They carry meaning that is connected with her experiences, her past. A translation is always incomplete. For instance, the English word *rain* means to her something quite different from the German translation *Regen*, because she associates *rain* with the coast in the United States, vaporized salt, youth, etc. Giving up one's native language can be like giving up a substantial part of one's past and, ultimately, one's identity, which—as in Lillian's case—could be fatal.

Dvorah, the heroine of Mitgutsch's last novel, *Abschied von Jerusalem* (1995; *Lovers and Traitors*, forthcoming in 1997),[9] is also trying to find a place where she can grow roots. Because she is partly Jewish and spent some time in Israel twenty years ago, she returns hoping to make this country her *Heimat*, or homeland. Finding a home would provide her with a new identity. She states two reasons for doing so: "It was the turning back which my grandmother was no longer capable of, and it was the return to something inexplicably familiar as if there were a blocked remembrance, even if the clear images and words were missing" (AJ 151). Her grandmother had lost all Jewishness since she had to live in a Chrisitian world, and the result was that she had lost her own identity in the process. The other reason for Dvorah's return is more difficult to explain—it seems to be an inner force operating on the subliminal level which fills her with the desire to go back to Jerusalem.

During the first week in Israel, she meets an Armenian, Sivan, who is twenty years younger than she and who becomes her lover. She grows ashamed because of their age difference and their affair. When in the Arab part of Jerusalem, she sees the following graffiti: "There my shame is on the walls, glaring and obscene. I even found a young man who translated it for me. 'We fuck your women' is written there as unsurpassed humiliation of the enemy" (AJ 11). In a flashback she surmises that their getting together was not by chance but planned: "And he, a bait for female tourists with the right passports, a professional feeder, a pimp with a political order, he saw at once that he would have an easy game with me, provided that he complied with my desire for a romantic return of my youth" (AJ 59).

In this atmosphere of hate, it is difficult to imagine that Jews and Arabs are rooted in the same soil. One Arab merchant explains the situation as follows:

> We are similar to each other, the Jews and we...only no one wants to see it. If a Frenchman emigrates to America, he will become American in ten years, the same is true for Germans, for almost every nation. But we, Jews and Palestinians, have our roots here and we cannot tear them out and transplant them elsewhere, and it does not matter how much time passes, we are unable to exist somewhere else, we would die. And if we

have to live in the diaspora, we are here with our thoughts and with our entire desire, in Jerusalem. (AJ 110)

To show that having common roots does not preclude the development of hostile attitudes, Mitgutsch includes a simile which is reminiscent of Lessing's famous ring-parable, only that in her novel it has turned into the reverse: "Directly in front of me a blooming climber suffocated a cedar, one could hardly see anything more of it. Both were growing out of the synagogue's ruins, or maybe it had been at one time a mosque or a church. The only remains of it were the lancet windows" (AJ 111).

Mitgutsch does not write only about the political problems of the Middle East, but also includes in her novel observations about her homeland Austria, present and past. Mentioned also are the deportation of Jews from Vienna in 1941 and the pro-Nazi attitudes of Dvorah's hometown inhabitants. The story of a Bavarian immigrant woman who is looking for a nanny demonstrates that these attitudes have not changed much. Dvorah applies for this job and one day she sees the woman looking at a photo showing a relative, maybe her father, in an "SS-uniform with the usual smooth face, a large size photo, an armband, insignia of rank, medals" (AJ 177). It seems that this war-bride cannot shake her past just as in the case of the German teacher who tells one of his pupils named Edelstein: "You surely have Jewish ancestors. It was years after the war, but I felt the threat, and she also reacted at once with bewildered defense, no, I am Catholic, my grandfather only bought the name" (AJ 116). Soon Dvorah finds out that the whole city has a Nazi past which it tries to hide unsuccessfully:

> Soon I saw them in the entire city, the faces, the names which had meaning in the documents, and I did no longer put aside the mistrust which I had even begun to harbor against myself. I looked into their eyes: What do you think today, where were you in the past, what do you have on your conscience? Not even of my father do I know this, he remained silent, and I was not close enough to him and never had the courage to insist on an answer. (AJ 122-123)

This incident is once again reminiscent of Mitgutsch's belief: Radical change does not and cannot occur in a short time. This applies not only to women seeking their self-identity after a long period of oppression, but to political attitudes as well. The Nazi ideology when ingrained deeply in people's minds and hearts may take generations to change.

Will women reach the goal they seek? Mitgutsch does not tell her readers, but doubts arise if Dvorah's fate is considered. Dvorah discovers in the end that her lover Sivan is an "activist" or terrorist who is killed by the Israelis during an attack. She is detained by the Jewish security guards and questioned about her relationship with him. Thus, Mitgutsch's Dvorah is a woman who set out to look for a place to settle, a place where she could breathe freely and where people would be accepted on the basis of who they are. This place she has not yet found.

Syracuse University

Notes

1. Maria-Regina Kecht, "Gespräch mit Waltraud Anna Mitgutsch," *Women in German Yearbook 8. Feminist Studies in German Literature and Culture*, ed. Jeanette Clausen and Sara Friedrichsmeyer (Lincoln: University of Nebraska Press, 1993), 133. All translations were made by me.
2. Ibid., 134.
3. Waltraud Anna Mitgutsch, *Three Daughters*, trans. Lisel Mueller (San Diego/New York/London: Harcourt Brace Jovanovich, 1987); German title: *Die Züchtigung* (Düsseldorf: Claasen, 1985). Subsequent references to this text will be marked with Z and the page number. All quotes from Mitgutsch's texts were translated by me.
4. Mitgutsch, *Das andere Gesicht* (Düsseldorf: Claasen, 1986). Subsequent references to this text will be marked with G and the page number. All translations of this text are mine.
5. Mitgutsch, *Jakob*, trans. Deborah Schneider (New York/ San Diego/London: Harcourt Brace Jovanovich, 1991); German title *Ausgrenzung* (Frankfurt: Luchterhand, 1989). Subsequent references to this text will be marked with J and the page number.
6. Mitgutsch uses here the German term *Fotze* (cunt) which is stronger than *bitch*.
7. Mitgutsch, *In fremden Städten* (Vienna: Buchgemeinschaft

Donauland Kremayr & Scheriau, 1992).

8. Karl-Markus Gauss, "Heimkehr in die Fremde. Der vierte Roman von Waltraud Anna Mitgutsch," *Literatur und Kritik* 27 (June 1992): 90.

9. Mitgutsch, *Abschied von Jerusalem* (Reinbek: Rowohlt, 1995). Subsequent references to this text will be marked with AJ and the page number. All translations of this text are mine.

The Possibilities and Limitations of Language: Elisabeth Reichart's *Fotze*

Linda DeMeritt

Secondary literature focuses almost exclusively on the historical background of Elisabeth Reichart's oeuvre and on its significance for contemporary Austrian political reality. Reichart's first novel, *Februarschatten* (1984; *February Shadows*, 1989), is based on the so-called *Mühlviertler Hasenjagd* (The Rabbit Hunt of the Mühlviertel), during which Soviet prisoners of war escaped only to be murdered by the National Socialists aided by local inhabitants. Reichart was heralded as one of a growing number of young Austrian authors whose books revisited the question of Austrian victimization by, as opposed to collaboration with, Nazis during World War II. The novel was seen as evidence of increasing willingness among writers to confront the political past and present of Austria.[1] In Reichart's subsequent novel, *Komm über den See* (1988; Come Across the Lake), a young woman slowly approaches a past circumscribed by the loyalties and betrayals among women resistance fighters. This novel, published on the anniversary of the annexation of Austria and two years after the election of Kurt Waldheim as President, was viewed as a critical mirror of Austrian society. Critics concentrated on its portrayal of contemporary Fascist tendencies, resurfacing now because of past repression.[2]

In an interview with Christina Schweighofer, Reichart identifies the motivation behind her first two novels: she felt compelled by a sense of personal responsibility and duty to give voice to the real victims of Fascism, in particular to the women whose (her) stories have been largely excluded from public dialogue to date.[3] Juliet Wigmore points out the importance of making the content of these personal lives public. Works such as Reichart's challenge historical accounts which exclude women or relegate them to a traditional role in the home.[4] Just as important, however, as Reichart's stories themselves, is the telling of those stories. In giving voice to her female characters, Reichart consistently thematizes the possibilities and limitations of language. *Februarschatten* documents a conflict between competing and opposing words: "forget" from Hilde's past versus the words of her daughter urging her to remember—silence versus language. The protagonist in

Komm über den See, a gifted translator who realizes that her talent extends only to others' words, embarks upon an existentially threatening journey in order to find a language of her own. And Reichart's most recent work, *Sakkorausch* (1994; Foreign), is replete with unmarked quotes by its "coauthor," the historical Helene von Druskowitz, thereby questioning the very notion that language can be original or express the individual.

A perspective focusing solely on historical content is particularly problematic for Reichart's work of 1993, *Fotze*.[5] The generally favorable reception that welcomed her first two novels is muted or even silenced here. While the sexual topic, anticipated in the provocative title, undoubtedly accounts in part for this lukewarm to nonexistent critical reaction, complaints are also raised repeatedly about the work's lack of realism. Klaus Bellin's review is typical of the puzzled reaction to *Fotze*: he is disturbed by the many unanswered questions concerning plot and by the lack of concrete details that would define the narrator.[6] Even commentators favorably disposed to the text point out the absence of a realistic level and admit the difficulty of determining the storyline; at times they present inaccurate assumptions and at other times apparently simply throw their hands into the air with resigned bafflement: "Everything is possible."[7] While many critics praise Reichart's language, none investigate it with seriousness. Yet the work documents, in both its content and form, the search for a personal as opposed to public discourse, a feminine as opposed to masculine voice.

The concrete event that induced Reichart to write *Fotze* was the war in Yugoslavia (108), or, more specifically, the rape and brutality against women committed daily in the name of that war. The narrator inhabits a similarly war-torn landscape, its suppression of women reflected and perpetrated mainly through language. The narrator, who is a writer, explores the relationship between language, sexuality, and violence. She experiences both first-hand the effect of this language of domination and seeks an alternative.

The opening pages of the work focus on a relationship between the narrator and a man she calls her lover "with calloused hands." This man gives her a word—"Fotze"—for her previously unnamed sexuality, thereby allowing her to rediscover her sensuality. Reichart's description of the relationship emphasizes the senses: smelling, seeing, touching, and hearing. This is the importance of the man's calloused hands, for they scratch the narrator's skin and emit a distinctive odor. He presents to the narrator a word for smells: "word smell." However, the author's neologism is ambiguous: it expresses oneness between the head ("word") and the body ("smell"), but also foreshadows the eventual subordination of the senses to language, their annihilation through the power of abstract thinking. The calloused hands of the lover become soft and lose their smell. As the word replaces the senses the union of head and body is revealed as illusory, prompting the narrator to relabel her lover "word addict," obsessed with "word power." She realizes that the language granted her is not hers, but his, and that therefore these words do not provide access to the experience of her body, but rather supersede that experience. Only words remain: "...in my desire to embody his words, I disembodied myself, without noticing / land of words / no land in sight, only this map..." (38).

Throughout her text, Reichart shows how contemporary language prohibits unmediated experience of reality. For Reichart, language is defined as any picture, concept, or symbol that has become so naturalized that it reduces or prevents our ability to perceive its artificiality, let alone challenge its authority.[8] In today's society, language has become an inflexible system of signs disconnected from the person. The author criticizes the language of technology as empty phrases incapable of communication: "Air charged with electrical current, daily more current, daily more cordless telephones, bodies sleepwalking among networks and magnetic fields, word endings cut off and word beginnings swallowed, language in decline, replaced more and more by its transmission devices" (58). The narrator's girlfriend, who approaches the smells of life armed with perfume bottles, who collects hundreds of pornographic videos but never climaxes, typifies a society severed from its physical reality by the proliferation of words emptied of personal meaning. This society values its pictures and preconceptions as a means to silence individual questions or alternatives, thereby guaranteeing the efficient perpetuation of the system. The ever-increasing accumulation and slippery meanings of public discourse find metaphoric representation in the "slime" which is deepening around the narrator, threatening her with suffocation.

To escape, the narrator must render language personally meaningful. She locks her lover's words in a closet, throws the key away, and sits down at her writing table. In the ensuing silence ("wordless trust," 34), she returns to her memory of a bunker wall painted with the word "Fotze." Her childhood experience represents her initial encounter with the word, and by recalling the experience, she strives to reclaim the word from her lover. For Reichart, the search for language is simultaneously a search for personal memory, sexuality, and identity. Her narrator is involved in a quest to determine personal meaning prior to societal definition. She rejects the words and wars of contemporary male-dominated society and endeavors to return to an earlier time and place marked by the language and cooperation of her grandmother, mother, and sisters.

The narrator's attempted pathway of escape transports her from the fifth family house back in time to the first. Each of the five houses in the text designates a different period of Austria's past and present. The fifth house, built in the middle of a nettle patch with materials left over from concentration camps (31), clearly represents the continuing state of war in postwar Austria. The first house, with its yellow color (46), alludes to the Austrian Habsburg monarchy.[9] It depicts a type of idealized society in which various peoples can live together harmoniously, peacefully, and with their diversity preserved: "...just look at this Schönbrunn-yellow and all these countries and the splendor of these colors..." (52). As the only house with a basement and nestled among other houses, it suggests a sense of permanence and community lost in contemporary reality. Headed by the narrator's grandmother, this society of women has remained embedded within the "magical nexus," where nature and (wo)man, thought and the senses, intuition and rationality still coexist. In this house the union of man and woman was still possible, as indicated by the narrator's relationship with her first and only real love, the "lover from Vienna" (51).

The harmony of the first house is destroyed by the narrator's mother, who betrays the female community to seek salvation in her husband and, later, in her sons.[10] The grandmother's language is lost; the narrator's mother adopts the language of the male world she joins. The narrator thus turns to her sisters who, held captive in the second house, have remained isolated from the words and society of men. The sisters' inability to function within the structures of today's world is indicated by their language, described as "these incomplete sentences" (75). One sister, with a harelip, merely mimics the other, who talks in sentences without subjects. This language, sounding helpless or defenseless at first in comparison to the smooth rhythms of societal discourse, is potentially liberating precisely because it refuses to recognize a subject/object hierarchy. It nullifies the power of the "I" to dominate the other: "And I would learn the compassionate language of my other sister. I would ban all subjects from my language, first and foremost this 'I'. All of my sentences began with 'I,' expendable, omnipotent, it brings about harm" (78).

Reichart's text can be read as a search for an individually expressive language, but it also makes certain assumptions about the masculine and feminine. The narrator's quest for a non-binary, non-hierarchical language can be understood within the context of feminist calls since the late 1960s for an *écriture féminine*. In recognition that language is the medium through which experience is organized, French feminists such as Julia Kristeva, Luce Irigaray, and Hélène Cixous propound a new poetics that allows for the articulation of difference or otherness. This poetic language celebrates the unconscious, the body, multiplicity, ambiguity, openness, and the pre-symbolic or instinctual realm; it plumbs desire and pleasure as sensations beyond societal control. Writers of an *écriture féminine* strive to invent the words, to fill in the gaps of a language and mode of thinking that exclude the feminine.[11] In many ways the narrator of *Fotze* embodies such a writer. She explores her desires and attempts to recapture the world of her grandmother, a world in closer proximity to the instinctual and natural. She deplores the paucity of descriptive terms for her sexuality and strives to fill this void, to reclaim it. The capitalized phrases in the text express the namelessness of the narrator's sex: "It hurts DOWN THERE. Don't touch IT. I felt a prickling sensation BETWEEN MY LEGS" (15). Such sexual anonymity invalidates her existence just as surely as the number and nature of the words for penis constitute male potency: "word potency" (43). Inversely, by naming her sexuality, Reichart's narrator endeavors to assert herself, to affirm her presence within both linguistic and societal structures.

However, the narrator's search fails. She cannot escape the thought patterns and language structures of her society; she is too conditioned to break out of her prison; she cannot adopt her sister's language. It proves senseless to ban the subject from her language after the fact, and it proves impossible to unthink this subject: "If I could think just one sentence in their language without first formulating it in mine and only then striking the subject. Nothing's gained by that, no discovery and no new perception, no borders are overcome and no compassion won" (78-79). Even if she could speak her sister's language, their realm, isolated from men and society, is not viable. The narrator's failure seems to echo criticism of *écriture féminine,* which questions the existence of a presymbolic realm, or at least denies access to members of contemporary reality. If language predetermines our perception of reality, how can women perceive or create an alternative? Is there such a thing as unmediated experience? Is it possible to resolve the contradiction that, in spite of the fact that societal language excludes women, leads to violence, and censors experience, it is the only language we currently possess?[12]

Reichart's narrator ultimately must assume contemporary discourse. Her appropriation of societal structures—linguistic, social, and sexual—is apparent in the subjection of her sisters to the same brutal depersonalization that she underwent earlier. By forcing them to parrot the sentences of her lover the "word addict" lover before acknowledging their sexuality (70), the narrator perpetuates the hierarchies of society, with the difference that the previously suppressed has become the suppresser. Instead of using her desk to pen an alternate writing, the narrator ascends the podium to embrace masculine language: "I...will mount the podium of guilt, and I will enjoy being his equal" (96). She subordinates her feelings to the overpowering strength of her thoughts, reducing sexuality to "word orgasm having nothing to do with the body" (96). In the final passage of the text, the narrator sinks into the slime of societal, masculine discourse: "But then [the slime's] embrace is complete. I want to perish in this fulfillment. One with it, I again belong to you, fulfilled in my wordless existence" (124).

In an essay titled "Die Grenzen meiner Welt sind die Grenzen meiner Sprache" (The Limits of My World Are the Limits of My Language) Reichart describes contemporary reality in terms reminiscent of her protagonist's world. She depicts the victory of the masculine in today's society as the suppression of intuition by rational thought and authority, the dismissal of experience in favor of conceptual projections, and the subjugation of the body to technology: "We no longer give birth from the earth, our stomachs, but rather from our heads."[13] Instead of assuming responsibility for life, we allow language—"doctrines," "theories," "computers," all those systems that function without question and without our agency—to usurp authority. Simultaneously, however, Reichart posits literature, with its potential to overcome dichotomies and instead provoke endless possibilities of otherness, as a means, however ineffectual, to subvert the predictable, emotionless language of the theoretical:

And the literature—it's our most foolish hope, and that's what makes it so precious. Each day it becomes more important in its impotence, when computer language has settled into our brains, when we can do nothing but theorize endlessly, uniformly, predictably, numbly, then literature will become our treasure chest, it will preserve the memory of totally different languages, totally different people, endless possibilities for life and for failure and above all for death and someday, while the first snow is falling, a longing for an understanding of the world other than our simple "right-wrong" one will again awaken, and at that moment literature will be there, and great amazement will pass through our heads and make room for it.[14]

The tension apparent in this essay between hope and resignation, between the importance but impotence of literary language, also underlies Reichart's *Fotze*. The above passage, while contending the rigidity of language, undercuts that inflexibility with its unusual and alienating punctuation and line breaks. Similarly, but much more radically, *Fotze* depicts the failure of its protagonist to escape the conceptual systems imposed by language while its own words stretch and bend that language to the point of potential liberation.

Thus, although the final image of the work is one of apparent stasis or closure negating individual or feminine expression, Reichart's poetic language itself strives to reassert possibility by playing with the syntax, meanings, progressions, and rhythms of contemporary language. The title of the work introduces such play. In Austrian German, "Fotze" not only means a derogatory term for the vagina, but it also signifies the mouth as well as a slap in the face or on the mouth. This single word encapsulates the topics of Reichart's work: sexuality, language, and violence.[15] Its use anticipates the word-plays, the multiplicity of meanings, the interconnectedness and circularity, and the ambiguity characteristic of her language throughout.

Reichart's language works above all to overcome the boundaries artificially erected and maintained by a hierarchical, linear, and rational societal discourse. The plot traces the forward development of the narrator, but it does so in a circular fashion whereby a picture, face, or event surfaces, fades, and then resurfaces later within a different but related context. Key words, for example "bunker," "map," "slime," "war," "closet," "word addict," and of course "Fotze," serve to structure the narrative.[16] Each time the narrator's thoughts return to a particular image, the reader receives further clarification; however, clear definition within an individual circle and sharp distinction between circles remain illusory. The sequencing of the circles is determined by the narrator's thought associations, resulting in leaps which frustrate the reader's search for ordered, linear causality. For example, the narrator moves from the outbreak of the most recent war to thoughts of war in general, to her neighbor who comes to borrow coffee for her sick husband, to the coffee package falling, to the lost key to her memory (13). Such a progression ignores the boundary between real and imagined, between reality, fantasy, dreams, and memory; it transcends the limitations of time and space. The author plays with possible scenarios and imagines what could happen: "This, or maybe something else, would happen to the closet if only I could find the key to it" (13). The circles seem to float, similar to the "state of suspension" with which Christa Wolf described the language of Reichart's first novel, *Februarschatten*.[17]

Many of the images or pictures contain multiple levels or reference points, heightening their indeterminacy and plurisignation. Since her debut, the most prevalent and typical are those in which the political and personal are inextricably intertwined. "The state of wars" refers to the historical and concrete wars in Yugoslavia and under Fascism, but it also describes interpersonal relationships between the sexes; the "map," filled solely with names and words devoid of life, denotes Austria as well as the narrator's own lack of body. Here, as in her previous works, the effect of history on the individual, the interaction between the political and private, is thematized.[18] In addition, the author imbues concrete objects—frequently very ordinary, even household things—with figurative meanings that defy realism. The common, everyday closet comes alive and, as a memory which the narrator wishes to ban, instead threatens her and usurps authority (11-13); tomorrow's newspapers contain yesterday's news, indicating the banality and predictability of mass communication (103). The text flows back and forth between these various levels without obstacle or warning, and meaning is derived only by combining the multiple reference levels, not by dissecting or separating them.

Reichart's attempt to overcome boundaries and encourage interconnection is reflected in the text's unique punctuation. Commas substitute for periods, encouraging a flow of thought without interruption, occasionally for pages on end. The lack of periods obscures the conclusion of one thought and the beginning of the next and can result in initial confusion as to the contextual placement of a phrase. Reichart frequently utilizes suspension periods to conclude a paragraph or, less commonly, a sentence (see 6, 7, 8, 11, 13, 14, etc.). Thoughts do not end, but rather trail off. Such ellipses invite the reader to spin the thread further on the one hand, but on the other hand they also demand acknowledgment of language's limited ability to encompass and present neatly for consumption. Finally, the author incorporates the slash as a standard vehicle of punctuation. It serves to connect two associations directly, without mediation (see 6, 8, 10, 16, 17, 21, etc.).

The choice of punctuation marks is directed to a great extent by the sound of language. Reichart's text is richly aural; it engages the reader's sense of hearing. Its rhythms trace the path of the narrator and therefore constitute a necessary comprehension tool. When she attempts to follow her sisters into the "nature's labyrinth," into a realm of the sensual, chaotic, and natural, for example, her inability to do so is communicated through a discontinuous and choppy rhythm which contrasts sharply with the otherwise wavelike flow of the text. The narrator cannot escape the logic and order of her world; she cannot speak her sister's subjectless sentences, as expressed in her short subject-driven sentences and search for explanations and certainty:

> I am surrounded by a labyrinth of vegetation. My thoughts have not changed form. I remain the center of the earth. And these sticky leaves disturb only me, these branches block only my path. I am the intruder. Suddenly I knew again what was happening to me. I had fallen asleep under the pear tree and I must still be sleeping. There was no other explanation. (77)

The ear is further activated by means of the author's word choice, resonant with repetitions, rhymes, and alliteration. For example: "...desired brothers who knew nothing of my desires, their thoughts were already elsewhere, they roamed unknown realms / absent eyes, brothers' eyes, I didn't want to let them go..." (6); "...my innocence excluded me, secluded child they said..." (9); and "in the pulpits they still long for quiet / disquiet dismissed/ along with its instigators" (10). The provocation of the ear works to overcome the dichotomy between head and body lamented by Reichart's narrator and by the author herself.[19] The rhythms and resonances of Reichart's language demand active participation of both the intellect and the sense of hearing.

Other senses are activated by means of a sentence construction in which the connection between subject and predicate is broken, exposing the subject and rendering the language very concrete or object-centered. The first two sentences of the work emphasize the hands of the lover: "Soft, warm hands with the recurring calluses from the years they bore bricks, mixed mortar. Callused hands, rubbed together, never touching me." The focus on the feel of the hands or, in the following example, on smells and sounds, is typical for such constructions: "Perceptible quiet. The door locked from the inside, the final stale drops of beer drunk from bottles lying around, a few cigarette butts smoked, a jacket left carelessly behind, to put it on and rub my nose in it. Wordless sojourn" (7). By evoking the senses and freeing the object from a subject/predicate linguistic hierarchy, Reichart's language counteracts the abstraction and mediation of contemporary technological discourse.

Reichart's language even undercuts the apparent resignation or closure of the final picture in *Fotze*. The narrator acknowledges defeat; she states that she must join the game, but her participation continues to violate the rules, this time through the employment of irony and exaggeration. The structures and vocabulary of her masculine environment are taken to the extreme: language is stripped of its prettifying elements to reveal the consumer nature of sexual relationships which leads to antipathy and debasement:

> I'm coming, men, I'm coming! Unleash your cocks, I'm out for a joy ride, I'm buying cucumbers, watering cans, pistons, plungers, dicks, pricks, spikes, straps, can openers, love bones, spears, horns, poles, posts, bars, bayonets, stakes, pipes...I'll pay in cash, I'll pay for performance, I demand stamina and stiffness, dignified silence and the tenderness which you bestow upon your stamp collections or upon the butterflies you kill and mount... (120)

There is little room left here for ideal pictures; these "naked words" (108) expose the reality behind the images perpetuated by society. Irony and contradiction also negate the narrator's final confirmation of complicity with power: "Power wants to be loved. I denied it love. Well, now I submit. I will leave my land of embarrassment and enter your land of love: 'The lake was whipped by the wind and its water emptied'" (123). The repetition of and variations on the word "love" convey that the realm she enters is anything but one of love. Furthermore, the narrator states that she will comply with the demands of power and impart final words upon her departure, but the words she delivers contradict this seeming acquiescence, for they contain no societal relevance or message. She quotes herself; her words are meaningful only in a purely personal context. Tension exists between the content and the form of the narrator's thoughts. Even in agreeing to assume societal discourse, the narrator's words reflect upon and criticize this language. And even in succumbing ultimately to silence, the final word—"being"—loudly proclaims existence.

Does Reichart's language then revisit the question of an *écriture féminine* and constitute a positive example of its existence? As we have seen, public discourse with its boundaries between the mind and body is characterized as a language of men. Reichart's language strives to approximate the "magical nexus" represented in the house of the feminine. In its ambiguity and overlapping levels of meaning, it works against reduction; with its openness to possibility, its evocation of interconnectedness and provocation of the senses, this language challenges a discourse which, as a reflection of society's authoritarian structures, is divisive, resistant to change, and inimical to the body. The "treasure chest" of language has been opened and serves to subvert the functionality, one-dimensionality, abstraction, and truncation of societal discourse.[20] Reichart's language epitomizes in numerous ways the demands of a feminist aesthetic for "connection, flow, interrelation, and therefore equality."[21] Yet it is not created in a void, i.e., in the absence of the dominant discourse. Like her narrator, Reichart cannot simply unthink the prevalent societal structures. What she can and does do is use—and abuse—these very structures in order to provoke awareness of their existence.[22]

Reichart writes against a discourse that functions so smoothly, so naturally that we no longer are aware of it. We have become deaf and blind—not only to the objects, sounds, and smells of our bodies and of the world around us, but also to each other and, in the sense that language becomes petrified in ideologies and false ideals, to the truth of past and present. Linguistic play is the key to reawakening us; it is "the attempt to speak beyond the realm of the natural, i.e., beyond what we take for granted."[23] Reichart's confirmation of ambiguity and plurisignation foils the assumption of one-to-one correspondences. The inclusion of fantasy and dream opens the text to manifold possibilities, leaving questions rather than answers. The unusual punctuation and breaks in syntax are not easily consumed, and engagement of the senses thwarts or at least counterbalances the intellect's monopoly on comprehension. The language of *Fotze*, its attempt to imitate the "incomplete sentences" of the narrator's sister, alienates and subverts reader expectation in the hope that the boundaries and dichotomies of language, mirroring societal reality, be undermined. Although Reichart's narrator fails in her attempt to find a new language, Reichart's own literary form challenges the old. It cannot posit a concrete counterforce, but awareness and longing, what Reichart has termed "a longing founded in knowledge"[24] for other possibilities.

Allegheny College

Notes

1. Regina Kecht, "Faschistische Familienidyllen—Schatten der Vergangenheit in Henisch, Schwaiger und Reichart," *Austrian Writers and the Anschluss: Understanding the Past—Overcoming the Past*, ed. Donald G. Daviau (Riverside, CA: Ariadne Press, 1991), especially 313-316. See also Juliet Wigmore, "'Vergangenheitsbewältigung' in Austria: The Personal and the Political in Erika Mitterer's *Alle unsere Spiele* and Elisabeth Reichart's *Februarschatten*," *German Life and Letters* 44.5 (October 1991): 477-487, who orients the discussion more toward women's positions.

2. Jürgen Koppensteiner points out that the book was judged almost exclusively on the basis of "historical and political references," but only to argue that the criticisms of Austria apply to the majority of countries today, in "Zwischen Anpassung und Widerstand: Bemerkungen zu zeitkritischen Prosawerken von Peter Henisch, Elisabeth Reichart und Gerald Szyszkowitz," *Modern Austrian Literature* 25.1 (1992): 53-54.

3. Christina Schweighofer, "Wir haben uns selber betrogen: Steyregg, Wien, Tokio, und retour: Annäherung an die Dichterin Elisabeth Reichart," *Die Presse* (June 16-17, 1990).

4. Wigmore, 477-479.
5. Reichart, *Fotze* (Salzburg/Vienna: Otto Müller, 1993). Subsequent references to this work will be cited in the text by page number.
6. Klaus Bellin, "Die Last der Bilder," *Neue deutsche Literatur* 3 (1994): 175-177.
7. Walter Vogl, for example, in an otherwise insightful and positive review, nevertheless (incorrectly) hypothesizes that the narrator was sexually abused by her father, that she is a masochist, and that nothing remains of her ultimately except for a throbbing vulva: "Das Bett der Gewalt," *Die Presse* (October 2, 1993).
8. Criticism of a societal discourse that has become naturalized or "unquestioned" is a recurring theme in Reichart's works. For example, in the short story "How far is Mauthausen?" the narrator quits her job as a guide for the former concentration camp Mauthausen after realizing that her sentences no longer shock her, that they have become "complete" and therefore unquestioned: "I am afraid of complete sentences," *La Valse: Erzählungen* (Salzburg/Vienna: Otto Müller, 1992), 154, 162.
9. In a conversation with the author, Reichart indicated to me that the remaining three houses were meant to signify the First Republic, Austrofascism, and Fascism. A general pattern of decline from one house to the next characterizes the progression through time, with the first house contrasting sharply with the fifth. Although the historical reference of the first and fifth houses are clear in the text, Reichart herself admitted that the other three are more obscure.
10. The theme of salvation and its impossibility except within the self occurs in other works by Reichart, for example, in *Komm über den See*, "I should have known that salvation cannot come through someone else..." (Frankfurt: Fischer, 1988), 67.
11. This brief summary is based primarily on the balanced discussion of *écriture féminine* by Susan Sellers, *Language and Sexual Difference: Feminist Writing in France* (New York: St. Martin's Press, 1991) and on the anthology of primary sources by Maggie Humm, ed. *Modern Feminisms: Political, Literary, Cultural* (New York: Columbia University Press, 1992), especially 193-226, 367-388.

12. Sellers, 37-38, 96-97.
13. Reichart, "The Borders of My World Are the Borders of My Language," *Wespennest* 82 (1991): 114.
14. Ibid., 141.
15. Gerhard Moser, "Die Nacktheit der Wörter: 'Fotze'—eine Erzählung von Elisabeth Reichart," *Neue Züricher Zeitung,* Fernausgabe 34 (February 11, 1994).
16. Some of these words' circles, most notably "lake," "moor," and "slime," extend even to other works, in particular to *Komm über den See.*
17. "To have set it all down as if it were made of stone, of flesh and blood, while simultaneously inscribing it as fiction and thereby keeping it in suspension—this, in my opinion, is the real artistic contribution made by Elisabeth Reichart. As well as the fact that she does not proclaim the necessity of a social intercourse more humane than the murderous type so obvious in her book. Instead, she weaves it into the innermost structure of the book itself; it is apparent in the attractiveness of the author to her characters": Christa Wolf, "Nachwort: 'Struktur von Erinnerung,'" Reichart, *Februarschatten: Roman* (Frankfurt: Fischer Taschenbuch, 1989), 108; new edition, (Salzburg/ Vienna: Otto Müller, 1995); English translation, *February Shadows* (Riverside, CA: Ariadne Press, 1989). Bellin acknowledges a similar suspension, although he criticizes its radicalness: "Once again [Reichart] demonstrates her artistic ability to allow the subject material to float; she refuses to depict things too fastidiously, too clearly, and allows her story to maintain some of its mystery...And yet some things remain so vague and obscure that one cannot decipher characters and connections with finality" 176.
18. In an interview with Achim Roscher, Reichart states: "I am particularly interested in how history affects the individual person...How does the individual react to historical processes and how do they influence that person." In "Elisabeth Reichart im Gespräch," *Neue deutsche Literatur* 35 (1987): 129.
19. See Reichart's *Wiener Poetikvorlesungen.* This dichotomy is also a topic in other works, especially in *Komm über den See.*
20. Reichart, "Die Grenzen meiner Welt sind die Grenzen meiner Sprache," 141. Reichart refers to literary language in similar

terms in an interview forthcoming in *Modern Austrian Literature*: "'Für mich ist die Sprache eigentlich ein Schatz': Interview mit Elisabeth Reichart," with Linda DeMeritt and Peter Ensberg.

21. Marilyn French, "Is There a Feminist Aesthetic?" *Aesthetics in Feminist Perspective*, ed. Hilde Hein and Carolyn Korsmeyer (Bloomington, IN: Indiana University Press, 1993), 73.

22. Rita Felski offers convincing arguments against both a feminist aesthetic founded solely in reflection theory and, at the other extreme, the *écriture féminine* propounded by the French feminists. She agrees with structuration theory that existing structures are both "constraining and *enabling*," similar to how Reichart uses and abuses them, in *Beyond Feminist Aesthetics* (Cambridge, MA: Harvard University Press, 1989), 60.

23. Vogl, "Das Bett der Gewalt."

24. Roscher, "Elisabeth Reichart im Gespräch": 129. This is the same "longing" described by Reichart in her essay "Die Grenzen meiner Welt sind die Grenzen meiner Sprache," 141.

Elfriede Gerstl: Understatement

Konstanze Fliedl

For the satirist, reality is both too much and too little. Satire exaggerates, that's its way—so they say, at least. It exacerbates a bad situation, creates a grotesque image, enabling us to see what might occur unless... In this unspoken "unless" lies the utopian change which is not delineated, but ardently yearned for by the satirist. The more malicious his/her means, the more moral is his/her end; a commonplace perhaps, but one that does not go without saying. Even today, satirists are accused of indecency when they use their distorting mirror to reflect current obscenities. The most recent example is that of Elfriede Jelinek's play *Raststätte* (1995, Service-Stop), which attacks perversions of all kind; the lecherousness does not even spare young girls and boys. And long before the premiere, Elfriede Jelinek had been made to look like a child-abuser herself.

However, it seems that such exaggeration is no longer necessary to satirize reality. On the contrary: reality is busily catching up with the most radical satire. Karl Kraus only needed to use literal quotations to pillory the press in the most merciless manner. The extreme cynicism pervasive in real society can no longer be outdone; that is something that the satirist must now recognize. In 1962, Hans Magnus Enzensberger asked, how "a reality, which ridicules all exaggeration could feel injured by satire."[1] Clever satire, by contrast, is able to incur a change, reverse the course; undercut the force of fact.

The Viennese author Elfriede Gerstl has been doing just that for a long time. She has ignored the solemn moral stance of enraged social criticism. Her texts reverse the satirical process: reality is made to look so trivial that it becomes ridiculous. Understatement counters a bad situation. From this reversal arises the satirical effect. This art of understatement is, of course, quieter, more subtle and more precise than an indignant lashing-out in all directions. That is why Elfriede Gerstl's voice has often gone unheard.[2]

The Minimum of Narrative

It is no coincidence, therefore, that the novel *Spielräume* (Rooms to Move), written in 1968-69, was only published in 1977.[3] Grit, a student, moves from Vienna to Berlin, where she lodges with the Bartsches, a petit-bourgeois married couple. She has contact with the *Szene* and engages in various relations with married men. She reads Wittgenstein but fails to reach a decisive political stance. That in itself would be an exciting story, a feminine *Entwicklungsroman*, or a parody thereof, however, that is precisely not the contents of *Spielräume*. Gerstl's book is peculiar in that it does not allow itself to negotiate with the demands of "an audience (of critics) which is accus-tomed to, and which has become addicted to, plot" (Sp 17). The work acquires "room to move" by putting an end to that "tatty old game of 'searching for meaning'" (Sp 20). The influence of the Wiener Gruppe on the text is unmistakable; yet nothing in it reminds us of the sometimes ideological overemphasis on language and functionalism which Gerhard Rühm mentions in his history of the group.[4] *Spielräume* does not present a bravura critique of language. There is no self-conscious experimentation with prevailing thought and speech patterns. The novel's fragmentary narrative and its miniature perceptions and reflections attempt something else, namely: the diminution of all literary, philosophical and political discussion (whereas its negation is still dependent on it). Even the most subversive concrete poetry needs the canon it perforates to achieve the intended shock; even anti-authoritarian thought recognizes the authority of those it seeks to oppose. Gerstl's "Grit" does neither; but is a figure-of-speech that runs away from this trap. As far as "Grit" functions as a "realistic," psycho-logically and politically motivated person, she will not succeed in finding a perspective: "I probably have some kind of mental illness preventing me from making myself warm and comfortable in one of those ready-made, inexpensive ideologies" (Sp 31); "when I talk to reactionaries, I'm pressed to argue from the extreme left-wing corner; when I'm with the lefties, I feel the urge, for example, to criticize their practice, that cannot be justified by theory" (Sp 70). Even when "Grit" speaks with the voice of poetological consciousness, she does not take sides:

> Cue: but where's that small connection—
> in my head of course, darling, if I want, I'll make one for
> myself,
> if not not
> yes of course I could put things in a teeny bit of mathematical
> (or epic) order (if I wanted to), that's true enough. (Sp 81)

"Grit" evades both the norm and emotional protestation. Her unraveling of this "epic order" is no theory-loaded revolt. Philosophy may disguise itself as comedy: first, Grit quotes her "doyen" Disney—"sensier, sensier"—then "doyen" Wittgenstein. Passage 4.116 of his *Tractatus* is presented in several new variations, one of which goes: "Everything that can be said, can also be said in passing" (Sp 60f.). Grit specializes in the incidental; she writes micrograms of all that is poetic, philosophical, political, and in her tiny caricatures, such great discourses appear small. It is this reduction that makes the text "political"; Andreas Okopenko called it one of the few political novels of postwar Austria, "no Viennese contricks, no rumen-Kafka, none of this nostalgia shit."[5] The subversive wit of *Spielräume* lies in the way it shows us the boastful rhetoric of epistemological, linguistic and capitalist critique.

Diminutive Perspectives

The novel minimizes narrative sequence, but does not preach a nonnarrative program. At the same time, it introduces to us an Austriacism, on the "airlift of grammar" (Sp 26), an Austriacism that has always brought before the high and mighty a degree of skepticism, namely: the diminutive. The Austrian diminutive suffix (*-l, -erl*) has tradition. Back in the time of the monarchy, particularly in dialect folk plays, this "longing for the zero-grade" was marked; their distrust of politics and intellectualism led authors from Nestroy to Horváth to dwarf words such as *Freiheit* (freedom) and *Vater* (father) to *Freiheitl* and *Vaterl*.[6] Those great concepts we knew when they were still in their infancy are brought back down to size by means of an infantile tag. Above all, Gerstl gives new forms to the passwords of heightened consciousness. A "little-thought addiction" (Sp 82) leads to nothing much, at most perhaps, "leftover-bits of awakened consciousness" (Sp 39). What remain are "emotionettes,...possibly a philosophette for supermen." Grit's objection to enlightened Marxist thought is that its psychologism is "still only one of many little dead-ends," thus suggesting that *every* ideology is marching up a blind alley (Sp 37). According to Grit, the left wing wants the working class's wages to be at starvation level, so that they can be brought "through a slight historical swing, backwards (via impoverishment) forwards (to revolution)" (Sp 84). But when Gerstl trivializes, she does so in order to show in what pretty little packages capitalism comes; its special offer is particularly small: "When someone comes along and thinks he can will may might buy me up as a bit of labor, or intends to do a bit of bartering with me, 1.2 months labor and a little-lifetime..., o yessie" (Sp 90).

Trivialization functions as anti-dogmatic strategy. The lower the perspective slides, the more absurd all categorical assertions seem. The star-studded heavens above us vanish on a summer's day, and Elfriede Gerstl lures out the lap dog from behind the "idealistic tiled stove:"

A MORAL LAW SEEN FROM UNDERNEATH

Beneath a swinging shopping bag
            full of summer

waddles the asthmatic Pekinese
and may not
                  after the perfume of the ladies

turn around,
for high above,
just beneath the heavens,

such behavior is called
unfitting.

But every time it asks,
what it is it doesn't fit,
it gets no answer.[7]

The poet who asks in such a way is for Gerstl a somewhat down-at-the-heels "dog of its age." No emblem of poetry or place, no monument of national importance remains the same when observed practically, or from the periphery:

The Eiffel Tower

                        is among the towers and not a
tower at all but rather a pillar; although Mr. Eiffel was called
Mr. Eiffel when he built it, for sure, and at all other times too.

Mr. Eiffel is therefore the surest thing about the Eiffel tower.
The Eiffel Tower as a pillar supports children, fish cutlery,
watering cans and other sensitive rooms in its superstructure:
the Eiffel Tower is therefore (apart from Mr. Eiffel) a kitchen
maid.

It is only that on the periphery, usually, but nevertheless of
Paris... [8]

Even then, in 1959, Gerstl spoke out against the dignity of towers; she
would do it again. In the light of the symbolism of depth psychology
she was able in 1975, to present a report on psychoanalytical theory in
such a way that small differences became even smaller. Her perspective
this time was that of the female periphery: "It is not written in the
stars, but rather in our genes, whether we will belong to the master
class of penis-holders, or to the servant class of those who hold
nothing."[9] However, it was not with the heavy pathos of the victim
that Gerstl set about dismantling the so-called phallocentric discourse.
She perforated the self-important aura of psychoanalysis, as well as that
of its originator, with solid common sense. Without Freudian license,
she compared Viennese bars to "smoky (not disreputable) uteri; and the
fact that everybody wants to get into somewhere, like a roast piggy
under the grilly, big Siggy didn't invent."[10] In 1981, she examined the
poems of H.C. Artmann, and like a jack-in-the-box, regressive and
aggressive images of women sprang out as puppets for one's every
need.[11] But it was not from above that Gerstl gave such musty male
fantasies a good dressing down; rather, she dug at them from underneath. She set the pains of men to the accompaniment of ditties, in this
case the hits of the fifties—and the voyeuristic, infantile and sadistic
affectations in H.C. Artmann's poetry came down to the level of "only
dolores's legs will do that" or "do you know the sugar-babe / in the
belly-dancing band." Perhaps not the texts themselves, but their clichés
of femininity, could be rediscovered in the *souterrain* of the entertainment industry. This type of satire hurts no less than politically-
correct veto, but it does not bestow on its object the importance it
claims for itself. Gerstl deals with the taboo of cultural significance by
means of its opposite.

Essays on the Small Things

Gerstl has also attacked the culture industry itself, expressly and frankly. A premise of Gerstl's work is the problem of the author, who, as a petty-businessman receiving charity from the public dole, necessarily enters into a closer relationship with the state he is criticizing than is comfortable for either of them. The distribution of grants and bursaries does not, according to Gerstl, depend on literary achievement, but rather on pertinent social conduct. She describes in vivid detail the way in which the Austrian author internalizes these schizophrenias and dependencies. She cites the names of Hertha Kräftner (suicide 1951), Walter Buchebner (suicide 1964), and Otto Laaber (suicide 1973), as examples of how public disdain is redirected towards the self and pushed to its furthest and most desperate consequence.[12] Only rarely does heedless megalomania compensate for such narcissistic offense. But Elfriede Gerstl would not be likely to choose such a grandiose solution. She votes, quite programmatically, for options that other writers would only choose with a guilty conscience: industrial sponsorship, jobs in advertising and on the radio. Gerstl's essays are aimed at the persistent (auto) suggestion that an artist should not want to make a living. Her pleas are didactic with all the hopelessness of the didactic aim: neuroticizing pressure from outside is analyzed in detail, and thus reduced. Such a long-term therapy can only hope for slight success; this, however, does not make it superfluous.

In her radio plays, Elfriede Gerstl has attempted to square the circle further. In the fifties, the radio play had come to be nothing more than a sad parable in many cases. The nuclear family was its presupposed audience, and that audience it sought to instruct, via its one-way communication, to keep quiet. As a stage play reduced to the single acoustic element, the radio play demanded passive identification on the part of the audience. Sounds illustrated the plots, just as nineteenth-century novels had included illustrations.[13] Although the medium's technical possibilities could be exploited in the sixties, especially in experiments with verbal material, the dilemma of the silent audio-consumer remained; he/she did not have the reader's most basic freedom, namely: to determine himself/herself the speed of the reading. Gerstl's radio plays focus on the paradox of making audible the incapacitation engendered by the medium itself. "You are not alone or ORF, your loyal companion"[14] allows the mute listener to speak by proxy. Merely by quoting from everyday recordings of women's, sports', or children's programs, this pseudo-enlightenment, offering cosmetic, fitness or educational morsels, is parodied. The voices of the listeners react by asking about their own history:

L 1:	and where is the history
	the history that calls me
	the history in which we're
	known to one another
L 2:	none of us has much but
L 3:	we all have a history
L 4:	if only I would talk
Female L:	if only I could talk
L 4:	I could write a book. [15]

The radio play "Gudrun, die Geschichte und ihr Unterricht" (Gudrun, History and Its Teaching)[16] also refers to Brecht's *Fragen eines lesenden Arbeiters* (Questions of a Reader-Worker). "Gudrun" opens as a question-answer game between teacher and children, before commencing a rapid sweep through history. The sites of historical catastrophes, "Biafra" and "My Lai" and "Nagasaki" interrupt the teacher's ordered sentences. By means of acoustic editing, history is divided between men's foolish crusading and women's endless waiting.[17] By muddling up retrievable historical facts, the play pursues the method and the contents of history teaching *ad absurdum*. The small subject of history, peasant and beggar, may then emerge in the gaps between the sentences. And there it must stay: in this medium Gerstl's plays can only be presentation, not practice. By calling on the listener to tell his/her own history, or even history itself, the radio plays function as models of their own abolition. The fact that the genre of the radio play was abolished by the colorful world of television shows that the history of mass media retains its own irony.

In the essay form, experiments on the small can be carried out time and time again. Determining the form and contents of the essay is still a crux of literary studies. Not much can be gained from generic analysis, other than revealing that the essay playfully circumscribes its theme, unsystematically and associatively. Its strength is that it has still eluded definition, and that it will not define itself either; this situation Gerstl uses for her own purpose. The essay is not apodictic; it has neither program nor main theme; that which is fragmentary suits it.

It is the ideal form for Gerstl's understatements.

The Author's Old Clothes

One of Gerstl's characteristic understatements is her emblem for writing: the junk shop. Gerstl is referring neither to post-modernism nor to its critics (who like to talk of a "self-service shop"). In *Spielräume* Grit considered how to serve the "culture officials' junk shop" (Sp 57). But in the poem "in der sprache wohnen" (living in language) the image has become a means for the author to express herself—where Karl Kraus's metaphor of "the old house of language" has been transformed into the diminutive "language-maisonette:"

> ...In my cobbled-together
> > language-maisonette
> stands and lies my vocabulary
> as cabbage and turnips
> as in a junk shop
> we often find what we're looking for
> but sometimes not. [18]

The "junk shop" is Gerstl's most ironic poetic tool—and her bastion against the ultimate demand of (literary) fashion: seasonal ware. Everything must be new, down to the quotation of past fashions. Gerstl is both a theoretician and practitioner of fashion; she has written essays on the rise and fall of various items of clothing, of the parka, for example.[19] She even could have done the sociology of the Loden-coat, a topic suggested by Heinrich Böll back in 1962[20]—and she herself owns a historical clothes collection. The ambivalence of fashion for Gerstl's work, between conformity and differentiation, is neither surprising nor wholly inconvenient. On the one hand, it is clear that even those who refuse to participate cannot fully escape the dictate of fashion. The "well-advised clothing industry" reacts accordingly, even to anarchism and nonconformism, with off-the-rack garments (Sp 67). Even that old, *un*fashionable dress, protesting its originality in the face of market forces, is assimilated into the repetitive cycles of fifties, sixties, and seventies styles. A second-hand outfit could be seen as an ironic foil to the latest autumn look. But on the other hand, the ephemeral nature of fashion resists all cultural claims for durability and atemporality. "The power of fashion," writes Elisabeth Lenk, "is momentary power, temporary tyranny. That which conflicts with today's fashion will tomorrow be taken up with passion. But does this continual reversal of oppositions not prove the relative nature of even the most fundamental elements of our philosophy?"[21] If we take Gerstl's writings on fashion to be cunning commentaries on the culture industry, then she is seen to travesty its "intellectual values." The industry itself chases after current fashion, but then, under its cultural pessimism, disparages it as mere superficiality. That is precisely what Gerstl does not do. She proceeds exactly the other way round: she narrates history as quick changes of fashion. The title chapter of her most recent book, *Kleiderflug* (Clothes Flight), is a review of six decades of fashion.[22] The ridiculous promises of happiness in advertisements, "chic belongs to happiness," and the compulsory measures taken against the body, "you too can be centimeters slimmer," are the two opposing images of women they proffer. But between these sentences, Gerstl slips in memories, moments of life; these are equally images of certain eras. The head-scarf of a woman amongst the rubble of war, the first nylon tights, the "sober" little black dress for apartment-hunting—these are all signs and traces of what woman has to achieve, or what she can afford. The subtitle is "lost clothes": in Gerstl's texts the loss of wardrobe through journeys and house-moves represents the loss of the multivalency that familiar things acquire. Later, she speaks of the possibility of mixing and matching, of selecting her own signs within the frame of a semiotic game. Text becomes material; a dress becomes text: "My basic equipment grows according to plan and chaotically / some will be eliminated—others found / it grows as a text grows / literature and collecting arise from deficiency / fullness defiantly put against some deficiency."[23] At least the "stone-age" habit of collecting and exchanging avoids the necessary exploitation of selling off the unsold merchandise at the end of the season. It is about the freedom of *picking something up*—and even that is an anachronism in our throw-away society. When Gerstl compares writing to the old junk shop, the poetic demand remains a modest one; she limits it to the arrangement of bits and bobs. But the ridiculousness of aiming for literary originality is made evident. Gerstl also picks up the tension between a writer's archaic means of production and the market, which is geared towards the speedy change-over of goods. Gerstl herself has never published quickly: her work has often been labeled "slim." It is obvious that such a way of working will fail to secure her market success.

Poetry in Motion

Near or inside the "junk shop" Elfriede Gerstl finds a second poetological metaphor: that of non-sedentariness, of coming and going. The short prose piece "Carolines unordentliche Wohnsitze" (Caroline's Disorderly Domiciles) has as its heroine a woman who is reproached for "not knowing how to live."[24] Caroline spends her time at railway stations, on staircases, in cafés, carrying her possessions around in plastic bags and occasionally depositing them with waitresses or toilet ladies. Caroline must first find for herself, in niches in public places, that which other people can take for granted, namely: a home. Each temporary settlement will do until the next move. In the quatrilingual book of poetry *Vor der Ankunft* (Before Arrival), the texts are collected in such a way as to reflect the agitation of movement. There is no sure destination, and no sure home: "Forwards backwards / I journey on this trip."[25] In certain cases, the journey becomes a circle, a tour around a vacuum of uncertainty:

new york and return

was bewildered
felt afraid
traveled far
courted danger
gained courage
returned heartened
able to tell
high towers
deep gorges
gained courage
courted danger
traveled far
felt afraid
bewildered as ever.[26]

These sentence fragments, all missing a subject, tell of a flight of panic. Settling is only halfway and only occasionally possible, not "at home," but in a social gap. Elfriede Gerstl has written a homage to something that is called *Krätzl* in Vienna, a dialect expression for living-space. Strolling and quick visits to bars give rise to a provisional feeling of familiarity: "Whoever, like me, has never learned to live, lives here."[27] *Here* lies Gerstl's literary topos: poetry as something that comes and goes. This poetic program enables her to get around the whole ideology of possessing a home, of being anchored in a literary domain. Style is something ambulatory, something that simply circumnavigates theoretical labels. Slow tempo is part of flanerie and it resists the dictate of mass production; the flaneur pieces together fragments of a reality. Walter Benjamin's chapter on this subject begins with the sentence: "But the great reminiscences, the historical shudder— they are the junk that he (the flaneur) leaves for the traveler, who believes he can tackle the *genius loci* by means of a military password."[28] However, Benjamin's protagonist only appears as an ironic quotation in Gerstl's text. The self-stylization of the nineteenth century would be too much of a fancy dress for someone to whom it no longer occurs to want to transform the city into his interior.[29] Gerstl merely sets a figure of constant motion against the background of cultural affiliation and sedentariness, something presumed dead that has rearisen with astounding vitality. "but who's himself / who's at home / who's himself at home alone;" Elfriede Jelinek has answered Gerstl's questions by naming those who are reserved for home: "They never doubt that they are at home after cooking their food there...They do not have to learn what is peculiar to them, for it is they, and only they, who have produced it. Having to protect that which is peculiar from strangers, makes it, they think, all the more natural."[30] In fact, Gerstl understates how much of an effort it is not settling anywhere, not settling into a coziness of thought; she also understates the effort of writing. In motion, in passing, the fervor of all those new fanfares and anthems is satirized once again.

This inability to live somewhere has a very pragmatic background, however. Gerstl's Caroline does not walk about with her plastic bags just for fun. It is characteristic that Gerstl, in her essay about Hertha Kräftner, mentions one of her stories, *Das Liebespaar* (The Lovers), in which she showed a man and a girl who have no place of their own and who go into exile on park benches and in desolate houses.[31] It is not only the serious housing shortage of the fifties that Gerstl recognizes in this story. As a child, Elfriede Gerstl had to hide from the Nazis in a number of houses.[32] Those small, outer flights conceal the threatening image of that one great flight; because of that, the *Krätzl* offers relative security: "At last, one can live here by coming and going as everywhere else and needn't go away immediately—as before."[33] As Andreas Okopenko writes in his afterword to *Spielräume*, Gerstl has always scorned the idea of "transforming her political childhood (Jewish U-boat) into an Anne Frank who survives" (Sp 101). Her description of this time is as brief and unsentimental as possible:

> The bad thing was that we had to be so quiet, (you could do almost nothing but lie on your bed), and that it was so dark when we wanted to read the few books we had (e.g., "Leatherstocking" or Schiller's ballads). Only on really sunny days did enough light come through the holes in the blinds, reflected in regular gaps all the way down and on both sides.[34]

Whoever has had to read like that will write differently. They will bore small holes in the pompous facade of the literature shop.

University of Vienna

Translated by Angharad Price

Notes

1. Hans Magnus Enzensberger, "Satire als Wechselbalg," *Einzelheiten* (Frankfurt: Suhrkamp, 1962), 220.
2. Literary criticism has reacted to the work of the author (born 1932) almost wholly positively; Elfriede Gerstl has received the *Staatsstipendium für Literatur* (1973), the *Theodor-Körner-Preis* (1978), the *Würdigungspreis* (1984) and the *Preis der Stadt Wien* (1990); nevertheless, she is still regarded as the "great unknown" of the Austrian literary scene.
3. Gerstl, *Spielräume* (Linz: edition neue texte, 1977); (new edition with an afterword by Heimrad Bäcker, Graz: Droschl, 1993). Cited in the following as (Sp).
4. Gerhard Rühm, ed. Vorwort, *Die Wiener Gruppe* (Reinbek: [Rowohlt, Paperback 60], 1967), 28.
5. Andreas Okopenko, Nachwort, *Spielräume*, by Gerstl, 101.

6. Cf. Wendelin Schmidt-Dengler, "'O wär ich eine Maus,...' Zum österreichischen Selbstverständnis in der österreichischen Literatur," *Romanistik integrativ. Festschrift für Wolfgang Pollak*, ed. Wolfgang Bandhauer and Robert Tanzmeister (Vienna: Braumüller, Wiener romanistische Arbeiten 13, 1985), 500.
7. Gerstl, *Gesellschaftsspiele mit mir. Wenig übliche Gedichte und Geschichten* (Linz: Wimmer, 1962), 13; cf. "Idealismus wärmt," 17.
8. Ibid., 20. Reprinted in: *wiener mischung. texte aus vielen jahren* (Linz: edition neue texte [Graz: Droschl], 1982), 30.
9. Gerstl, "Die Diskriminierung der Frau durch die Psychoanalyse," *International Art Conference of the Galerie nächst St. Stephan, 1975.*
10. Gerstl, "grüssen, gehen, stehen (beschreibung eines wiener ausschnitts mit gemischten mitteln)," *Friederike Mayröcker et al.: Blauer Streusand,* ed. Barbara Alms (Frankfurt: [=st 1432], 1987), 11.
11. Gerstl, "Frauenlob bei Artmann und im Schlagertext," *Unter einem Hut. Essays und Gedichte* (Vienna: Edition Falter/ Deuticke, 1993), 170-181.
12. Cf. ibid. the essays "Hertha Kräftner, ein Beispiel weiblicher Selbstaufgabe," 157-161; "Flüstern mit Otto Laaber oder Leben auf Sparflamme," 182f.; "Zwei österreichische Dichterschicksale oder Wie der Kulturbetrieb seine Opfer macht und in posthumen Ehrungen sich selber feiert," 189-194.
13. Cf. Evelyne Polt-Heinzl, "'...drehen Sie das Radio an...Die Stille tut ihnen nicht gut.' Die Hörspiele Marlen Haushofers im zeitgenössischen Kontext," *Marlen Haushofer: Die Überlebenden. Unveröffentliche Texte aus dem Nachlaß. Aufsätze zum Werk,* ed. Christine Schmidjell (Linz: Landesverlag, 1991), 116-138.
14. Gerstl, *Berechtigte Fragen* (Vienna: Jugend und Volk; Edition Literaturproduzenten, 1973), 15-28.
15. Ibid., 23.
16. Ibid., 39-47.
17. The hero of the medieval *Gudrunlied* waits thirteen years for her fiancé.

18. Gerstl, *wiener mischung*, 16. Cf. Karl Kraus, "Bekenntnis," *Gedichte* (Frankfurt, [=st 1319; Schriften 9], 1989), 93: "I am only one of the epigones, / who live in the old house of language."

19. Gerstl, "Aufsteiger Parka," *Unter einem Hut*, 205f.

20. Heinrich Böll, "Keine Träne um Schmeck," *Gesammelte Erzählungen*, vol. 2 (Cologne/Bornheim-Merten: Kiepenheuer/Lamuv, 1981), 235-255.

21. Elisabeth Lenk, "Wie Georg Simmel die Mode überlistet hat," *Die Listen der Mode*, ed. Silvia Bovenschen (Frankfurt: [=es 1338], 1986), 442f. This unusual essay, not coincidentally, deals with the essay and the flaneur.

22. Gerstl, *Kleiderflug* (Vienna: Edition Splitter, 1994), 7-25.

23. Ibid., 15.

24. Gerstl, *wiener mischung*, 16.

25. Gerstl, *Vor der Ankunft. Auf Reisen entstandene Gedichte, Before Arrival* (trans. Beth Bjorklund), *Avant l'arrivée: poèmes nés au cours d'un voyage* (trans. Renate Kühn, Christian Prigent and Yasmin Hoffmann), *Prima di arrivare: poesie scritte in viaggio* (trans. Gerhard Kofler) (Vienna: [= Freibord SR 24], 1988), 25f.

26. Ibid., 85f.

27. Gerstl, *grüssen, gehen, stehen*, 13.

28. Walter Benjamin, *Das Passagen-Werk*, ed. Rolf Tiedemann, vol. 1 (Frankfurt: [= es 1200], 1983), 524.

29. Rather its "interior" into its "exterior." Franz Schuh, in the afterword to *Kleiderflug*, writes: "The house is, as it were, the 'outer' interior design of the stroller, who is not in her element at home"; "Irgendwo im Nirgendwo oder über das Dasein," *Kleiderflug*, 68.

30. Elfriede Jelinek, "Ein- und Aussperrung [zu Elfriede Gerstls Gedicht 'Wer ist denn schon']," *Frankfurter Allgemeine Zeitung*, (June 30, 1993); cf. *wiener mischung*, 60.

31. Hertha Kräftner, *Das Blaue Licht. Lyrik und Prosa*, ed. Otto Breicha and Andreas Okopenko, with an afterword by Peter Härtling (Darmstadt: [= SL 334], 1981), 78-84; cf. *Unter einem Hut*, 160f.

32. Cf. Gerstl, "Individuelles Wohnen," *Kleiderflug*, 55.

33. Gerstl, *grüssen, gehen, stehen*, 13.

34. Gerstl, *Das kleine Mädchen, das ich war. Schriftstellerinnen erzählen ihre Kindheit*, ed. Ingrid Strobl (Cologne: Emma-Verlag, 1982), 37.

Elfriede Czurda: Poison and Play

Kristie A. Foell

Elfriede Czurda's work is full of productive tensions that go beyond the inherent contradictions of being an Austrian feminist living in Berlin. Her use of language is inventive and playful, particularly when one hears her read aloud with her full-voiced Austrian vowels; yet she can carry through a literary device or an intellectual conceit with scientific accuracy. The rigorously analytical structure of her works is tempered by humor; occasionally the two come together in gleeful sadism. Czurda combines a seemingly apolitical "linguistic play" with a deep commitment to women's history and emancipation.

Born in 1946 in Upper Austria, Czurda "always wanted to become a writer";[1] realizing that the life would be difficult and that there was much to learn, she first studied art history and archaeology in Salzburg and Paris. After earning her doctorate in art history with a dissertation on Eugène Fromentin, she worked as an art historian. In 1975 she began working as general secretary of the *Grazer Autorenversammlung*, a position that allowed her to pursue and promote her interests in women's literature and the representation of women.[2] In Linz, she worked as an editor for *Edition Neue Texte*; after her divorce, she moved to Berlin in 1980.

Czurda does not cultivate a personal mythology of connection between her life and work. Commenting on an artist figure in one of Gerhard Roth's plays, she laconically describes "an exciting biography such as only mediocre writers have ever enjoyed."[3] Still, some aspects of Czurda's biography shed light on her creative work: she is both Austrian and cosmopolitan, an academically trained, intellectual writer who writes theoretically informed criticism as well as literary texts. Her own negative experience with marriage interacts with her criticism of the experience and the idea of marriage, and with her insistence that this bond is often destructive for women. It would be quite wrong-headed to dismiss her critique as that of an embittered woman disappointed by love (a popular anti-feminist argument), for Czurda is anything but embittered. On the contrary, she radiates vitality, curiosity, self-confidence, and a playfulness, both sophisticated and innocent— qualities that come through in the experimental aspects of her writing.

It will be important to keep these distinctions between work and life in mind during the following discussion of Czurda's most programmatically feminist work, *Die Giftmörderinnen* (The Female Poisoners), an experiential journey through the world and mind of a Weimar-era woman who slowly poisoned her husband. I have recently been reminded how difficult it is for feminists to discuss women who murder in terms of social situations and psychological exigencies specific to women without having the analysis misunderstood as an amoral endorsement of murder.[4] It is a great contradiction that, in an age so marked by the acceptance of real and fictional violence against women, there should be such visceral outrage against women who become violent. Against this background—in both Europe and America—Czurda's fictional revisiting of a 1920s murder is both courageous and necessary.

Die Giftmörderinnen

Die Giftmörderinnen exemplifies Czurda's complex commitments to (women's) history and aesthetics, feminist engagement and linguistic play. The plot is based on historical events that were first worked into literary form by Alfred Döblin in his 1924 *Die beiden Freundinnen und ihr Giftmord* (The Two Girls Who Poisoned Their Men).[5] The action of Czurda's novel is simple to recount: Else marries Hans and the two move in with his mother, a situation that soon threatens the new wife's sanity. Even without this external difficulty, the couple is not well-suited; the wife's sexual coldness provokes the husband into sexual violence, which soon becomes their primary mode of interaction. The wife turns for support to a new female friend, the unhappily married Erika; their friendship soon escalates into passion, expressed not only sexually but in a compulsive, voluminous exchange of love letters. After several unsuccessful attempts to leave the marriage (Else's parents refuse to acknowledge the gravity of her marital situation), Else decides to prove her love for Erika by poisoning Hans through slow but steady doses of arsenic. She nurses her husband for weeks as he slowly deteriorates, expelling his corroded guts through vomiting and diarrhea. This is the most gruesome phase of Döblin's account, but not of Czurda's: she paints the husband's preceding physical and psychological abuse in more detail. A brief look at Döblin's rendering will highlight the literary innovation and incisive feminist analysis that distinguish Czurda's novel.

The actual 1922 murder and 1923 trial were covered extensively in the press; the relatively light five-year sentence the historical Elli Link received, a precursor of the still controversial battered-wife defense, provoked outrage and fears of social decay on the right, while the lesbian relations between the two women fed into the debate on the origins of homosexuality. This became the central question for Döblin: did the two women engage in lesbian relations because of the frustrations and brutality in their marriages; or was an innate lesbianism one of the causes of the marital dissatisfaction? In the spirit of the early Weimar years, either interpretation would tend to exonerate the murderess. Döblin vacillates between the two views, seeing the friend (the historical Gretchen Bende) as "developmentally a child" and "too weak to hold a restless man like him, let alone rule over him with her womanly wiles" (BF 21). Döblin implies that the failed marriage and the husband's philandering were Gretchen's fault, her homosexual behavior a poor attempt to compensate for this failing, the new friend, "a substitute for the rotten man she couldn't hold onto anyway" (BF 22). Döblin's repeated references to childishness on the part of both women echo Freud's description of homosexuality as a fixation on an earlier stage of development; they also play into old thoughts about women's moral inferiority.

Throughout his narrative, Döblin has two stated goals: on the one hand, he attempts an "objective" recounting of events, in keeping with the crime series for which he wrote the account;[6] on the other hand, he wants to portray the motivations of his subjects convincingly. Döblin's attempts at combining scientific objectivity and persuasive subjectivity lead him to recursions into naturalism that appear laughable today, as when he writes of Hans, "he was tremendously deranged. The signs of epileptic degeneration were much in evidence" (BF 41), or of the jurors in the trials, that they "saw themselves confronted with the necessity of pronouncing a uterus, an ovary, guilty, because it was formed one way and not another" (BF 85). Döblin tries to communicate the feelings and inner states of his characters, but concedes the failure of his own language: "First there are the horribly unclear words one must use to describe such processes or causal connections...The curt, stupid words for the description of inner processes: attraction, aversion, disgust, love vengefulness" (BF 93). Of course, it was precisely the stenographic transcription (not description) of inner processes that brought Döblin his lasting fame with his 1927 *Berlin, Alexanderplatz*, whose main character, Franz Biberkopf, is the male equivalent of Elli Link insofar as he beat his prostitute girlfriend to death. Döblin's early literary disappointment might be understood as part of his artistic development, a step towards learning to make the most outcast members of society comprehensible. On the other hand, perhaps one reason for his failure in this case was that the male writer could not understand the female murderess; to understand her motivations was not only too threatening to him personally, but also would have required him to take a critical view of the patriarchal society from which he profited, even as a writer.

Czurda succeeds where Döblin falls short because she views her protagonist not as an isolated "interesting case," but as representative of the female condition under patriarchy. As Kathleen Thorpe has noted, the name "Hans" is "the generic name for men," just as Else is "'every Else'—the female analogy to Hans."[7] Czurda's description of Else's marriage, then, does not rely on convincing the reader of how abnormally abysmal this particular marriage is; instead, her portrayal is grounded in a feminist analysis of how the structure of any traditional marriage oppresses the female partner.

The objectification of people, who are labeled and forced into roles within the family (provider husband, industrious wife), contributes to Else's ability to see Hans simply as an obstacle to her own freedom and to murder him. The chapters "Die Arbeit und die Haus Arbeit" (Work and House Work) and "Die Ehe" (Marriage), with their programmatic titles, offer Czurda's uncompromisingly feminist analysis of marriage. Only Hans has exchange value, and this allows him to occupy the central role in the family:

> Hans's surplus value within the family is significant. He raises the nutritional value. Hans gets this from his potency. Explosivity. A Hans Rinx can explode at home anytime he wants to. Then there are protuberances! At work he becomes the central cog. The colorful ribbons of power and surplus value flutter around every word that slips from Hans's lips. Swaddled in these glowing bows, Hans is the fancy-fancy mumbo jumbo of Mamma Rinx and Else.[8]

The image of the maypole both underscores and ridicules this phallocentric world, within which Else is an eternally indebted recipient and beneficiary: "Else the brain sparrow must pay lengthy installments until this happy fate is paid off" (G 57). Else's "fortunate fate" as a housewife consists in her ability to be a consumer with Hans's money:

> A husband pays a housekeeping allowance. With the household gold Else buys the world. 1 chrome skillet, 1 knife block solid wood, 1 glass fruit bowl white with pink glass flowers, 1 ornamental cushion embroidered with roses, 2 brushes turquoise always come in handy, 2 pink plastic mixing bowls always come in handy too, 1 ornamental watering can copper color. Just like that Else goes shopping. A married woman has it so good. Now Else is a factor in the world. (G 60)

This is Else's only participation in the world of exchange, however. She is precisely an "element," a thing, not an actor: "Else is an integral component of the Rinx property" (G 61). The arguments against Else entering the world of commerce through work can still be heard in the 1990s: "Else can be glad she doesn't earn anything. Just think of the expenses and outlays. And taxes. Else would have to pay a Cleaning Woman, a Washing Machine, a Dish Washer, a House Keeper, a Seamstress, a Cook, Stoker, Painter, Glazier and the whole list" (G 62). The list, of course, also describes the real value Else brings to the family unit. Her value is consistently denied, however, in favor of the myth of female dependence and subservience. Else is to be kept apart from the public world and belongs to Hans alone: "Far within the intimate marriage Else efficiently keeps house...In Else only Hans abides or bites" (G 62-63).

Czurda shows Else's environment as personified by Hans and his mother, Frau Rinx. Although Hans's negative behaviors following their marriage—especially his alcoholism and sexual violence—are important factors in driving Else to murder, Czurda hones in first on his language. Initially a language of seduction, his words are like a flattering mirror: "Elsesparrowsoprettyareyou like a humming bird I saw at the zoo. Has every feather a different color, not just like a peacock, which has many colors, but the same on every feather. That's how special you are to me, Elsesparrowsoprettyareyou, every spread out feather extra bright"(G 11). These phrases, repeated and varied throughout the novel, carry a narcissistic danger: when a woman derives not just her social position, but her inner sense of worth, from her relationship to a man, she gives away her own identity. What Hans gives to Else in this regard, he can also take away:

> Hans swiftly finishes the interior of his fortress...And around the outside, too, Hans keeps his eye on the whole inept Else, who has something wrong with her everywhere. Hans doesn't want other people to talk about her. Else can be grateful that good-as-gold Hans will have her with all her limitless faults. (G 12)

Once Hans has gained his goal through flattery, he secures his property further by robbing Else of her self-confidence. Else cedes her competence (only Hans is capable "*kann's*") and the power of speech itself.

The main villain in Czurda's novel is neither the brutal Hans nor the murderous Else, but the patriarchal structures that reinforce the oppression of women, even by other women. Hans's mother, Frau Rinx, is the clearest example of women pitted against one another by the patriarchy; this figure, peripheral to Döblin's telling, is central for Czurda.[9] Frustrated and unsatisfied, her situation is interchangeable with that of many "former mothers": "First a mother works out a child. Once the work is done, such a woman is no longer good for anything. Only for pleasure. Seduction. But nature does not intend this for a former mother" (G 155).

The chapter "Die Wünsche" (Wishes) introduces Frau Rinx along with an interminable list of her desires: "Out of obstinacy, Mrs. Rinx especially wants: Happiness! A Pressure Cooker! A pair of black pumps for special occasions" (G 19). Even though continuing to have material desires is an act of rebellion for Frau Rinx, they are merely the substitute the consumer culture offers women for real fulfillment:

> The real wishes are refugees. Mrs. Rinx does not write them on any list. No human ear will ever hear them. She will take them with her to the grave. She has always aborted them immediately. No law can forbid that. Hans is her Wish Vault. Before him, Hans's father was the Family Grave for the female Rinx Wishes, before him the Papa of Mrs. Rinx nee Rappel. (G 19-20)

This older woman's dilemma is not simply that she has unmet desires, but that she has no legitimate path for fulfilling these desires herself. The mere fact of being a woman makes her dependent on father, husband, and son for her needs and wishes.

Frau Rinx's unnamed wishes seem to include power first and foremost, even if it comes in the petty form of power over her daughter-in-law and household. Frau Rinx also wishes to preserve her sexuality and even fertility. At one point, she expresses her continuing sexual needs in a socially acceptable way by wishing for "a nice retiree to stroke her breasts. To carry her heavy bags up to the second floor like the departed Mr. Rinx" (G 19). But her desires focus instead on the man most accessible to her, the one who can already be considered her property: "Thus does she gild her golden rod Hans. She made him turn out right. If she had her way she'd swallow him. And birth him again. He ought to turn out just as well the second time, her enchanting affair. He sprouted in just the right place. It's too silly that Mama has to lose this member" (G 20). The incestuous relationship that develops is Frau Rinx's only entry into the commerce of daily life. Family dynamics would otherwise require that she give way to the new, young wife unless she retains her hold on the economic engine and source of patriarchal power in the family. Czurda thus establishes a certain sympathy, or at least understanding, for the motivations and exigencies of this destructive, manipulative, and cruel figure. This balances the horror of what the mother's actions mean to Else, and Czurda hence avoids the danger of misogynistic representation inherent in a negative mother-in-law figure.

The incest itself is portrayed ambiguously, in keeping with the technique of the rest of the novel, which often switches time frame or perspective with little or no signal. The reader must take an active role in reconstructing linear causality (or choosing not to and accepting the interpenetration of past and present, thought and action). For example, in the middle of a tortured marital sexual encounter between Hans and Else, we read:

> The door opens. The light clicks on. The radio is turned on. Mama Rinx is standing in the room. She is naked. She dances a waltz. Her Hip Bones grind. She props her leg up. She swivels her pelvis...She stretches her toes. She does a few knee squats. She stretches her breasts. Fondles them with her

fingers. She spindles her teats. Drink, Hans Lover Son.
(G 33-34)

The scene quickly becomes so grotesque that it is hard to accept it as
reality within the narrative. When Hans, responding to his mother's
appearance, attires himself in diapers and pacifier, the scene slips even
further into the realm of phantasm rather than narrative event. The scene
then repeats itself in Else's mind: "Else's eyes are inner flood lights.
Even when Else closes her eyes, it never turns dark...A glistening
bright Mrs. Rinx wanders through every darkest night...In Else's
memory this is hell" (G 34-35). Whether Mamma Rinx "really" breaks
into the marital bedroom and seduces her son in front of his wife is less
the point than the shocking image's emotional impact on Else and
subsequently on the reader.

   Another scene in which Else appears to discover the incestuous
relationship is more straightforward in terms of action, but distanced
this time through the means of representation: a photograph. Else
chances to find a color picture on the floor and cannot decipher it:
"Underbrush? a withered meadow? a sand trough?" Only when Hans rips
the picture from Else's hand does Else recognize its content:

> But that's. Else gulps. But that's a horrible. It shoots through
> Else like a shot.
> No trespassing.
> Else stares at the stone gray genital of an old woman.
> ...An Epiphany. (G 71)

This clear moment of discovery might be the climax of a traditional
murder mystery or psychological thriller. In combination with the
previous passage, however, it could be confusing to the reader
accustomed to linear narrative: has Else repressed the first event, only to
"discover" the seductive relationship between mother and son a second
time? It may not matter whether either event "really happens" within
the novel: both are shocking possibilities of how Else *could* discover
this relationship. The portrayals of a taboo represent a *psychological*
truth; the graphic images underscore the dramatic effect the living
situation has on Else.

   Language and communication are central to Czurda's portrayal. As
one critic has written, "the background to this story, which knows that

victim and perpetrator are caught up in one and the same system, is women's centuries-old struggle for a suitable language of their own."[10] Language is both subject and tool in the telling of this tale. In a parody of Christian theology, Hans sees himself as the "Word," while Else is a blank piece of paper: "Elsesparrowprettyareyou like an innocent white sheet of paper, upon which I am the word. You are around me in all your purity. You are like the Void, which only I can blot out, since I have words to put into the emptiness. Because I am the Word so to speak" (G 13). As Else sits in her jail cell at the beginning of the novel, she finds that Hans's words remain even though he himself is gone: "Hans is gone now, to be sure. But his words still stick in Else's body. They remain. They grapple in this abandoned tract of land. They have stamped Else. They have rubbed her with lard. Her skin is an ulcer of words" (G 14). Czurda demonstrates what her blindly driven protagonist does not realize: namely, the feminist problem is never one individual man, husband, rapist, but the entire system of signification and set of social expectations that put women collectively into situations that can produce an Else.

However, not only Hans and the male world treat Else as a passive receptacle for their words. Erika, Else's lover, also directs her stream of words *at* Else rather than *to* her: "Then, in gratitude and love, Erika pours forth her many feelings. These flow into letters that fly to Else. Only when Else is at Erika's house does the rivulet empty directly into Else" (G 112-113). If Hans's "Word" stands for phallocentric power, Erika's words are formless feelings: "His command of a single word. Toots, a broken record, love love love love. Unswerving love, the groove. This underdeveloped female memory has expelled all rationality with a catapult" (G 16). Erika's stereotypically feminine flaw is a lack of intellectual distance. Thus, Czurda does not offer an easy retreat into matriarchy or lesbian separatism as a solution to Else's problems.

Czurda literally deconstructs language by taking apart the compound nouns that are so abundant in German. By splitting a familiar word like *Hausarbeit* (housework) into *Haus Arbeit,* (House Work), she makes the reader more conscious of the content of signifiers that can become worn and empty through use. In a phrase like *das Schlag fertige Antlitz von Hans* (G 31), literalization actually changes the meaning of the disassembled word. The sentence with *schlagfertig* not separated would mean "Hans's quick-witted (clever) face"; with the word separated, it can be read: "Hans's face, ready to strike." Czurda thus makes the reader aware that an everyday word for "clever" has its roots in aggression: *schlagfertig* literally means "ready to hit." Czurda often allows poetic association to carry thoughts in new directions through language, resulting in both humorous and critical impulses. The free associations, which appear in all of Czurda's writing, may occur from any character's perspective, as when she writes of Hans, "A craving slings its noose out of the Alcohol Morass called Hans Rinx. From the Depths of the Swamp there lustily rises a captivating Whip. Cot. Crevice. Hans isn't sure exactly" (G 31-32). The word play here may reproduce Hans's drunken state; since he is exerting his sexual control over Else, however, the words "cot" and "crevice" also resonate with the situation.

When Frau Rinx notices Else getting "uppity," her thought-words are almost musical in their direct expression of emotion: "Stop. Only huMANity allowed. Change signals immediately. Notch Sign. Secure the Traffic Lane Satin Border Stone. Cats Eye Radio! Glow Filter Defense traraaa!" (G 84). Shock, outrage, and an urge for military discipline come through in both form and content of this passage. *Männschheit* is a good approximation of how an Austrian with a thick accent might pronounce *Menschheit* (humanity), but the spelling also points out what feminist linguists have long said about the word "man" in both German and English: that this word and other supposedly generic terms for humans are often slanted towards the masculine. Else is excluded from humanity, which, the spelling reveals, is male.

Else's relationship to language and creativity is foregrounded in her friendship with Erika. For pages on end, Else simply affirms what Erika tells her. In her lovemaking, however, Else invents new and mostly senseless compounds as pet names: "Oystersteeringwhile... bear'searlegwarmers...adrenalinehoneyarrow" (G 105-107). Else is the poet, not Erika, despite the latter's long letters, which are full of banalities. Else's use of language for love is the opposite of Czurda's deconstructive method: instead of taking apart familiar words to make their meaning conscious, she creates unheard-of combinations without meaning. This may be a first step in the direction of women's language, or it may be part of Else's flight from consciousness with Erika.

Perhaps Czurda's greatest achievement in this novel is her portrayal of Else's state of mind, which is far more convincing in its subjective, disjointed prose-poetry than was Döblin's hyperrealistic "portrayal of a milieu." Else's estrangement from her own body and her appropriation through language are central to this account. As painful as the portrayals of Hans's violence is the following rendering of the couple's lack of sexual communication:

> Her body does not speak...It dams up rigidly around the bones, far removed from very Else...There! There is a hand. Seeking the thighs. Will find them any minute. Has five frightful fingers for burrowing. Has fingers that bore. Like moles. Like worms. Draw a Mucous Trace. Foul the whole region with mucilage...Hans pants. Hans shivers. Hans sweats. What's coming now happens, thank God, in a past an Else can't remember. Thank God Else wakes up in a future, in which what's coming now is over. (G 32-33)

This scene alone, appearing early in the novel, makes Else's act understandable. When a woman is so estranged from her own body, it is no wonder that she can see another human being as an obstacle to be removed, especially if he intensifies and forces her to experience her own estrangement. "Else is unwittingly confronted with the choice between losing herself and murder. That she chooses the latter has symbolic meaning for the author."[11]

Other Works

Since none of Czurda's work has yet been published in English translation, a brief discussion of her other writings seems in order. (Perhaps this article will alert potential translators, who would need strong poetic gifts in English to do Czurda's work justice.) Of Czurda's five volumes of poetry,[12] *Duh Voik* (You People) deserves special mention both because of its technique ("ethnographic stenogram of an ordinary day")[13] and because the period in question—October 10, 1989 to December 29, 1990—fell during the year German reunification became a reality. In this volume especially, Czurda engages in a kind of automatic writing: "I sit there passively—as passive as a receiver can be—and pick up the currents; in all its fragmentation I register whatever appears on my membrane."[14]

Elfriede Czurda's first prose work, *Diotima, oder, Die Differenz des Glücks* (Diotima, or, the Difference of Happiness)[15] was influenced by Watzlawick's *How Real Is Real?*[16] Its themes of physical and emotional distance, differences in perception, and the impossibility of communication under those conditions are taken up again, with more humor, in *Signora Julia,*[17] a satirical novel that begins with the loving couple, Julia and Arkadius, in a *locus amoenus,* only to have them separate physically, both because their utopia is impossible and because Arkadius must search for his past. Throughout most of the novel, Julia plays the Solveig or Penelope role of waiting female (with increasing impatience) and Czurda satirizes the man's need for travel, adventure, and self-involved investigations; eventually, however, Julia tires of this and embarks on a journey of her own. The novel thus allows itself a generous satire of masculine ideals, yet avoids letting the woman fall into the disempowered role of passive sniping.

The novel *Kerner: Ein Abenteuerroman* (Kerner: An Adventure Novel)[18] seems to be a complementary prelude to *Die Giftmörderinnen* in its portrayal of male brutality. Kerner is a petty bourgeois who seeks the physical challenge of mountain climbing in order to forget about molesting his teenage daughter. Like *Signora Julia, Kerner* satirizes the male thirst for adventure, seeing it not only as self-aggrandizement, but as a means of escaping unpleasant truths. The fact that the female protagonist of *Signora Julia* discovers her own need for adventure saves Czurda's oeuvre as a whole from buying into essentialist gender stereotypes in its critique of masculinity.

Czurda is an exciting avant-garde feminist author. One should perhaps not be surprised, then, by her situation: while her life outside of Austria is by choice and she has received much critical acclaim,[19] her economic situation remains challenging: "My monthly income is that of a sales clerk...Fifteen percent of my subsistence needs are met by my books; the rest I have to earn with readings and radio work."[20] One can only wish her as much success in practical matters of popular exposure and earnings as she has already achieved in her artistic productivity, creativity, and critical acclaim.

Bowling Green State University

Thanks to Kathleen Thorpe for communication at a critical moment and to Elfriede Czurda for giving freely of her time and her texts.

Notes

1. Conversation between Elfriede Czurda and Kristie Foell in Berlin, July 1994. All translations were done by me.
2. For example, together with Elfriede Gerstl, Czurda organized a conference and edited a special number of *Wespennest* devoted to "Beispiele zeitgenössischer Frauendarstellung in der Literatur," *Wespennest* 44 (1981).
3. Czurda, "Roths Sucht sich zu sehnen. Zur männlichen Selbstherrlichkeit in Gerhard Roths Theaterstück 'Sehnsucht,'" *Wespennest* 44 (1981): 20.
4. Here I am referring to the 1995 murder case of Susan Smith, a woman from South Carolina who received the life sentence for drowning her two young sons.
5. Alfred Döblin, *Die beiden Freundinnen und ihr Giftmord*, orig. Berlin 1924 (Frankfurt: Suhrkamp, 1971). Subsequent references to this text will be cited with BF and the page number.
6. The series was titled "Außenseiter der Gesellschaft. Die Verbrechen der Gegenwart."
7. Kathleen Thorpe, "Undine revisited: *Die Giftmörderinnen* by Czurda," *Lesen und Schreiben. Literatur—Kritik—Germanistik* (Tübingen/Basel: Francke, 1995), 249-254.
8. Czurda, *Die Giftmörderinnen* (Reinbek: Rowohlt, 1991), 56-57. Subsequent references to this text will be marked with G and the page number.
9. Conversation between Czurda and Kristie Foell, July 1994. Czurda emphasized that the explosive potential of Frau Rinx and her desires was one of the main attractions this story held for her (the other was the secret code Else and Erika developed with their geranium pots).
10. Silvia Volckmann, "Wörter im Leib," rev. of *Die Giftmörderinnen* by Czurda, *StadtRevue* (Cologne, November 1991): 156.
11. Ibid.
12. Czurda, *ein griff = eingriff inbegriffen* (Berlin: Rainer, 1978); *Falschungen: Anagramme und Gedichte* (Berlin: Rainer, 1987); *Fast 1 Leben* (1987); *Das Confuse Compendium* (1991); and *Voik: Gehirn Stockung Notat Sturme* (Graz: Droschl, 1993).
13. *Voik*, 6.
14. Ibid., 5.

15. Czurda, *Diotima, oder, Die Differenz des Glücks* (Reinbek: Rowohlt, 1982).
16. Paul Watzlawick, *How Real Is Real?* (New York: Random House, 1976).
17. Czurda, *Signora Julia* (Reinbek: Rowohlt, 1985).
18. Czurda, *Kerner. Ein Abenteuerroman* (Reinbek: Rowohlt, 1987).
19. In addition to positive reviews in the press, Czurda received the Austrian "Förderungspreis für Literatur des Bundesministeriums für Unterricht und Kunst" and the "Theodor-Körner-Preis" (both 1984); she has also read and lectured widely in Germany and abroad.
20. Quoted by Günther Nenning, "Voixtümlich notiert: Elfriede Czurdas schwerwütige Gedichte," rev. of *Voik. Gehirn Stockung Notat Stürme* by Elfriede Czurda, *Die Zeit* 37 (Hamburg, 1993): 69.

Med Ana Fraundintn: Critical Dialect Poetry: Lesser Known Poetic Ventures by Christine Nöstlinger, Annemarie Regensburger, and Anna Nöst.

Klaus Zeyringer

1. Discourses

In the past two decades the term "women's literature" has become standard. Although useful from a practical perspective, the term has proven hard to define. Generally, definitions entail a notion of authority. In a signifier-signified-equation, this authority has a limiting and excluding effect, because it tries to bring disparate ideas under one umbrella and subsumes them into a rigid classification system. "It is the act of defining itself which determines and selects. As a result of this standardization process, some texts are included under the term 'women's literature,' others are not," Sigrid Weigel writes.[1]

In light of the substantial literary output by female Austrian authors since the early 1980s and their subsequent reception by the media and literary scholars, it has become clear how difficult, or even hopeless, it is to find an all-embracing term for such a wide array of literature without having to perform interpretative somersaults. It is utterly meaningless to include texts by female Austrian authors such as Jelinek, Mayröcker, Fritz, Kerschbaumer, Gerstl, Treudl, Helfer, Wolfmayr, Frischmuth, Mitgutsch, Reichart, Ganglbauer, Seidlhofer, Mühringer, Schwaiger, etc. under one literary roof. However, it should be pointed out in what ways this complex process of canonization leaves some texts and female authors out in the cold. Since we are concerned with an *open* study of literature—open towards the multi-faceted spectrum of literary production and critically reflecting upon traditional canonization mechanisms—we would like to focus on critical dialect poems which have so far been excluded from the canon due to the selective process of classification. In general, critical dialect poems have had to overcome two obstacles: first, the publishing industry has considered them of limited appeal on account of their regional character. Second, the almighty powers of canonization have looked at critical dialect literature askance because it occupies a literary space that seems to border on the trivial as well as the national in form and language. If the discourse about *écriture féminine* is a.) not to stop at elite forms of expression, b.) not solely to react to (and against) "higher" forms of language, and c.) to differ from usual authoritarian systems, it cannot exclude dialect literature a priori.

2. A Common Denominator for Three Different Literary Examples

In the past decade, female authors have mostly examined their position in society through their writing. *Écriture féminine*, based on American and French theory by Luce Irigaray, Julia Kristeva, Hélène Cixous and Michel Foucault, was partially influenced by the discourses of the women's liberation movement(s). One mode of expression was to construct a "subjective inner view" and thus criticize exterior conditions. As a result, literary fiction has repeatedly tried to illustrate the process of overcoming female speechlessness and subsequently, aim at and express various forms of resistance on different poetic and social levels.

From the mid 1980s onwards, numerous female Austrian writers have reacted and criticized Austrian conditions and events in an increasingly ardent way. Some of them have acted as "warners" in a public forum. For instance, in June of 1987 Elfriede Jelinek, Barbara Frischmuth, and Marie-Thérèse Kerschbaumer held a vigil in front of St. Stephen's Cathedral in Vienna to commemorate the Austrian Resistance Movement. These Austrian women writers have also considered writing as an act of resistance and put it in a political context. Elfriede Jelinek, for example, has stressed her "political credo," which became manifest in her play *Nora* (written as early as 1977 and first performed in 1979). Jelinek says that "a woman's movement cannot be conceived of without a political context."[2]

Fiction written by and about women in the 1980s focused on the self-exploratory processes involved in writing and reflected women's attitudes towards a male-dominated society, their upbringing, and their own mothers, the mediators of rules and norms.[3] This attempt to position oneself both personally and publicly serves as a common denominator for critical dialect poems by Christine Nöstlinger, Annemarie Regensburger and Anna Nöst. These three authors and their texts are also examples of the differences and considerable wealth of female literary expression in Austria. Christine Nöstlinger, who was born in 1936, can boast of a wide-ranging body of work. She has become known for her children's books and for television work. She lives in Vienna and uses Viennese dialect in her three volumes of poetry, which were published in 1974, 1982 and 1987. Born in 1948, Annemarie Regensburger lives in the Tyrolean town of Imst, where she uses a Tyrolean dialect for her work and adamantly refers to herself as a "dialect poet." Anna Nöst, who was born in 1961 and grew up in the eastern part of Styria, works as a financial controller of the *Abfall Service Austria* (Waste Disposal Service Austria). Because "dialect is a spoken language,"[4] her South Styrian dialect poems are recorded on a CD.

3. A Historical Survey: Dialect Literature

Ever since the sixteenth century, regional dialect literature has been known to deviate from the standard literature of German-speaking regions. In the nineteenth century, dialect speech patterns were used for the *Dorfgeschichte* (village stories), which was considered a part of socio-critical literature until 1848.[5] The *Dorfgeschichte* used dialect patterns to create a realistic mood through language. Even then, authors were faced with the dilemma of fulfilling their realistic mission—to enlighten and educate—but only using dialect language to such an extent that it would not interfere with the intended propagation of the work. Since their topics stemmed from a regional source, standard language did not suffice to convey their messages: language was thus not only seen as "an aesthetic mode of expression, but also perceived to have a social function."[6] Although the *Dorfgeschichte* in the early 1800s augmented dialect to the status of a literary language, in the second half of the nineteenth century, the *Dorfgeschichte* lapsed into the realm of the idyllic and trivial. In addition, dialect folk plays by authors such as Anzengruber, Schönherr and Morré were excluded from standard literature by a canon which considered the national element to be synonymous with "eternal beauty" and "eternal beauty" tantamount to the national element. Regional speech patterns were thus increasingly associated with nativist and nationalist ideas. In his play *Die letzten Tage der Menschheit* (The Last Days of Mankind), Karl Kraus described dialect as the formulaic masks of nationalist and nativist larvae and lemurs which revealed itself to be of an aggressive nature.

Ever since the emergence of "blood and soil" literature, literary scholars have denigrated dialect poems. Dialect literature has had to defend itself against the reproach of "dulling the masses." This opinion prevailed as late as the 1950s when the Wiener Gruppe started to blaze new trails. A plethora of self-described "regional" and "popular" poets is still carrying on this nationalist and conservative tradition, though. They continue to rhyme the name of the state "Steiamoak" (Styria) with "grouß und stoak" (tall and strong). Just like "Christian idiots from the Alps" (Joseph Roth), these regional poets are fully aware of their stance as "We Austrians" and thus entitle their works "Dahoam is dahoam" (Home is Home).

LEBENDIGES WORT, the forum for publishing literary texts provided in the Graz *Kleine Zeitung* newspaper with the highest print-run, is subsidized by various provincial governments. It uses a "folkish" language and wants "its readers to remember the virtues and special qualities of regional forces in troubled times such as these."[7] This idealizing regional literature is blooming all over Austria, in order to adorn the country and keep it clean and tidy. Authors like Auguste Müller who write under the pseudonym Binder-Zisch industriously stick to the cliché of the pure and chaste dialect: "A barefoot girl with a face like milk and blood / for real, not painted /.../ that's how I see the dialect!"[8] These regional forces naturally will not permit strangers to reach for a flower which grows on native soil. (Ever since the publication of the *Bekenntnisbuch* in Austria in 1938, we know the meaning of this "brown" national-socialist metaphor. In the *Bekenntnisbuch*, national-socialist authors celebrated Hitler and the annexation of Austria into the German Reich with spring metaphors).

Steffi Gleichauf wrote in her poem "Kärntnarisch" (Carinthian) in the magazine *Die Kärntner Landsmannschaft* in 1986: "Why one is / as one is? /.../ It is because of the roots / that are growing so deep into the good soil. /.../ We cannot explain / how it is / when the hand reaches for a flower. Only / we don't like it / if the hand is a foreign hand."[9] The poem's false pretenses even go down to the level of word notation with verses fluctuating from standard language to dialect—once using regional expressions—"dö so tief" (these so deep)—and then again adhering to standard patterns—"die Wurzn" (the roots). This kind of literature "puts on a folksy mask and can be closely associated with infamous blood-and-soil idealizations, which point in the direction of a national defense service and a 'brown-and-blue' (National-Socialist and Nationalist) preservation of regional traditions."[10]

Dialect literature has been examined and judged in light of these developments and of the constant presence of a national-conservative tradition. Works by the Wiener Gruppe, critical texts from the sixties, seventies and eighties, and poems by Nöstlinger, Regensburger and Nöst stand in stark contrast to this background. They still have to defend themselves against a reception which is marked by one-dimensional expectations and overshadowed by negative images of a false folklore.[11] In order to receive recognition, dialect literature has to overcome the combined obstacles of regional limitations and preconceived notions.

Dialect and avant-garde were first combined by the Wiener Gruppe in Austria in the 1950s. Friedrich Achleitner, H.C. Artmann, Konrad Bayer, Gerhard Rühm and Oswald Wiener looked for new ways of expression and thus ridded regional speech patterns of their standard and dialectic clichés. They considered dialect a "fresh material" and skillfully combined the spoken language with surrealism, dadaism, and constructivism. In 1956 Gerhard Rühm published an article on the new dialect literature in the magazine *alpha* :

> We have discovered dialect for modern literature. We are primarily interested in its phonetic variety...Even one single word can assume different tones and thus be individualized ...while in standard language—dialect is a "spoken language" —every word seems to be objectified and rigid...Although surrealism constantly refers to the subconscious, it has overlooked the important fact that dialect plays an essential role in our "daily" thinking and therefore also in our subconscious mind. On account of its realism and immediacy of expression we stand a good chance of alienating and thus reevaluating words by contrasting them with each other.[12]

These authors were not concerned with remembering the voice of national-socialist forces or with taking "Vienna literally" as Josef Weinheber did in *Wien wörtlich* (Vienna Literally). Rather, they wanted to take dialect literally and use it as an autonomous linguistic tool for their avant-garde mission. Dialect had thus become a totally new art tool which could disturb common usage: it was considered innovative, subjective and provocative. The best known example is H.C. Artmann's volume of poetry *med ana schwoazzn dintn* (With Black Ink) of 1958, which was also the biggest commercial success. The Wiener Gruppe, therefore, set a tone for dialect literature, which has been resonating from works such as *Laut und Luise* (1966) to *stanzen* (1992) by Ernst

Jandl, and which has recently appeared in works of male and female Austrian authors such as in Walter Pilar's poem *An sanften Samstagen* (1987; On Soft Saturdays) and in some of Elfriede Czurda's poems in the volume *Voik. Gehirn Stockung Notat Stürme* (People: Brain Stoppage Notation Storms) of 1993.

Authors of the generation of 68 expressed their political activism through "new dialect literature." In plays by Wolfgang Bauer, Peter Turrini, Gustav Ernst, and Heinz R. Unger, dialect itself became part of the voice of protest. In their works, these authors continued the tradition of the folk play, viewed dialect language as a part of everyday reality and looked at life "from the bottom up." (Michael Scharang's experimental radio plays of the 1960s based on documentary literature can also be included in this group). These authors tried to liberate dialect literature from preconceived notions and contrasted it with a phony and false "folk culture."[13] By quoting speech and thinking patterns, their texts reveal the political functions and social effects inherent in them; i.e., in *Der Herr Karl* by Carl Merz and Helmut Qualtinger (1961)—which is hailed as a classic of "new dialect literature," second only to Artmann's renowned volume of poetry.

So far, dialect language has not figured prominently in works of female Austrian authors. Apparently, they prefer to express their political activism, social criticism and thoughts on women's liberation exclusively in standard German. When their reflections have been expressed in dialect, they have been received and reviewed less intensively.[14] One interesting example is Nöstlinger: while her works in standard language were massively reviewed, her volumes of dialect poetry did not attract much attention. Yet, the increasingly subjective perspective of Austrian women's literature from the early to mid-1980s must be seen within the framework of subjectiveness expressed through dialect patterns. A well-reflected linguistic work can thus be contrasted with a problematic immediacy[15] which does not deal with experiences on a linguistic and literary level. Nöstlinger, Regensburger and Nöst contribute to the emancipatory potential of women's literature by using dialect language according to Gerhard Rühm's postulate and by applying dialectal patterns in an innovative, subjective and provocative way. Even though they shift and change accents, they create a link between the avant-garde position of the Wiener Gruppe and the activist forces of "new dialect literature."

4. "Iba de gaunz oaman fraun" (About the Very Poor Women): Christine Nöstlinger

In 1974 Nöstlinger published her first volume of dialect poetry entitled *Iba de gaunz oaman kinda* (About the Very Poor Children); the sixth edition (1988) confirms its popularity. In 1982 she published *Iba de gaunz oaman fraun*[16] and in 1987 *Iba de gaunz oaman mauna* (About the Very Poor Men).[17] Although its poetic "I" is shifted, the same title attests to the same literary program: she describes an everyday reality "from the bottom" and "from the inside" in Viennese dialect. This new linguistic pattern requires the male or female reader to pay special attention. Nöstlinger shows her readers snapshots of blue-collar workers and the lower-middle class. Their linguistic and dialectal roots also imprison them in their world.

Situated in the center of the trilogy are "de gaunz oaman fraun." Their images are also reflected in the poetic mirror of "de gaunz oaman kinda" and later of "de gaunz oaman mauna." Nöstlinger presents images of women of the lower classes and describes the experiences and feelings of women living in the Viennese municipal housing projects.[18] She tells their "sadly comical and madly depressing"[19] tales: a woman wants to drown herself, but does not want to walk all the way from the district of Ottakring to the Danube; while cooking spinach, a woman realizes that "municipal housing projects" have become "municipal prisons"; a woman has children by three men; a woman threatens to take revenge on her husband by becoming obese—he would be punished by having the fattest wife in the entire project. The only way they can express their anger at the unfair order of their small and big worlds is through an inner monologue.

The women are not allowed to articulate their pain and complaints, for their protest and resistance is prevented by the patriarchal dictum: "Nua ned drau rian" (Don't rock the boat!). This is also the title of a poem and the first verse of each one of eight stanzas. In the ninth and last stanza one truism is wedged between two expressions of incomprehension: "Kennt's des vaschdee? / Eh gloa—/ des kennt's ned vaschdee!" ("Can you understand that? / Of course—/ you can't understand that!") (F 8). The only way women can oppose male violence is through their silent suffering and fragmented daydreams. One formula says that this is cleverness on their part, which, together with other linguistic and mental clichés, safeguards peace in the housing project: "Schlau muasd sei!" (You must be sly!) is the title of a poem in which a woman uses some truisms to explain her passive attitude towards her husband's brutality: When he slaps me / I have never / blinked an eye /.../ but to really object / and to fight him / that isn't worth it (F 13). Dialect is written in a seemingly new form: for example, in "Waunama" (If He to Me) three words of standard German are contracted. Nöstlinger finds rhymes for a brutal and absurd reality. Her text contrasts with its title and shows how ridiculous all empty clichés are: the woman says that she is stronger than her abusive husband: "That I / don't smack him, / that I don't / punch him/—it really / would be possible /—because I am / stronger" (F 13). She is fantasizing about being the one in control by subverting the established order. Yet due to the patriarchal dictum and its empty clichés, she does not act out her desired aggression and thus reveals her weakness. The title "Schlau muasd sei!" is meant as a challenge, which the woman cannot meet.

Some poems deal with female stereotyped behavior passed on in the mother-daughter-chain, for instance, "Glane Greiss-Soi Gedaunkn" (Little Labor Room Reflections) (F 11f.) and "D Mutta weids Madl ei" (The Mother Informs the Daughter) (F 21f.). Women daydream about matriarchy and visualize it according to a male totalitarian pattern in "Olle Mauna" (All Men):

All men	Olle Mauna
All men are crazy,	Olle Mauna haum an Huscha,
All men are idiots,	olle Mauna haum an Spreck,
All men are fools,	olle Mauna haum an Duscha,
To marry one does no good!	sie an nema, hot kan Zweck!
All men are sadistic,	Olle Mauna san Sadisten,
All men are losers,	olle Mauna san aum Saund,
All men are fascists,	olle Mauna san Faschistn,
I want a manless country!	i wü a männaloses Laund!
All men should be castrated,	Olle Mauna muas ma kastrian.
All men should be cast out,	Olle Mauna muas ma vatreim.
All men should be banished,	Olle Mauna muas ma faschian.
Only women should remain!	Nua d Fraun diafn übableim!

(F 61)

The title of the volume is illustrated poem by poem (and with photos by Barbara Pflaum). However, it also is relativized and, in the end, sounds slightly ironical: women toil along, but also get caught in indoctrinated cliché traps. The women are imprisoned in their little worlds together with the "gaunz oaman mauna." Men experience impotence when they build new houses, commute to work and toil equally hard. They work off their frustration through alcoholism, xenophobia and violence towards the "gaunz oaman fraun." Men's daydreams are also tinged with resignation and violence, as becomes apparent in the poem "Ana aus bruck" (A Person from Bruck), which has an ending reminiscent of H.C. Artmann's "black" poems: "and I dream / that / within a year / I will have slain / my whole / family."[20] A commuter from the small town of Bruck can release his aggression only on his family. His isolation is expressed in a few words which appear in the poem in an isolated form.

Nöstlinger presents a world in which the interior view becomes a prison where dialect language is the adequate form of expression. Yet it also hides and represses any form of covert, though inarticulate protest. The language "from the bottom" can hardly be considered innovative or, as avant-garde artists such as Rühm described it, "a fresh material." It is not used for montage purposes, but as a more detailed expression of a social reality and a provocative tool of critical activism.[21]

5. "Stolperer" (Stumbler): Annemarie Regensburger

After *All Ding a Weil* (All Things Take a While), Regensburger published her volume of poetry *Stolperer, Kritische Mundartgedichte* (One Who Stumbles, Critical Dialect Poems)[22] with the small Haymon publishing house in Innsbruck in 1988. In his epilogue to *Stolperer*, Karl Mussak points out that Regensburger initially used poetry "to come to terms with her own life" and refers to her "harsh childhood and youth in a rural environment," "substantial professional burdens," as well as "her obligations as a mother of three children":

> Just like many other women, she suffered from the narrowness and speechlessness of everyday life. When she started writing, she threw the doors and windows of her house wide open to take an active interest in everything that happened in her closer and broader environment. She has tried to shape society with the means that are at her disposal…She contrasts rigid mental

patterns and traditions with a critical examination of the status quo. She demands renewal and change. Dialect poetry thus becomes a social ferment.[23]

From its narrow boundaries, a world-view is formulated in the language of the examined world, i.e., in Tyrolean dialect. In the beginning of this volume of poetry is "the word"—the poem "'s Wort." Three groups of mostly short poems follow: "Sig salber Stolperstua" (To Stumble Over Yourself) (17 poems), "Stolpern über d'uan" (To Stumble Over the Others) (49 poems) and "Stolperer zun Sinn" (One Who Stumbles Towards Meaning) (28 poems). The first part, which calls a person his/her own stumbling block, describes the upbringing as a school of rules and roles. All positions are basically determined from birth, as the title of the first poem—"Lei" (Only) demonstrates. If a girl is born, the cliché goes: "It's just / another / girl" (S 10). While a formulaic pedagogy indoctrinates women with societal standards, it also exorcises an awareness of identity: "If you are / not allowed / to be the one / you really are / then it is / no wonder / that it'll / come out / in your sleep" (S 12). In contrast to Nöstlinger's women, who voice their protest in daydreams about violence, Regensburger's "heroines" can only refute their upbringing by wetting beds or stammering (the poems "Bettnässer" (Bedwetter) and "Stotterer" (Stutterer) are printed next to each other, S 12, S 13). They follow norms that other people impose on them. These norms become their life-motto:

Norm	Norm
As long	So lang
as you act	de tuasch
like everybody else	wie alle
as long	so lang
as you are	de bisch
like they	wie sie
want	dih
you	habm
to be	wellen
that is how long	so lang
you can	kannsch
exist.	sein. (S 22)

This "norm" displays a well-structured form: the poem's three-part rhythm grows from repeating the time-limiting condition "so lang": the first part consists of three verses, the second of six and the third again of three. "Dih" (you) is in the center of the second part and thus of the poem. It is an isolated representation of a personal identity. In its structure, the first part corresponds to the third, which, seen from the end, sets the tone for the indoctrination of norms: "Sein wie alle" (to be like everybody else). *Sein* (to be) holds an isolated position in the last verse; it is not further described, except for the comparison "wie alle." *Sein* has a time limit ("so lang" is a threat in the end) and is only possible if it is the same as that of all others ("allen"), i.e., "wie sie dih habm wellen" (as they want you to be)—at somebody else's will.

The second part of the volume primarily deals with the relationship to the others and thus to society, whose double standards of morality Regensburger unveils. In "Doppelmoral" (Double Standards), a poem comprised of few words, she exposes hypocritical structures, for example: "You can do / whatever you want—but it should not / become public" (S 39). "Obrigkeit" (Supremacy) (S 43) bases its "Autorität" (Authority) (S 45) on a power of definitions and formulas:

Power	Macht
Power	Macht
wants	mecht
that everybody	daß jeder
does something	macht
and	und
not that we	nicht mie
want something	mecht
	(S 46)

In this poem, the principle of power is expressed by a combination of dialect language and the techniques of "concrete poetry," i.e., a structure of three words. Not only can words be "reevaluated" by "being contrasted with each other," as Gerhard Rühm suggested, but they can also reveal a societal structure through their brief and precise format. "Macht" also connotes a male authority which puts a question-mark after "gleichberechtigt" (Emancipated): "When you have done it all / after you cooked / mended, done the wash / ironed, cleaned up /.../ then

/ inbetween / you can do / what you want" (S 18). Again and again, Regensburger puts her poetic finger into the wounds inflicted upon women by outside forces which determine their identity and constantly limit their autonomous scope of action. He gives the orders, she follows; he demands, she is at his will.

In the third part of her volume Annemarie Regensburger asks some fundamental questions. In various poems she criticizes the Catholic church by revealing a religious authority which uses a formula of suppression. Incidentally, the Tyrolean author Margareth Schöpf describes the same phenomenon in the dialect of the Ötztal Valley and also stresses the authoritarian formula by resorting to standard language:

"Thy Will Be Done."	"Dein Wille geschehe"
I cannot be tamed	I bin nit ze zämen
You can't take anything	konnst mir nö sövl
away from me	nemen
I will always	i wear olm
rebel	au begern
because I cannot	weil is oafoch
learn that	nit derlearn
"Thy Will be Done!"	"Dein Wille geschehe!"[24]

In this context, Regensburger also refers to power positions which can be indoctrinated in empty clichés: "Can a Chair be holy?...To be a Chair has made people, and people want power" (S 64)—the poem "Stuehl" (Seat) explains her attitute by taking the expression "Heiliger Stuhl" (Holy Seat) literally and analyzing it.

Regensburger, like Nöstlinger, does not consider dialect language a charming expression of a phony idyll of the native country. Rather, the native country is bared of its idyll through a precise linguistic process. Dialect language is an original and personal form of expression which, contrary to the formulas and authoritarian concepts of standard language (in Nöstlinger's and Regensburger's texts, they mostly appear in titles), makes critical questions possible: dialect brings subjects up for discussion.[25] As is the case in many texts of "women's literature," female authors attribute a repressed and disturbed life to societal structures by describing personal life and speech patterns.

In contrast to Nöstlinger, Regensburger strikes an avant-garde note in some of her poems by slightly deviating from a "realistically plausible" speech pattern and by using the approaches of the Wiener Gruppe. The structure of Regensburger's thirteen-liner "Still" is similar to the first seven lines of Achleitner's dialect poem "auwe" (Ouch): "still / still / still / stoop / still / still / still /..." (S 65).

6. "Linzer Kipferl" (Linzer Croissants): Anna Nöst

In 1993 the company *Abfall Service Austria* recorded a CD of its financial controller Nöst. It was entitled *Linzer Kipferl. 30 Gedichte und Litaneien im Südoststeirischen Dialekt.*[26] When the CD was presented in Graz in 1993, Deputy Mayor Ruth Feldgrill-Zankel held a "ceremonial speech," in which she paid tribute to Nöst "as a mouthpiece of women."[27] In the Ursuline boarding school in Graz, under the authority of the Catholic church, which Nöst attended in the early 1970s, a sophisticated standard language was the norm; dialect language was only used on holidays and during vacation time.[28] While studying in Vienna for an M.B.A. degree, she began to write dialect poems. Together with the group "Literarische Eingreiftruppe des Club Brou Ha Ha. Gesellschaft für Niveaudiskussion mit beschränkter Häufung [*sic*]" (Nils Jensen, Gerhard Ruiss, Sylvia Treudl, Johannes A. Vyoral), Nöst organized a "reading for fish" in Klagenfurt in June 1986. This reading was meant to be a provocative counteraction to the Bachmann Literary Contest (Bachmann-Wettbewerb). In 1988 Nöst won the Award for New Dialect Poetry at the Kloepfer Contest in the city of Köflach, named after the national-socialist author Hans Kloepfer.[29] The audience, however, reacted negatively to her texts: "Nöst's strange scribblings don't even rhyme," one protesting voice in the audience remarked.[30]

In Nöst's texts, dialect is a spoken language, which is partly organized in rhythmical patterns, in theses and antitheses and in repetitions and variations: a certain speech melody is intoned, interrupted, broken and then played in a new way. Dialect is the material of linguistic attempts to resist standard language and its demands, as Ernst Jandl's favorite music group *Attwenger* does it. One example is "lous du i" (Listen To Me): "do you listen / I / do / listen / I mean you listen / do I mean I hear you / do I mean me / do I mean hear / I mean hear / do I hear me / I don't know" (LK 2). In this text, Nöst definitely follows the tradition of the Wiener Gruppe, whose notions about dialect as a spoken language she adopts.[31] One single word can take on many different nuances. By contrasting words, Nöst succeeds in creating an alienating effect: "innovative, subjective and provocative," just as Gerhard Rühm postulated it.

Anna Nöst's litany of swear-words is particularly provocative. Reminiscent of goliardic poems in Catholic litanies, she offsets a pleading and praying chorus with a speaker. The poem draws on the linguistic wealth of dialect language, which cannot be matched by standard language: "du" (You) is one of the longest texts on the CD: "you, you, you, you jerk you, you idiot, you fool, you dope, you klutz, you hick, yokel..." (LK 20-22). She mounts, varies, repeats, reorders and modifies about fifty swearwords. In this text, as in the poem "lous du i," Nöst uses rhythmical figures that follow the rules of rhetoric (change of ascending and descending bars, polyptoton, epanalepsis, anadiplosis, anaphora, epistrophe). For this, she uses a *ductus* of reduplication typical of dialect language. Advocates of a pure and "chaste" dialect can only be very suspicious of this text; they and their "regional forces" must consider it a provocation.

Nöst composes South Styrian images and speech patterns by using changing rhythms. Although the speech melody sometimes conceals the contents, all of Nöst's texts have critical implications and, as Nöstlinger and Regensburger, voice protest against "die da oben" (The Ones On Top) "von unten" (from the bottom):

> The Ones on Top
>
> you can't do anything anyway
> can't change anything anyway
> what do you want to do
> the men on top do anyway what they want to do
> the men on top
> do anyway what they want to do
> on top the men
> (LK 14)

In Regensburger's poem "gleichberechtigt" (Equal Rights) women's volition is subject to one condition—social submission. Free will thus shuts itself off from ever becoming reality. Nöst investigates those who can do what they want and who are able to make people work for them: "dei hearn do oubm" (the men in leading position).

Nöst's overarching topics include the gloominess prevalent among outsiders, especially among women, the power structures under which they suffer and difficult communication—all existential questions raised in rural areas. For example: a farmer marries his "last" daughter, who is "rechdhowarisch" (self-righteous), off to a mechanic, with whom she won't get a word in edgewise...has no rights said the Holzbauer (LK 3); a seventeen-year-old girl is pregnant and her parents complain that she has brought shame upon them ("ins des oundua") (to bring us shame) (LK 4); at a country festival all young women are waiting to be asked to dance ("feisd") (provocative) (LK 5); different ecological sins stink like hell ("do schmeickds") (Does it taste?) (LK 11); weeks pass by, the same way, monotonously ("z moundas") (every Monday) (LK 17). The only way out—by saying no, by talking, by leaving, by resisting, is expressed in a conditional mood:

If I could	wann i kunnd
...	...
If I could	wann i kunnd
I would leave	dad i gian
I would leave	dad i gian
If I could	wann i kunnd
I would talk	dad i reidn
I would talk	reidn dad i
I would say no	dad i na sogn
say no	na sogn
no I would say	na dad i sogn
if I could	wann i kunnd
...	...
	(LK 26f.)

7. Conclusion

In their critical dialect poems, Nöstlinger, Regensburger and Nöst create images of a woman's world "at the bottom" of society. Their language is one "of the bottom" and "from the inside." They show how women are taught societal norms and how behavioral patterns are passed on from mother to daughter. The most marked example is Nöstlinger's poem "D Mutta weids Madl ei" (The Mother Informs Her Daughter) in which a mother instructs a daughter about the rules of life:

The Mother Informs Her Daughter

...
A woman
who reads a book
when her husband
the poor guy
sews on the shirt buttons himself
should be killed.
Because she is not honorable
to our sex!
A woman
has to live for her husband
and the children
...
Why that is so
is another question
that one simply doesn't ask
because one's opinion does not count
(F 21f.)

It is exactly this question—why conditions are as they are—that Nöstlinger, Regensburger and Nöst urgently ask again and again and in many ways. In their poems, this question is tied into an aesthetic and literary program with an avant-garde touch. As in Elfriede Jelinek's, Maria Merthen's, Waltraud Anna Mitgutsch's and Marianne Fritz's fiction, the mother makes sure that her daughter adheres to the rules. The mother represents a male authority and passes on behavioral patterns. She teaches her daughter the obligation to be and remain silent: "nua ned drau rian" (not to complain) (F 7) with Nöstlinger, "schluckn" (to swallow), "s Maul haltn miaßn" (to shut up), "still / duckn" (quiet and stoop) with Regensburger,[32] and "wous reidn hoad is" (where speaking is hard) and 'I say nothing / I think I won't say anything / I think' in Nöst's "fraunlied" (Women's Song).[33]
    Critical dialect poems are directed against this silence. They "talk about" and "touch upon" prevalent conditions. They do not stay behind the trivial bars that constitute the prison of pseudo-aesthetic regional literature, which is forced into false rhymes and tries to create a "We Austrians" feeling by imitating a folksy tone. Rather, critical dialect

poems show us ways to voice discomfort by resorting to new speech patterns in image and sound. As Gerhard Rühm has noted, they are based on twenty-six letters which in their novel composition can shake up established habits of reception. The phonetic richness of dialect language as well as its eminent role in routine and subconscious mental processes that aroused the interest of the Wiener Gruppe also attracts Nöstlinger, Regensburger, and Nöst. The three authors mount and reproduce routine mental processes in their formulaic, contradictory and cliché-indoctrinated form. They use three different kinds of Austrian dialect: in Nöstlinger's Viennese, we find words such as "mei lem" (my life), "mauna" (men), "mutta" (mother), "madl" (girl or daughter), "ned" (not); in Regensburger's Tyrolean it is "lebm" (life), "manda" (men), "mama" (mother), "madele" (girl or daughter); and in Nöst's South Styrian dialect it is "leibm" (life), "muada" (mother), "nid" (not)...

These three authors take recourse to distinct experiences and feelings and thus reveal fundamental structures and positions of society—in an innovative, subjective and provocative way.

Université Catholique de l'Ouest, Angers, France

Translated by Gudrun Bauer

Notes

1. Sigrid Weigel, *Die Stimme der Medusa. Schreibweisen in der Gegenwartsliteratur von Frauen* (Dülmen-Hiddingsel: tende, 1987), 22. See also Margret Eifler, "Postmoderne Feminisierung," *Frauen-Fragen in der deutschsprachigen Literatur seit 1945*, ed. Mona Knapp and Gerd Labroisse (Amsterdam/Atlanta: Rodopi, 1989), 1-35 (=Amsterdamer Beiträge zur neuren Germanistik 29). This is not the place to discuss the term "women's literature." I am fully aware that it is a problematic issue. Like Sigrid Weigel, I consider "women's literature" a discursive event.

2. "Elfriede Jelinek: Interview mit Kurt Palm," Burgtheater. Zwölfeläuten. Blut. Besuchzeit. Vier österreichische Stücke, ed. Kurt Palm (Berlin: Henschel, 1986), 231: "...daß eine Frauenbewegung ohne einen politischen Zusammenhang nicht denkbar ist."

3. For more details see chapter 9 and 10 in Klaus Zeyringer, *Innerlichkeit und Öffentlichkeit. Österreichische Literatur der achtziger Jahre* (Tübingen: Francke, 1992). See also Klaus Zeyringer: "Österreichische Literatur von und über Frauen in den achtziger Jahren," *Frauen in Österreich. Beiträge zu ihrer Situation im 19. und 20. Jahrhundert*, eds. David F. Good, Margarete Grandner and Mary Jo Maynes (Vienna/Cologne /Weimar: Böhlau, 1993), 247-272.

4. Anna Nöst in: Michael Tschida, "de woasd e de va doud," *Kleine Zeitung* (December 31, 1993).

5. With Franz Michael Felder this form of expression continued until 1869.

6. Uwe Bauer, *Dorfgeschichte. Zur Entstehung und gesellschaftlichen Funktion einer literarischen Gattung im Vormärz* (Munich: Fink, 1978), 105.

7. Quoted from a brochure, Hans Haid, "HOAMATL so keusch und rein und braun. Bemerkungen zu Mundartreimern und 'Heimat'-Pflegern," *Lesezirkel* 3.18 (1986):14.

8. Ibid.

9. Ibid.

10. Ibid.

11. See for example Gerhard Moser, "Wien im Wort," *Volksstimme* (November 27, 1987): "Whoever knows the state of Austrian dialect poetry—from lay to KHD poets (KHD=Carinthian Home Service)—will be able to appreciate Nöstlinger's work."

12. Gerhard Rühm, ed. "Dialektdichtung," *Die Wiener Gruppe. Achleitner. Artmann. Bayer. Rühm. Wiener. Texte. Gemeinschaftsarbeiten, Aktionen.* (Reinbek bei Hamburg: Rowohlt Taschenbuch, 1967) (=Rowohlt Paperback 60), 20.

13. A broad public audience witnesses this contrast in the realm of Austrian folklore music, where critical musicians such as the Styrian band Broadlahn, the Upper Austrian duo Attwenger and Hubert von Goisern have to hold their own against pseudofolkloric mega-concerts of the band Zillertaler Schürzenjäger.

14. Hans Höller, a scholar of German literature from Salzburg, told me the following about the Upper Austrian Literary Award: there are many critical female poets who write in their native dialects. Most of the texts have not been published yet. For the wide variety of critical dialect literature see *Dialekt. Anthologie 1970-*

1980, eds. Bernhard C. Bünker and Manfred Chobot (Vienna: Internat. Dialektinst., 1982).

15. Weigel, 108.

16. Christine Nöstlinger, *Iba de gaunz oaman fraun* (Vienna/Munich: Jugend und Volk, third edition 1988; first edition 1982). Further references to this volume of poetry will be cited with F and the page number in the text.

17. Nöstlinger, *Iba de gaunz oaman mauna*. (Vienna/Munich: Jugend und Volk, 1987).

18. One year after Nöstlinger's volume of poems *Iba de gaunz oaman fraun* was published, the Austrian daily *Kurier* advertised her columns with the following slogan: "The woman who finally writes about what concerns every woman." Today Nöstlinger writes for the tabloid *täglich alles*, among others.

19. S.L. (Sigrid Löffler), "Gaunz oame Fraun. Die Kinderbuchautorin hat Dialektgedichte gemacht," *Profil* (March 29, 1982).

20. Nöstlinger, *Iba de gaunz oaman mauna*, 20.

21. One reviewer criticized the "artificial character of a constructed lower class Viennese dialect." It would make it harder to find an access to "normal" people "who compensate their unfulfilled desires and dreams with violence and resignation" in: "Oama Mauna," *Wochenpresse* (October 9, 1987). In simplified terms, this article describes the dilemma of critical literature: "It is doubtful whether the speechless can be more easily accessioned through poems by the so-called upper classes, which are the only ones to buy books."

22. Annemarie Regensburger, *Stolperer. Kritische Mundartgedichte* (Innsbruck: Haymon, 1988). Further references to this volume of poetry will be cited with S and the page number in the text.

23. Karl Mussak, "Nachwort," *Stolperer. Kritische Mundartgedichte*, by Regensburger, 80.

24. Margareth Schöpf, "Dein Wille geschehe," *Tiroler Tageszeitung*, (April 14-16, 1990).

25. Mussak, 80.

26. I quote from the booklet enclosed with the CD recording produced by Abfall Service Austria. In some passages, the spoken text slightly deviates from the printed text. In addition, the CD comes with a translation of the poems. Further references to this enclosed booklet will be cited with LK and the page

number in the text.

27. See "Die Komik der Heimatsprache," *Neues Land* (January 2, 1994).

28. See "'Linzer Kipferl' zwischen Oststeiermark und Wien," *Neue Zeit* (December 14, 1993).

29. Like Franz Nabl, Hans Kloepfer was an informant and collaborator of the Kampfbund für deutsche Kultur (Combat Group for German Culture), the cultural organization of the illegal NSDAP party in the mid-thirties. In 1938 he contributed to the *Bekenntnisbuch österreichischer Dichter* and praised Adolf Hitler. In the same year, he published a poem entitled "Steirischer Bergbauerngruß" (A Greeting from a Styrian Mountain Farmer) in a National Socialist anthology: "Schreibm tuat er sie Hitler, / und uns so guat gsinnt, / wia ma weit in der Welt / net an liabern findt. /.../ Drum, o du mei Herrgott / und unser liabe Fraun, / tuats jo, wo er umgeht / aufm Hitler guat schaun!" (He calls himself Hitler / and he likes us as a friend / you can't find a nicer guy in the whole world!). Quoted from: Klaus Amann, ed. "Franz Nabl—Politischer Dichter wider Willen? Ein Kapitel Rezeptions- und Wirkungsgeschichte." *Die Dichter und die Politik. Essays zur österreichischen Literatur nach 1918.* (Vienna: Edition Falter/ Deuticke, 1992), 158. Like Nabl, Kloepfer was one of the poets the Nazi regime particularly promoted. To this day, the Graz Institute for Styrian Literature is called "Franz-Nabl-Institut."

30. Tschida.

31. See texts by Friedrich Achleitner, *Die Wiener Gruppe*, 39ff.

32. Regensburger, *Stolperer*, 17, 58, 65.

33. Nöst, the CD booklet, 24.

Writing and Remembering—Acts of Resistance in Ingeborg Bachmann's *Malina* and *Der Fall Franza*, and Elfriede Jelinek's *Lust* and *Klavierspielerin*: Case Studies in Hysteria

Nancy C. Erickson

Like Nora's sisters, the protagonists in Bachmann's and Jelinek's writings trip across the stage in a presumptive envelope of middle-class respectability. Professional women, wives of millionaire industrialists or of socially prominent psychiatrists inhabit the fictional spaces created by the two women. Separated by ideological perspectives dictated by age and personal circumstance, Bachmann and Jelinek each write from the common vantage point of "women in contemporary Austrian society." Each calculatingly creates the illusion of "middle-class respectability" and then dashes any expectation evoked in the subsequent unfolding of the protagonists' experiences.[1] Bachmann, like Jelinek, strips away the layers of "respected" socialization to reveal the profoundly sickening reality that often constitutes the exigencies of women's lives.

This article deals with Bachmann's and Jelinek's aesthetic processes of uncovering the layers. It is precisely through understanding what each of the authors accomplish in the act of peeling back "den schönen Schein" (the beautiful illusion) that the reader comes to "recognize" the text.[2] The connections between Bachmann and Jelinek have been well documented in the critical literature over the past fifteen years. That Jelinek considers Bachmann a true "pioneer" in the development of a uniquely female writing is shown by her close professional association with Bachmann's work. More specifically, Jelinek wrote the screenplay for Schroeter's 1991 film adaptation of Bachmann's *Malina*. While Jelinek has chosen to distance herself somewhat from the film version,[3] critical reviews of her work continue to link the two authors.[4]

Elfriede Jelinek's connection to Bachmann is not only based on common philosophical grounding. If "misery breeds company," then the reception of the two authors' works recorded by the media and the critical literature has provided a second common link. While the critical reception has also included serious consideration of Bachmann's and Jelinek's writings, indeed, positive acclaim,[5] many critics' apparent obsession with what could be considered trivial aspects of appearance and person has worked to extend that trivialization in part to the discussion of their works.[6]

Bachmann was criticized for turning in the late 1950s and early 1960s from what analysts deemed her appropriate metier, that of lyricist, to take up the writing of prose. Although reprimanded, on the one hand, for creating "neurotic" characters, she was idolized, on the other, by journalistic media that created a Marilyn-Monroe-like figure for the literary world.[7] Introduced to the German speaking public in 1954, her picture was splashed across the cover of the August edition of *Spiegel*, along with the title story in which she was described: "Much blond hair, soft-brown eyes, her expression still and shy."[8] Jelinek has often been similarly reduced to a sum of her physical attributes in critical articles that have questioned the seriousness of her commitment to Marxist ideals given her penchant for designer clothing.[9] She has been asked to comment on her use of make-up, the implication being that any writer with a serious agenda for social revolution cannot and should not concern herself with personal appearance.

That a great deal of critical time and space has been devoted to delving behind the personages of Bachmann and Jelinek can be quickly substantiated with a review of the secondary literature. Bachmann's use of prescription drugs and alcohol, her late-night typing sessions which brought many complaints from her neighbors, her on-again, off-again relationship with Max Frisch; or Jelinek's own bouts with clinical depression, the details of her marriage arrangement, and her relationship to a demanding and overbearing mother have all been well documented.[10] All of that may be somehow peripherally interesting, but the effect of the critics' obsessive focus on the personal details of these two women's lives has tainted much of the critical literature. What has resulted is the equation of protagonist, behavior, storyline and denouement with the psychological state of the author, thereby trivializing the writing as merely an exercise in self-help psychoanalysis. Jelinek herself has pointed out "that the work of a man would never be confronted with the same collective malice and disdain as would a woman's work."[11] But the critical readings of Bachmann's and Jelinek's texts have continued to promote a type of one-to-one correspondence between their writings and their personal lives, bringing the renowned German feminist, Alice Schwarzer, to conclude that the "Father" section in *Malina* points toward the horrendous consequences of incest. The criticism leveled at Bachmann's creation of neurotic prose characters, Jelinek's purported lack of sympathy for the women in her works, and her use of the patois of the "enemy," that is pornographic language, have worked to subvert the message and punish the messenger. It is precisely these criticisms which will provide the focus for the remainder of this discussion, along with the above-promised analysis of how both Bachmann and Jelinek strip away the layers of lacquered socialization to write against "den schönen Schein."

When Ingeborg Bachmann's *Malina* appeared in 1971, the critics received it with stony silence, while the general reading public rallied to this new piece by the author whose last extended prose publication had been *Das dreißigste Jahr* in 1961 (*The Thirtieth Year*, 1963). The question of what to make of this split character, the narrator and Malina himself, which Bachmann identified as two sides of the same person,[12] was perhaps the most puzzling aspect of the novel. Then too an apparently hysterical female character who in the end disappears into a fissure in the wall, committing suicide in the process, yet attributing her death to a willful act of murder—"It was murder"[13]—could have left many readers slightly bewildered.

Malina was the first part of a promised cycle of works which Bachmann entitled *Todesarten* (Ways of Dying) to draw attention to her claim in the "Foreword" to *Der Fall Franza*:

> It [the fragment *Franza's case*] tries to make something known, tries to uncover that which has not vanished from the world. For while it has become immeasurably more difficult to carry out acts of violence today, it is for that reason these acts against people are so much more difficult to detect, so difficult that we are hardly aware of them being carried out even though they occur daily in our environs and in our neighborhoods. Indeed I believe and will try to prove that even today many people do not simply die, but rather are murdered.[14]

Der Fall Franza was never completed and it appeared posthumously in fragment form in 1973. The planned cycle would have described the lives and trials of a variety of protagonists, ground to destruction under the wheel of social relationships. For the "virus" of Nazism which Bachmann had experienced as a young child in Austria was very much at work in the general social fabric; indeed, it was an elemental force at the very center of men's and women's interactions. She believed, like Judith Fetterly, that men's and women's relationships were not only adversarial, but murderous.[15]

The evidence for that belief constitutes the storyline for the fragment *Der Fall Franza*. A young Austrian woman experiences a physical and mental breakdown at the sadistic hands of her prominent psychiatrist-husband, who reduces their marital relationship to a case study of the manipulation of a human being to the point of exhausted hysteria. His systematic destruction of her person leaves her a shell of a woman, disheveled, unable to function and barely able to speak.[16] Such is her psychological state when Martin arrives (FF 360-361). Franza recovers partially under the watchful care of her brother and is able to accompany him on a trip to the Middle East. But the damage wrought by her husband and the society to which he belongs is so far-reaching that her recovery falters, she is attacked by an unknown stranger, and the resulting wounds cause her death (FF 465-469). She registers for the reader the fact that the man was "a white man" and incorporates that refrain into the thoughts that constitute her drift into unconsciousness and subsequent death:

> Martin
> The best of all brothers.
> The desert exists.
> The edge of the Arabian desert.
> Made up of the broken, the smashed, the shattered.
> White people.
> My head.
> The white people, they should.
> They should be damned. He should be.
> The whites. (FF 469)

Franza's senseless and brutal death marks the end of a senseless, brutalized life. The "schöne Schein" of respectability and propriety stripped away in Bachmann's telling of Franza's story lays bare the worm-infested truth. Bachmann's narrative perspective in *Der Fall Franza* keeps a distance between protagonist and reader, occasionally allowing the reader to move into Franza's psychological space as evidenced in the quotation above. But for the most part, the reader remains outside of the inner workings of the main characters' actions and the storyline is apprehended through the lens of the omniscient narrator. That stands in contrast to the narrative line in *Malina*.

Although Bachmann planned to publish *Malina* as the first in the *Todesarten* cycle, she had, in fact, written this highly experimental novel after *Der Fall Franza*. In the writing of *Malina*, Bachmann ended her lifelong quest for the protagonist who inhabits the pages. In an interview with Toni Kienlechner on April 9, 1971, Bachmann describes how she arrived at the idea of creating this "Doppelgänger:"

> For me that is one of the first, almost entirely submerged memories. I always knew that I had to write this book, *Malina*, very early, while I was still writing poetry. I was always searching for this main character somehow. And I always knew that this main character would be masculine, that I could write only from a masculine point of view. But I continually asked myself, why? I did not understand, not even in writing the short stories, why I had to use a masculine "I." It was as though I could find my way to myself, that is not to deny the feminine "I," by placing the primary importance on this masculine "I."[17]

Ingeborg Bachmann had neither models nor references for her search. What she wrote, she created out of a storage of images and impressions that she had recorded during her forty-five years as daughter, schoolgirl, victim of Nazi oppression, lover, companion, friend, political activist, literary scholar, lecturer and woman. The result was *Malina*. What Bachmann described in the above statement is the common inability of women authors to find an authentic voice through which to describe women's experiences in societies patriarchally structured, a phenomenon that French feminist linguists would later define as the struggle of female "voicelessness" in a world logo-centrically ordered.

The relationships among the three main characters, Ivan, Malina and the "Ich"-narrator, constitute the surface storyline. The Ivan-character assumes the role and attributes of romantic lover; Malina that of rational, pragmatic partner who works, predictably, in a museum, preserving a pre-established view of history. The "Ich"-character lives with Malina but carries on an intensely erotic relationship with Ivan. She moves between the two men, recognizing her dependence upon each and her connection to both. Bachmann constructs the breakdown of the relationships with each of the two men and in so doing strips away the "Schein" of "normal" domesticity, that is, the female protagonist caught in a typical *ménage-à-trois*. The author portrays the breakdown in the narrator's relationship with Ivan through a gradual disintegration in their ability to communicate with one another. That disintegration evident in the recorded dialogue reflects the separation of the "worlds" that the two characters represent and underscores Bachmann's fundamental disbelief that language use as presently constituted can result in real or true communication, that is, "wahre Sätze" between and among people. Thus the reader eventually "hears" only the protagonist's rehearsed sentences on the phone and must speculate as to the content of Ivan's responses on the other end. Those telephone conversations become a metaphor for the gradual distancing and intentional disruption of communication on the part of Ivan and the protagonist,[18] and the ellipses that occur point to the characters' inabilities to articulate their true thoughts and feelings, to communicate.

The second chapter of *Malina*, "The Third Man," serves as an intermediary stage, linking the protagonist's recognition of the futility of the relationship with Ivan to her decision to "leave" Malina. The dreams and resulting discussions that the protagonist and Malina have with one another provide Bachmann with a means by which to make evident the distance between the protagonist's world view and that represented by the father in those dream sequences, and, by extension, Malina. The figure of the father in the second chapter assumes the role of torturer, destroyer, rapist, murderer, and, ultimately, silencer. The figure's face is that of the father, but the mother figure is implicated as well by her inability or her unwillingness to defend her child against the attacks initiated by the father. Both male and female are to blame, for the murderer resides within us all, as Bachmann herself pointed out in the interview with Ekkehart Rudolph.[19]

The "remembering" which results from the dreams leads to night wakings, to fretfulness and to generally hysterical behavior on the part of the protagonist. Malina, therefore, executes his role as rational advisor; sitting at her side, he attempts to convince her to behave "logically," to continue to see to his physical needs, to clean up her work space, to move on, and to stop looking back. In the final scene, one of seeming domestic tranquillity, Malina and the protagonist sit across from one another, sipping their coffee. He is distracted and does not see as she stands up and moves toward an opening in the wall of their apartment: "I get up and I think, if he does not say something immediately, if he does not stop me, then it is murder and I leave because I can no longer say it" (M 354). She is unable to speak to Malina and as she slips into the open space before her, she holds her breath and thinks: "I should have written a note; it was not Malina. But the wall is opening up; I am inside the wall, and Malina can only see the crack that we have seen for a long time. He will be thinking that I have walked out of the room" (M 354). Her decision to move into the space that opens to welcome her proves her inability and unwillingness to continue life with Malina. Her action is deliberate, calculated, and, by the standards of Malina's world, hysterical.

The protagonist's carefully executed break with Malina's world, that of the father, is not to be understood as the capitulation of the broken victim, but rather as the calculated decision of a "rational" being. The protagonist, recognizing the futility, indeed, potential destructiveness, of continuing to participate in a world of murder, hatred, destruction and disease, chooses the space beyond. Escape from societal bonds in an ultimately freeing way was unknown to Bachmann, as elusive then as it remains for us today. Therefore, instead of creating a false idealistic "happy ending," Bachmann posits the escape through the wall, away from the bourgeois norm of heterosexual relationships resulting in the type of "petty-bourgeois horror." Bachmann says that although it may appear that Malina has driven the protagonist to her death, that is, in fact, not the case. In an interview with Gunther Bergmann, Bachmann explains the situation in the following way:

> I would not say that Malina drives the protagonist to her death, although it could be interpreted that way. Because he makes clear to her only that which has already happened. She has already been "murdered" so many times or at least been driven to the edge. Here [in the end] she [the protagonist] merely takes the final step, causing the disappearance of a character, that is she, which can no longer function because she has been ultimately, completely destroyed.[20]

The insight to know when to stop was for Bachmann "a strength, not a weakness."[21] What appears as a hysterical act is, rather, the calculated decision of the rational protagonist to escape "den schönen Schein."

The seemingly neurotic behavior exhibited by the female protagonists in *Der Fall Franza* and in *Malina* is the effect of what Sabine Wilke has formulated as the mimetic consequences of cultural inscription on women's bodies,[22] and what I have chosen to identify in the title as "hysteria." This hysteria is the acting out, the violent reaction against inauthentic, culturally-imposed modes of behavior, indeed, of a patriarchally founded world view that lies at the basis of the acts of aggression toward those outside the patriarchal strictures. Elfriede Jelinek describes the conscriptive process of socialization that is imposed upon women as formulated by Bachmann: "To force women violently into the male order is shown as a crime and as such is called by name."[23] In *Der Fall Franza* and in *Malina*, Bachmann strips away these layers of socialization to expose the destruction that lies beneath the surface.

If *Der Fall Franza* and *Malina* are Bachmann's efforts to authentically describe women's experiences in a patriarchally ordered society, then *Die Klavierspielerin* (1984; *The Piano Teacher*, 1989) and *Lust* (1990; *Lust*, 1992) result from Jelinek's decision to willfully lay aside the search for an authentic woman's language, and to appropriate the language of the oppressor himself in order to expose its inauthenticity. Jelinek's language pulses with rhythm, like the heartbeat in the arm, then in the temple when a rubber chord is tightened around the muscle in preparation for the needle. The shock of release is felt and the drug screams into the brain. Unlike Bachmann's language which registers the subtle workings of consciousness engaged in discovery, Jelinek's texts pierce the ear like the screech of the cutting stone against glass or the rasp of rough metal across concrete. That abrasiveness shapes her style, jolting the reader to attention and demanding immediate action. Wilke formulates a comparison between Jelinek's and Bachmann's writing in this way:

> Jelinek's style does not allow in any way for mimetic interpretation as is the case of Bachmann's prose, but instead comprises mimesis itself. Her [Jelinek's] method of destroying and distancing the reader from familiar language serves the goals of making the readers aware, of enlightening them of bringing the political message home. At the same time, Jelinek portrays the female body as the point of violent inscription, a recognition with which she wants the readers to

be struck, forcing them to bring about the necessary changes in societal structures. (Wilke 152)

Jelinek locates the inscription of society's rules on the physical bodies of the women and uses that vantage point to create her harrowing tales of brutalization. In so doing, Jelinek moves the reader forcefully back from the text and prevents her/him from developing empathetic attachments to the female characters, all to make her point.

Jelinek finds herself writing within a perverted and brutal society. Her surrealistic rendering of human interaction stems from her belief that in the post-modern world "men must break the opposition of women with a new brutality."[25] This heightened application of force brings about a counteraction in the further brutalization of human interaction generally.

Jelinek meets this challenge of post-modern existence with the aggressive language of the culture itself, recorded in the endless descriptions of nauseatingly graphic scenes of sexual violations and masochistic humiliations in both *Die Klavierspierlerin* and *Lust*. The scenes repulse the reader, push her/him to the edge of tolerance and then invite the reader back to participate again in the continual role of voyeur. Jelinek plays with her reader and with her characters in ways that underline their common capacity for viciousness and destruction, grinding down both reader and characters with the repetitive nature of the physical, emotional and sexual violence—grinding to the point of "sensing," that is, reversing the inability to feel, to perceive. Jelinek pushes the reader to the abyss and then pulls her/him back again. But this mass-produced "senselessness" is, in fact, the point. For Jelinek writes with a vengeance against the numbing, multimedia-defined processes that have eradicated our ability to sense, to feel, to connect, to communicate, to care in the post-modern world. Deadened through sensory overload, the victims of this societal inundation search in increasingly sensational and increasingly brutal ways to feel again, to feel anything. It is that search that drives Erika to the peep shows, to engage in sado-masochistic bondage, to perform oral sex on her student Klemperer on the urine-stained floor of the concert hall.

Ultimately, the only "plausible" solutions become the razor thin lines drawn expertly down the inside of the wrists, the inner thighs, lengthwise between the labia, splayed open to the mirror—attempts to wrest back any level of sensation from the black abyss of "senselessness." For it is not out of a deeply imbedded, female masochistic need that the protagonists engage in harmful, dangerous behavior. Sabine Wilke explains the phenomenon in this way: "Self-inflicted pain does not happen because of a senseless lust for self-destruction but as a result of the inability to feel the body, an experience that is sought for at any cost" (Wilke 154).

Erika Kohut in *Die Klavierspielerin* and Gerti in *Lust* attempt to regain something they somehow know they have lost. Jelinek's ability to "mime the miming," to deconstruct the structures imposed upon women by others,[26] gives the readers new understanding of the human cost of these brutalizing practices. Reading *Die Klavierspielerin* and *Lust* neutralizes the "male gaze." Pornographic materials which objectify women lose their magical control over the reader's consciousness and open a space for her/him to rethink the fictions around which she/he builds her/his views of the world. Jelinek helps the reader recognize that the structures, systems and behaviors that create Erika's and Gerti's specific hells are neither inevitable nor immutable—no small task for someone Elfriede Jelinek herself has described as an inveterate pessimist.

Jelinek's texts remain fundamentally different from those of Bachmann. There are no cathartic moments of self-insight. There are no consciously-executed decisions of the will. There is simply Jelinek's relentless depiction of the hysterical behavior of her protagonists; Erika vacillating between razor and peep show, Gerti compulsively searching for destructive sexual liaisons. While reading Jelinek's texts, the reader struggles for air. The inundation of senseless violence and dysfunctional behaviors overwhelms. There is no relief in sympathetic renderings of the victims' plights, no empathy for these women caught in a system spinning them out of control, no moment of respite, no sanctuary for escape. There is only the indictment against women who promote the "male gaze," as does Erika; or who participate in the brutalizing system out of their own masochistic notion of sanctuary, like Gerti.

Yet Jelinek places herself firmly on the side of women caught in the web of patriarchy, not as innocent victims of a brutalizing system ("...women are also in command...")[27] but, rather, as participants because their involvement in this system has perverted their consciousness and converted whatever the women have done to the general benefit of men.[28] She further explains her use of characters in her works by saying:

> I do not write about real people, but rather about people as cliché or example. That which I am criticizing is always language which in its perverted form has made possible the present fascist cultural industry and has stymied a thorough denazification of the entire entertainment sphere. (Wilke 13)

The protagonists become the vehicles for language manipulation which work toward Jelinek's goal of revealing the real underpinnings of the society in which we live. The patina of societal respectability is thoroughly and systematically dissolved. The characters' motivations are laid bare as their "un-lacquered" actions come into full view. The monstrousness of societies founded on principles of male dominance and repression dances in the clear and piercing light of Jelinek's critical eye and, by extension, the reader's.

Reading the works by Ingeborg Bachmann and Elfriede Jelinek is analogous to being fitted with a new pair of glasses which intensify the light and sharpen the angles of what is viewed. There is no respite from the use of those critical lenses and there is no returning to a "pre-reading" state of innocence once the reader has been fitted. What is taken in through the lenses is sorted with what the reader already knows about his/her world. All future references are cognitively filed in light of the newly formulated world view which results from reading these texts.

This is the purpose in the writing and becomes the purpose in the reading: two women authors, aggressive in their search for what may count as truth, write in order to resist the terminating, silencing, and subduing forces that bear down on each. The voices are strong, the resistance calculated, the effect an elixir for weary journeyers. The authors are the oracles, the seers, clearing pathways for those who would follow: Elfriede Jelinek taking the reader outside the symbolic order by burying the reader, bombarding her/him with phrases and with words; Ingeborg Bachmann attempting to find a new, authentic code among the metaphoric splits and openings. These two writers work to move society and its members out of the shadows and into the clear light of day.

Bemidji State University

Notes

1. Jelinek's allegiance to Marxist ideals has not prevented her from creating mainly middle-class characters, or characters with middle-class ideals as the main characters in her writings.
2. The goal to write "gegen den schönen Schein" is attributed to Jelinek herself in an article entitled, "Jelinek über Bachmann," *Emma* (February 1991): 21-24. The 1991 version is a reprint of an *Emma*-article published in 1984. Another version appeared in *Kein objektives Urteil, nur ein Lebendiges*, ed. Christine Koschel and Inge von Weidenbaum (Munich: Piper, 1989).
3. This acknowledgment was relayed to me in a conversation with Margarete Lamb-Faffelberger who had recently interviewed Jelinek.
4. See among others: Irene Heidelberger-Leonard, "War es Doppelmord? Anmerkungen zu Elfriede Jelineks Bachmann-Rezeption und ihrem Filmbuch 'Malina'," in *Elfriede Jelinek. Text + Kritik. Band 117*, ed. Heinz Ludwig Arnold (Munich: Verlag edition text + kritik, 1993), 78-85.
5. Ingeborg Bachmann received the coveted Büchner Preis for Literature in 1964; Elfriede Jelinek was awarded the Heinrich-Böll-Preis of the City of Cologne in 1986, the Prize for Literature of the State of Styria in 1987, and the Prize for Literature of the City of Vienna in 1989, among others.
6. Margarete Lamb-Faffelberger follows Jelinek's reception in the Austrian press, along with that of Valie Export. See Margarete Lamb-Faffelberger, *Valie Export und Elfriede Jelinek im Spiegel der Presse* (New York, Bern: Peter Lang, 1992). The author includes personal interviews with both women artists.
7. For a discussion of the "Bachmann myth" created by the media, cf. Constance Hotz, *"Die Bachmann."Das Image der Dichterin: Ingeborg Bachmann im journalistischen Diskurs* (Konstanz: Faude, 1990).
8. Berd Witte, "Ingeborg Bachmann," *Deutsche Dichter. Band 8. Gegenwart* (Stuttgart: Reclam, 1990), 339.
9. See among others Riki Winter, "Gespräch mit Elfriede Jelinek," *Elfriede Jelinek*, ed. Kurt Bartsch and Günther Höfler (Graz: Droschl, 1991), 9-19, where the two women discuss the topic of "appropriate dress" for a woman writer.

10. Jelinek is quite aware of the dangers involved and has acknowledged: "I have always argued that the life of the author should not be brought into consideration when judging a literary work, as happened with Ingeborg Bachmann, the generalization of her death as a result of the burns she sustained in the fire as the filter through which all of her work is interpreted. In my case, that process has had the effect of causing me not to be able to say anymore who I, in fact, am; so that I end up throwing myself into my work with all the energy that I have, throwing it all into the text, so that the text becomes the "I" that I have lost sight of" (Riki Winter, "Gespräch mit Elfriede Jelinek," 9).

11. Quoted in Lamb-Faffelberger, *Valie Export und Elfriede Jelinek im Spiegel der Presse*, 165. Original in *Anschläge*, (May 1989).

12. Bachmann goes so far as to state in an interview with Ekkehart Rudolph, included in the series of essays and interviews in *Ingeborg Bachmann. Wir müssen wahre Sätze finden,* ed. Christine Koschel and Inge von Weidenbaum, 3rd ed. (Munich: Piper, 1991): "When I reread all of that while proofing the text, I noticed that the character of Ivan is also not straightforward, that he might be a two- or three-faceted figure himself" (Rudolph, 88).

13. Bachmann, *Malina* (Frankfurt: Suhrkamp, 1980), 356. Further references in the text will be indicated by M plus page number.

14. Bachmann, "*Der Fall Franza.* Die Vorrede," *Ingeborg Bachmann. Werke* (vol. 3), ed. Christine Koschel and Inge von Weidenbaum (Munich: Piper, 1978), 342. Further references to this work will be indicated by FF plus page number in the text.

15. Judith Fetterly, *The Resisting Reader: A Feminist Approach to American Fiction* (Bloomington/London: Indiana University Press, 1978), 45.

16. Christa Gürtler describes what she believes is the connection between Franza's husband, his methods and his "experiment" carried out at the expense of Franza's sanity. She connects Professor Jordan's tactics to National Socialism and states, "Ingeborg Bachmann's orientation appears to be similar to Theweleit's. She is also of the opinion that fascism manifests itself first of all in the relationship between men and women and that this way of thinking is very much in existence even today." *Der dunkle Schatten, dem ich schon seit Anfang folge*, ed. Hans

Ingeborg Bachmann. Wir müssen wahre Sätze finden, 99-100.

18. I would argue that it is not the case that Ivan unilaterally withdraws from the relationship with the protagonist. Rather, I would maintain that the protagonist herself is well aware of the impossibility of a meaningful and sustained relationship with Ivan from the beginning. See a conversation between the two at the beginning of Chapter 1 after which the protagonist analyzes the superficial nature of their communication (M 31-32).

19. Rudolph, 89.

20. Bachmann, "2. April 1971. Interview mit Günther Bergmann," *Ingeborg Bachmann. Wir müssen wahre Sätze finden*, 93.

21. Bachmann, "14. April 1971. Interview mit Otto Basil," *Ingeborg Bachmann. Wir müssen wahre Sätze finden*, 105.

22. Sabine Wilke, *Ausgraben und Erinnern. Zur Funktion von Geschichte, Subjekt und geschlechtlicher Identität in den Texten Christa Wolfs* (Würzburg: Königshausen & Naumann, 1993), 139f. Further references to this text will be indicated by Wilke and the page number.

23. "Jelinek über Bachmann," 23. Refer to note 2.

24. Christa Gürtler, "Einführung," *Gegen den schönen Schein* (Frankfurt: Neue Kritik, 1990), 7-15.

25. Jelinek, "Interview mit Gabriele Presber," *Frauenleben, Frauenpolitik* (Tübingen: Claudia Gehrke, 1992), 28.

26. I have borrowed this idea from Rosemarie Tong's discussion of Irigaray's undoing of "the effects of phallocentric discourse simply by *overdoing* them." That is precisely, I would argue, what Jelinek does in *Die Klavierspielerin* and *Lust*. Rosemarie Tong, *Feminist Thought, A Comprehensive Introduction* (Boulder: Westview Press, 1989), 217-233.

27. Winter, 13.

28. Ibid.

Bachmann, Jelinek, Schroeter: *Malina*. From Metaphoric Text to Encoded Cinema

Margret Eifler

Bachmann Criticism

Bachmann's 1971 novel *Malina* must be counted among the classics of feminist literature.[1] The narration rests on the relatively simple plot of an eternal triangle: a nameless but well-known authoress, roughly forty, lives with a level-headed, rational man by the name of Malina; she later falls head-over-heels in love with Ivan. The text gradually reveals Malina as the self-preserving, masculine side of this woman's femininity; Ivan, on the other hand, is the longed-for man of her dreams and the reality complement to her emotional and physical desires. But aside from some sexual encounters with her, he has very little to contribute to their relationship since he views love like playing a game of chess. Beyond this external frame and the hauntingly elegiac tone, however, the novel is rich in horrifying archetypal dreams, vivid utopian hopes, sufferings for mutual recognition and respect, and lucid in its presentation of the seemingly unbridgeable split between male and female existence. The novel's rendering of the female dilemma has ignited and sustained interpretive controversy since its publication.

In 1991 Sarah Lennox reviewed the large body of interpretations surrounding Bachmann's novel and summarized their various tenets.[2] The interpretations, as she points out, are bound to contextual climates that shift in perspective and provide an aggregate of changing critical nuances towards the same text. For example, *Malina* was first seen as an account of victimization, a case of the helpless female subjugated to man, consigned to a male-dominant culture. The next phase of interpretation (the late 1970s) was decidedly more emancipatory—the protagonist was seen as a defiant woman who chose the fate of self-destruction rather than submission to male principles. Readings of the 1980s placed the novel in a radical counter-cultural frame, no longer showing interest in equality but declaring women to be simply "different" from men. The next and latest theoretical basis, the minority discourse, classifies women's vilified existence among the outcast and the pariah, belonging, as it were, to "the tribe of the Papua," as Bachmann had termed it.

All in all, the 1991 film adaptation of Bachmann's novel[3] met harsh criticism—mostly from women experts who obviously revere this unique book as a cornerstone in the feminist canon—and thus resuscitated strong feminist defenses of the book.[4] In the minds of these women critics, the film version—produced and directed by men—could only be construed as yet another cunning appropriation. Their dismissals of the film rest on the suspicion that a male-construed bias had reverted the female protagonist to the old patriarchal mold for women: hysterical, masochistic, self-destructive and ill-equipped for rational behavior.

The fact that in the end credits of this film five women of the "Kuchenreuther" clan who had a strong hand in the choice of this particular novel for adaptation are especially acknowledged left no impression on the critics: after all, the film was much too artistically conceived for commercial success at the box office, too female-oriented in its concept and based too strongly on actions within the inner self for today's broad-scale viewing expectations. Yet, it cannot be considered mere "business-as-usual" that the brothers, Thomas and Steffen Kuchenreuther, invested eight million marks of public and private funding to produce this film—one of the most expensive in recent German cinema. Moreover, the independent artistic talents of the predominantly female film-team—the provocative screenplay by the Austrian writer Elfriede Jelinek, the unusual camera style of Elfi Mikesch, the carefully considered design sets by Alberte Barsacq, the effective editing by Juliane Loranz, or the informed character-role assumption by the French actress Isabelle Huppert—have to be seen as a guarantee for an uncompromising rendition of feminist self-interest.

The leading German feminist, Alice Schwarzer, delivered the most radical disparagement of the film. She maintained that Bachmann's main theme—namely men's brutality vis-a-vis women, and in particular the suffering inflicted by incestuous sexual abuse—had been purposefully omitted, and that the film thus failed to recognize that over half of all women will encounter sexual assault during their lifetime.[5] Although this aspect constitutes an important causal subtext in the novel, Schwarzer's polemic makes clear that she would have preferred that *her* reading of the book be foregrounded in order to advance her specific agenda of feminist activism. As valid as this demand might be, it remains but one perspective, one viewpoint, one interpretation, one reading among many.

The cynical mockeries heaped upon the film by the critic Iris Radisch obviously stem from a bibliophile who by definition finds any film rendition of a book undesirable. The slow and complex evolution of the psychic state of the protagonist and her environment within the book seems unattainable in the immediacy of the cinematic medium; in her opinion, it distorts both the character and Bachmann's concept. Radisch, therefore, criticizes Jelinek for having scripted Ivan and Malina (except for the father-complex) as two woman-devouring monsters locked into a gender war which does not reflect the inner pain and sadness intended by Bachmann. Radisch feels that Jelinek placed the female protagonist in a crass conflict between bed and typewriter simply to demonstrate her personal premise that sex and creativity are socially not permitted to co-exist in women. Film director Werner Schroeter, Radisch argues, is stuck in a film style of grand operatic gesturing, modulating the internal sufferings of the "Bachmann-woman" into the frantic movements of a nervous breakdown, thus casting a tragic diva who prepares her heavenward ascension from the very start.[6]

Dorothee Römhild also provides an intensely negative judgment of the film; she perceives the film adaption as an unacceptable reductionist version of the book. She condemns, for example, the distorted rendition of the Christian savior metaphor, which in her view accentuates the main character into a female Jesus rather than points to the female oppression underlying the biblical patriarchal criticism which she perceives in the novel. Römhild denounces the negative aesthetization which caricatures the female intellectual as a hysteric, without taking into consideration Bachmann's socio-critical depictions of fascist violence inherent in male history. Again, we are given highly valuable focal points to the book, but they remain personal interpretative preferences for many critics.[7]

Another vitriolic commentary was put forth by the scholar, Kathleen L. Komar. She argues that the crucial duality of Malina's existence as a projection of the traditionally rational "male" role as well as a male component of the female narrator is simply lost in the film version, and with it the core of the novel's message about women in modern society. Komar states that the two leading men in the film are given too much viewer appeal: "Malina spends all his time ministering to the poor woman and Ivan—as one of my fellow male viewers put it—was doing her a favor by having sex with her at all" (Komar 104). The audience, she maintains, thus sees only the woman's dependence and not the men's projections in her struggle for a female identity. Komar claims that the director had little interest in projecting Bachmann's intentions of her literary text onto the screen. She concludes that "if Schroeter sees himself as a bridge, he seems to have one piling firmly in the patriarchal master narrative and the other in his own filmmaking ego; even the space that he spans has little to do with Bachmann, who is only a name to serve as a pretext for portraying the director's 'brilliance'" (Komar 105).

The Adaptation Challenge: The Relationship Between Literature and Film

From these highly charged film commentaries one can sense the overwhelming aversion toward and suspicion of adaptations. The contention that film usurps its literary source has always existed; since the inception of film adaptation early in this century, it has been the awkward step child of literature and has carried a stigma of inferiority. Already at the outset of cinema—around 1909, when the film sector had made significant technological advances in improved cameras, projectors and permanent movie houses, and when it had become possible to adapt longer narratives to the screen—cinematographers turned to literature as a proven reservoir of material. Their claim of an inherent kinship between literature and film met, however, with resentment from the defenders of traditional cultural values against these proponents of a new mass entertainment. At the root of this controversy lay not only fear of economic competition and of the cinematic culture overtaking the book market, but also the bourgeoisie's angst in the face of the debasement and erosion of its cultural standards and class distinctions. Doubtlessly, these film entrepreneurs recognized that a "literarization" of the cinematic medium would lend legitimation to the new art form, and it would allow them to capitalize on a substantially expanded audience, even from among the bourgeoisie itself.[8]

In today's conservative corners these adaptation practices are still quite often denounced as coat-tail syndromes of legitimization. Negative terms heaped upon this presumed dependence of film on literary models run from reproduction and xerography to cinematization and replication; less disdainful epithets include renditions, transpositions, translations, commentaries, analogies, reenactments, reconceptualizations, and modernizations. In opposition to the filmmakers who want to see total fidelity to the source, there are those who hold that an adaptation carries with it no obligation of congruence, that the literary work from which it is drawn is already inevitably inscribed in the cinematic text. Film as such does not constitute a totally separate aesthetic phenomenon; narration overarches both text and film languages, two differing sign systems that have to be appreciated and understood on their own merits and terms. Film adaptations are not tantamount to usurpations of literary texts; rather, the visual idiom is an extension with its own continuity and a time-honored medium.[9]

There seems to be an unalterable premise which maintains that in the cinema, one extracts the thought from the image; in literature, the image from the thought. However, this observation should not constitute an unbridgeable opposition between a perceptual bias for imagery and a conceptual bias for words; it simply constitutes the basic difference between these two art forms. Whether apprehending words or pictures, the reader/viewer is engaged in a psychic/cognitive activity, a process of decoding the iconic or the symbolic system, and is as such involved in the communicative intent of reaction.

Of course, there are many more specific differentiations between these two media. For example, in the terminology of the semiologists, words are considered abstract or arbitrary signs or symbols which are meaningless in themselves, signifying only by conventional agreement. Pictures, on the other hand, are generally understood as natural signs or icons representing objects with some sort of veritable resemblance and which give—especially as in the case of photography—the illusion of being almost identical to what they depict. Both literature and film tend to be fundamentally representational arts with a natural tendency to reflect the "world-out-there." Yet even film from the very outset veered away from the direct recording of real life toward the mode of literary "realism" in which not life but its fictional representation is rendered credible via mimesis or simulation. Writing generally is seen to rest on fixed equivalences that make definition and translation possible; film, in contrast, has no permanent lexicality, has no fixed grammar, at least not to the degree of verbal syntax. Thus film expresses in an iconic, visual mode, literature in a symbolic, linguistic code.

Although literary words and filmic images may be different classes of signs, they both are nonetheless signs of representational fiction trying to communicate human experience and thought. And like words in literature, images in film are capable of both denotation and connotation, signifying not only literal, "objective" entities, but associations surrounding them as well. Most theorists tend to agree that images carry stronger denotative force and lesser connotative capacity than verbal language—and this aspect should not be overlooked: communicating mostly through several means at once (sound, image, color, movement, action), film naturally addresses the senses more directly than the descriptive succession in literature, even when film is practicing the abstracting "art that detaches." The plurality and immediacy of the visual will always irritate the retarding desire to reflect and contemplate what it sees; film does not allow for the same control which readers have over their book. Yet whatever the differences of their potential reception and impact, the language of literature and the language of film stretch to a large degree into each other's repertoire to make us, the readers and viewers, feel and think—sometimes both at once. It is beyond any doubt the common goal of their aesthetic endeavor to effect emotional response as well as to elicit some thought-reaction.

A strong similarity between cinematic and literary language lies in their mode of discursive construction, in the manner in which they arrange their signs. Film, of course, can render various "messages" simultaneously (via superimposition, voice-over, multiple or split screens), while literature does not have such flexibility. Film, as pointed out earlier, is not determined by general rules of grammar or syntax in its communication. Nonetheless, in the manner of verbal language, the filmic idiom usually orders its signs successively, adding one to the other in some relational sequence to transmit its narration. Verbal language is said to be more capable of generalization than visual language, but again it seems that the directness of film is matched by the details of verbal description.

In relation to portraying time, both media are capable of retardation (slowing down, stoppage) or ellipsis (omissions, leaps, short-cuts). Cinematic methods to retard can use long-takes or freeze-frames; comparable narrative devices are long descriptive or philosophical passages; elliptic visual structures can be given as fades or scenes in rapid succession to indicate time changes, while filmic jump-cuts are narratively equaled by leaps or sudden passages without logical connectives from one topic to another. Both media can manipulate several time-frames within a given narrative. Film, in part, derived its famous cross-cutting technique from the novel, particularly from Dickens's writings. As for the ability of literature and film to suggest tenses, it is generally maintained that film, unlike literature, can create only in a virtual present; indeed, past events in film are mostly given as awkward flashbacks. The fact is that the film viewer experiences the visual impact always as a "virtual presence," even when the action may take place in the past. But this phenomenon seems equally to be the case with reading a novel: the narrative imperfect of a novel does not necessarily distance the reader from the action, the literary imagination is equally captured in a virtual presence (maybe because we visualize narration as mental fantasy).

Both film and literature also share the capacity for metaphor. *Webster's Dictionary* defines the term as follows: "Coming from the Greek verb to transfer, meaning a figure of speech in which a word or a phrase literally denotes one kind of object or idea used in place of another to suggest a likeness or analogy between them, a figurative language." In literature, the metaphors seem to be a second language, an established code rooted in tradition for which the film medium is too young. Many metaphors, of course, such as a rose (= love), a scale (= justice), an owl (= wisdom) are also transferable by the camera. The pyrotechnical overlay in the last third of Schroeter's film intended to signal such a metaphoric element, but the fires of hell were perceived as too exaggerated by most critics.

The metonymic level works similarly in both media. Metonymy is generally defined as a figure of speech which uses the name of one thing for that of another of which it is an attribute or with which it is associated, or a part which expresses a whole: e.g, the sail referring to the boat, the lands belonging to the crown. In filmic terms it would be the shot of a moving train signaling the idea of travel, a hovering vulture signaling death; but also such means as a rapid camera movement which can liken man to machine, or a slowspeed motion to point to a person's dreamlike state, or a stop-motion as freeze-frame to give a sense of impending entrapment. This device was used by Schroeter to end the nineteenth scene in Jelinek's script, the group of bathers frozen in their forward-bending motion, turning into a human tableau of willow trees, referring to the Danube landscape of the Kagran tale.

The cinematic ability to combine the traditional forms and issues of literature with its own mode of realization may explain why film has emerged not only as the dominant narrative medium of the twentieth century, but its dominant artistic form as well. The symbiosis between book and film has meanwhile become the established norm. Scholarly research has tabulated that at least thirty percent of the annual film productions consistently rest on literary source adaptations. Today's marketing strategies are geared to synchronize book and film releases; film adaptations help to sell new editions of the original book (as was the case with Döblin's *Berlin Alexanderplatz*, when Fassbinder came out with his serialized eighteen-hour television version of it) or films that generate their own screen scenarios of adapted books into print (e.g., Fassbinder's work-journal to Döblin's *Alexanderplatz*; or as in the case at hand of Jelinek's film scenario of Bachmann's novel *Malina*). Such interaction of the two media has become an undisputed mutual business practice and an extended cultural interactivity, retaining or reaching out to the public via renowned or highly advertised print texts.

No category, no critical term, no scholarly assessment can precisely define what cinematic rendition is or should be, yet the efforts to distinguish it are significant and they share an important general premise: film adaptation is a paraphrase of sorts, a reformulation or transfiguration of a text into a new medium with a "certain allegiance" to the original. And maybe we should expect a filmmaker to treat the source with study, insight and intelligence, even though any director ought to be granted the right to produce alterations, restructurings, selections, additions and deletions. An adaptation should be a filmwork that considered its source; attention should be paid to the text and context of its original. This consideration might include specific recognition of the literary particulars used, such as form, genre, point-of-view, tone, metaphors, motifs—all devices that bring content into expression. For only after having taken these elements into account will a filmmaker's transposition become a unique and deliberate recreation. Changes cannot be labeled violations or betrayals, selective reformulation cannot be disclaimed as misunderstanding. Adaptation should not exclude artistic renovation. In this sense, filmmakers should seriously attempt a relationship with their literary source, but must also claim their artistic right at resymbolization. All of these artistic aspects seem fulfilled in making the filmic adaptation of Bachmann's *Malina*.

Ingeborg Bachmann and Elfriede Jelinek: Affinities between the Novel and the Screenplay

Schroeter's choice of Elfriede Jelinek as the screen-play writer of Bachmann's novel was not only fair but superb.[10] In 1984 she had written a short but succinct analysis of Bachmann (War by Other Means),[11] expounding the treatment Bachmann had endured within the male intellectual establishment and how poignantly she had analyzed the female position within this world. Jelinek, being Bachmann's feminist junior, took a much more radical tack in making her point; in fervent feminist terms she extracted from Ingeborg Bachmann's writing the revelation of a fascistically maligned female lineage which she sees continued in the Nazi extermination of the Jews; in this alignment with Bachmann Jelinek proclaims women as the eternal exiles from a dominant culture in which they have no part and no voice and which is determined to keep them subdued and controlled. Jelinek was obviously aware of the feminist implications in Bachmann's writing, and although a generation has passed between these two women authors, they share many literary affinities and the same thoughts concerning the situation of women.

Jelinek searches for appropriate aesthetic forms to denounce dominant thought practices, as in the discourse of politics or gender, or of various deconstructive literary methods. In particular she favors the revealing practice of creating an etymon (a word from which another word is formed or implied), such as the signifying name rescriptions in the screenplay of "Ivan—Naiv" or "Malina—Animal—Melanie—Anima—Animus" or "Todesarten—Todesraten,"[12] indicating that all speech acts and all normative language practices have to be laid bare to disclose who and what is behind the voice. In this sense, Jelinek is the genuine successor of Ingeborg Bachmann's language ethics, which called for human communication, integrity and truth.[13] Jelinek did not only integrate in her screenplay pointed word plays to indicate the inner despair of the female character or reiterate Bachmann's speech device of the love-distancing, shallow telephone dialogues but she also added clever Wittgensteinian reformulations that accurately reflect Bachmann's thought processes. Such sensitivity toward language shows that Jelinek shares with Bachmann the fervor for deconstructivist aesthetics rooted in the ethical demand to deinstrumentalize all communicative interactivity.

The text of Bachmann's novel is constructed around the haunting interior metaphors of an all-pervasive father, visualizing his killing spaces such as the cemetery of the murdered daughters, or the underwater lurking grounds for the preying rapist, or the fascist-like concentration camp atmosphere of victimizations. On the other hand, Jelinek's analyses of social deformations rest more on external depictions, with a clearly discernible exposure of normative quotidian language. Comparing Jelinek's most recent novel, *Lust*, to Bachmann's *Malina*, the heightened emphasis on narrative caricature and the linguistic disruption of conventional meaning become evident. Jelinek's writing in comparison to Bachmann's own has taken on a distinctly more abrasive tone in order to dislocate and alienate all patterns of male privilege. For her the logocentric position of a patriarchal world order has become the object of derisive puns and cynical allusions. As such, Jelinek's critical detailing of dominance, her exposure of mechanisms which debase woman, her hyperbole against any and all forms of oppression make her own texts, as well as the rewriting of *Malina*, much more radical, and certainly more provocative, than Ingeborg Bachmann's dream-oriented images.

Jelinek's screenplay no longer evidences Bachmann's utopian aspirations for communion; the elegiac tone of longing is absent.[14] Allegiance to men has become for Jelinek an intolerable act of female complacency. In a recent interview she identified the man as a megalomaniac species; women who do not realize their colonized complicity within such a male economy and make themselves available for male sexuality or participate in their economic power for possible better social gains, reflect a wrongful social consciousness.[15] With this opinion she continues to address Bachmann's postulate of the reduced female presence under male rule of reason, but she turns Bachmann's mournful account into a militant disclaimer. The gender schism will remain tragic in both women writers, but Bachmann's literary suicide and relinquishing of female emotions is escalated in Jelinek's writing to ascertain exclusive male power and logocentricity. While Bachmann delineated grief to the point of self-effacement, Jelinek lashes out aggressively at the brutal indifference of the male. She calls it murder, restating Bachmann's conclusion in no uncertain terms.

To render Bachmann's concept into the filmic medium with its specific directness and immediacy seemed to have suited Jelinek's anger just fine; not only was she able to extrapolate from the original text the most disruptive models of heterosexual warfare, but the cinematic mode of expression let her wield the axe (to stay within Jelinek's idiom) of intense pictures. The screenplay as such, due to the inherent kinship between Bachmann and Jelinek, is a faithful rendition of the book's spirit, even though accelerated in its feminist attitude. Of course, the narrative thought processes of the novel had to be much more exteriorized in the film scenario; Jelinek thus invented an immense amount of analogical imagery, creating 124 scenes, which in turn were for the most part faithfully taken over by the film director and the film team. Jelinek gave predominance to the intellectual dilemma of woman by effectively incorporating in the film script not only the male dislike for women's intellectual work (e.g., Ivan's and Malina's incessant harassment regarding her readings and her writing), but also integrating Bachmann's attempts at utopian writing, ingeniously conveying the Kagran fairy tale as an intercut vision in a cartoon movie that the female protagonist views with Ivan and his children. Women's intellectual endeavor is analyzed by Jelinek in a recent interview as follows: "Women's writing is seen as a violating act, because the female subject is not conceived as a speaking one; if she does it anyhow, it is considered transgression, a kind of aggressive act."[16]

Another prominent structure extrapolated from the novel for the film scenario is the disharmonious existence between the genders; this ranges from the dream scenes with the murderous father to the puppet-like dancing of his wife and daughter that he commands; but it is also exemplified in Ivan's deteriorating interest in the woman's non-aggressive chess games and her exclusive love expectations; and it is made evident in Malina's increasingly growing disdain for her emotional insistence and in his relief at finally getting rid of his incorrigible female half. The female self is ultimately murdered by the overpowering male ego with whom she could find no congruence; while this ending might have been altered from its novelistic counterpart—losing its original self-willed action to a more clearly indicated push toward suicide—the fact remains: it was murder in both cases.

Jelinek had already explicated Malina's role in her essay about Bachmann in which she wrote that his existence as a male partner slowly changes into that of a "cannibal," who step-by-step consumes the identity of his female alter ego, foregrounding himself more and more until the woman has disappeared into the crack of the wall and he as the male can fully take her place.[17] Ivan, too, is associated with maligning actions against her; not only does he "sleep around" and disparage her writing, but he also derides her femininity by pointing out the brown spots of her hands as those of an aged woman (35th scene in the scenario). Both male lovers are portrayed as increasingly negative forces.

The female persona disappears differently in the film than in the novel or in the script: neither in the patriarchal crack in the wall nor in biographical flames, but in the sixfold refraction of a mirror—the symbolic device which continues visually as a motif that Jelinek ascribes to the female character throughout the film. The female of the film appears over and over searching for her unstable identity in a small cosmetic mirror, poignantly explained in the third scene of the filmscript: "It is as if always another has to assure me that I exist and if it is only in this mirror!"[18] Another memorable mirror scene occurs in the high-class fashion store, in which for a short moment the female subject feels humorously in control of her reflection until it is cut short by the inescapable male gaze; a clerk, secretly watching her, turns her into the object of his desire as he comes up to kiss her on her shoulder. Nowhere is "woman" given distance and freedom from male designation, returning the viewer to the previous third scene where the female laments what Gabriele D'Annunzio had once said: for woman it is only important to be beautiful in men's eyes.

Another faithfully rendered major structure of the novel is Jelinek's prolific and adept arrangement of the patriarchal-oriented dream sequences. Although set into different imagery, such as ice or dance instead of underwater or cemetery, these dream scenes vividly signal the principle of the dominating brute. They also conjoin harmoniously the artistic style of film director Werner Schroeter. Through the medium of film, these same scenes make clear and underline the increasing psychic deterioration of the woman writer; transfiguratively they elevate the individual love tragedy into the universal affliction of woman's calamity. Schroeter's cinematographic decision to place the rooftop scene (82nd scene in the screenplay) at the beginning of the film is incisive because it confronts the viewer right off with the movie's intention, namely not to offer a mimetic narrative of the usual sort, but to engage the audience in deciphering of estranged visions which underly encoded cinema.

The many negative criticisms of the film have characterized this particular cinematic language as incomprehensible and esoteric. The film's many seemingly unconnected events doubtlessly challenge understanding, but reflection puts most of these arbitrarily arranged filmic scenes into a thought pattern or encourages the viewer to read the original book or filmscript to gain answers. Upon reflection, the viewers may begin to connect their experiences with filmic scenes and come to an understanding of the underlying meaning, e.g., the menstrually bleeding woman who is ogled by construction workers—a scene which alludes to the blood of woman's violation by the sexual stares of men; or the woman ashamed of being left alone by her own kind, like the mother in another dream scene who passively watches the incestuous rape of her daughter. Does this iconography not correlate to the metaphoric complexity of the original book and bring meaning forth through its interconnectedness of images?

Werner Schroeter: Additions of His Directorship

To commission Werner Schroeter to direct this film adaptation seems at first glance an odd choice, especially if one intends to reach a relatively broad audience. Although he has made thirty-seven films since 1967 and has a loyal following among film buffs, he is a virtually unknown cinematographer to the general audience of the New German Cinema and carries at best the vague reputation of making rather inaccessible, eccentric, opera-like, homoerotic movies.[19] It takes film experts, such as Timothy Corrigan, to credit Schroeter with at least "seminal presence in the New German Cinema,"[20] or somebody like the cutting-edge feuilletonist J. Hoberman from the *Village Voice*, who proclaimed him to be "the key West German filmmaker of the past two decades." It is also known that Hans-Jürgen Syberberg, (in)famous for his film *Unser Hitler* (Our Hitler), called him "one of the truly great revolutionary artists of our age," and the late Rainer Werner Fassbinder acknowledged him as a formative influence, having inspired him to his only documentary, "Theater in Trance," filmed in 1981 during the Cologne *World Theater Festival*.

Beyond these individuals, there is little critical discussion of him within academic circles,[21] probably due to the fact that his films cannot be readily found in the video distribution outlets which champion many other contemporary German filmmakers, among them Fassbinder, Wenders and Herzog. Since his last film *Der Rosenkönig* (1987; The Rose King), Schroeter had been conspicuously absent as director, devoting much of his creative efforts to stage directing. Obviously, he has been hard-pressed to find financing for more independent *auteur*-productions, as is the case for so many filmmakers of the New German Cinema in these conservative times. But the difficulty of funding notwithstanding, Schroeter's aesthetic interests continue in the same vein, exposing the theater public of Hamburg in 1993, for example, to a stylistically over-whelming adaptation of Tony Kushner's AIDS drama, *Angels in America*.[22]

Therefore, Schroeter's cinematic predisposition, his tumultuous filmic style, his imagistic hyperbole, his ecstatic polyphonic musical composites, his predilection for the excessive—all this did make him a likely choice to direct "Malina." Also Schroeter admires emotionally wrought individuals, whose compelling drive and self-destructive passion sets them apart from any norm. He seems frequently concerned in his subject matter with the passionate excess of female artists—as in his early biographical portraits of the prima donna Maria Callas or the melodramatic homage to the diva Maria Malibran,[23] one of Callas's most famous predecessors, who died in 1836 at the age of 28 in Paris and of whom it was said that she literally sang herself to death—Bachmann's torn heroine seemed a likely character for Schroeter's filmic presentation.

Most female critics rather vehemently hold Schroeter's particular fascination for self-effacement against him. Controversy raged especially around certain utterances that stressed his interpretative view of the novel's female persona as having a self-destructive drive, which limited his filmic focus to the female herself without any interest in the generic problems involved. Jelinek is reported to have said in the Vienna newspaper *Standard* that Schroeter wanted to cut the patriarchal dream sequences with the father, because he considered the self-destructive behavior of the woman more significant. Alice Schwarzer, quoting Schroeter from a German television interview in which he said that it would be awful to film the book as it is written and that such lament would find nobody's interest today, was outraged by his arrogance and demeaning attitude towards female victimization. She cynically compared his filming of *Malina* to allowing Riefenstahl to direct the *Oppermann Brüder* (Oppermann Brothers).[24]

In addition to alleged ignorance of or indifference towards the female plight, Schroeter was accused of wanting to exploit the biographical reality of Bachmann's life. Regula Venske claimed that the filming of the novel not only reduced the subject matter into yet another unfortunate story of female neurosis but also diminished it in equal measure to the same biographical indiscretions that were voiced when the book *Malina* first appeared.[25] Komar, too, sees the film as an attempt to turn the story into Bachmann's biography, thus limiting the broader sociological implications about the female search for identity.[26] The critic Hans Günther Pflaum, on the other hand, quite unabashedly confirms these biographical intentions by citing Schroeter:

Ingeborg Bachmann's novel is the process of a self-dissolution, written with a strong intuition because very shortly afterwards she actually had died. The images in the novel have much to do with fire and she herself burnt to death two years later. Ingeborg Bachmann was a lyricist of the first rank, to switch to the novel genre to express herself was stylistically a radical departure and rupture. The authoress was no longer herself, she attempted to eradicate herself by writing this novel. And this I find fascinating; if you appreciate Bachmann, this end-product is the most fascinating.[27]

Bachmann herself had credited her incomplete novel-cycle to biographical experiences. It is known that she had been involved in difficult relationships with two men, the composer Hans Werner Henze and the writer Max Frisch. In 1973 she died at the age of 47 in a Rome hospital of burn wounds. Exhausted by drugs, she had fallen asleep in her apartment with a burning cigarette, which then ignited her synthetic nightgown. These facts can be seen as a backdrop to the film, but they do not override the film's philosophical composite. Yet it would be unfair to accuse the director of having created an autobiographical pyre, a voyeuristic reconstruction of Bachmann's life and death. Fire, and the threat of being consumed by it, are prominent features of the novel as well as of the screenplay and the film (Bachmann included in her work the famous sentence: "Avec ma main brûlée, j'écris sur la nature du feu"; With my burned hand I write about the nature of fire), a motif which the filmmaker adopted generously. To derive the fire imagery from Bachmann's biographical background and from the many allusions in her work seems, therefore, not only an appropriate tribute to her known personal sufferings, but an ingenuous element of iconography to capture much of the essence of her conceptual conflict.

It is also highly unlikely that Schroeter intended to depict the dual constellation of the men in Bachmann's life; the film is constructed in multiple layers of meaning. Both male roles, that of Ivan and Malina, are cast with great care and consideration. Despite the differences between the characters, Schroeter depicts both males as somewhat similar in appearance and demeanor. Ivan, the cool lover with his recreational sex drive and understanding of love as a game does not come across as a stunning stud but rather as a medium-built, "normal" man. Malina who embodies the reality principle and protects the woman from herself with increasing indifference, resembles Ivan, only with a bit more graying hair. The director Werner Schroeter demonstrates his highly sensitized intellect towards Bachmann's concept of the tragic female figure who displays an enigmatic interior space, namely the androgynous split into a female emotional psyche and a male rational alter ego. Following closely Jelinek's pointed schism of animus-anima, his direction of the female persona strives throughout to produce intense reflection. Isabelle Huppert renders a credible portrayal of the rift between the romantic yearning for mutual love and the despairing realization of never being able to attain it. The female, albeit the hyperbole of her inner split, retains outwardly a normal, unassuming physical profile. None of the male-female androgynous or the male-male bonding components are exploited for homosexual voyeuristic purposes. Thus, the casting of the complex female character must be credited to the director, Werner Schroeter as an excellent achievement.

Given Schroeter's filmographical interests, it was typical for him to cast the female persona of Bachmann's novel as unconditional. In her relentless search for absolute emotion, he gives her the martyred extension of holy madness, in which her sufferings are transfigured by her proverbial head-banging against the wall or by the pyrotechnical projections of living in hell. Known for thematizing mostly oppressed women, Schroeter usually casts his protagonists as harried, tormented, unhappy characters. Again he chose to feature his lead actress in *Malina* as slipping more and more into a hypernervous state of frustration. She is depicted as working with hectic gestures at her desk, substituting her frustration with endless cigarettes, fiddling constantly with her small mirror and lipstick as a gesture of identity reassurance, or giving in to the many increasingly grotesque hallucinations.

All of these signs leave distinct clues for understanding the movie. The female's stations of pain do not become reflections of hysteria or masochism, nor do they degrade into a melodramatic morbidity; they rather retain and convey on the part of the female a merciless and persistent sequence of uncompromising behavior towards male rejection and abuse.

Schroeter not only cast and directed the erotic duels and dualities between the genders close to the book and script, but also knew how to enhance them filmically. He reformulated the symbolic leitmotif of the wailing wall in a variety of images. While keeping the hallucinatory crack in the wall, he ended the filmic disappearance of the female protagonist in the fracturing mirrors of the apartment doors. This departure from the book and the script was meant to literally reflect the female's final decision to break away from her torment of not being perceived as a whole identity by herself or in the eyes of the world. Other superb iconographic achievements are the effective renditions of the fantasy states and dreams to the screen. Venturing into the theatrically exalted set of a deadly ice-world or into the abstract performance of the woman, Schroeter exposed the father figure as a rotating eternal metamorphosis of judge, butcher and fascist. But he also gave life to the many additional visions of Jelinek, such as the hallways filled with hunting trophies of the Austrian aristocracy or the furniture moving scene with Lina. Schroeter did not restrict his talent by drawing only on his expertise of operatic stage and film work; his cinematography in *Malina* proved his high versatility in experimental style.

The preeminent mark of his directorship is unquestionably present in the music he set to this film. He took up Jelinek's suggestion of indicating the split between harmony and disharmony as outlined in her Beethoven-Schönberg dialogue in scene 2, except that he made it audible through many interspersed music pieces and genres. He featured the avant-gardist music of the Italian composer Giacomo Manzoni; the discordant soft background tones convey distinctly the disturbing, restless, unstable states of affairs that evolve. Equally haunting and painful are the inter-cut arias by Carl Maria von Weber (Oberon: Aria of Rezia: "Ocean Thou Mighty Monster," sung by Maria Callas) or by Ludwig van Beethoven (Fidelio: Aria of Leonore: "Komm Hoffnung" (Come Hope), sung by Lotte Lehmann). At another juncture Schroeter interjects the bawdy "Wer schmeisst denn da mit Lehm" (Who Throws with Clay) by Claire Waldoff, highlighting the fact that the sound-track is a purposeful jump-cut composite of diverse music pieces; the avant-gardistic is not only permeated by the classical but interjected by the cabaretistic. Yet regardless of what context the music is taken from, it is consciously designed to transmit discord, the split that runs through time, place and people, and as such provides for this film and its inharmonious theme the analogous inconsonant background.

Conclusion

After twenty years, the film version of the book necessarily took a somewhat different perspective; not only had the adaptation taken a different direction, but also a different symbolization. The progress of time dictated alternate forms of the same problem: feminism had moved into another generational perception, and the change to another medium demanded an alternate encoding. Bachmann's use of an undeniably larmoyant, elegiac tone to portray the female's fate was changed to feminist militancy in Jelinek's scripting; Bachmann's postwar fascist imprint of patriarchal history gave way to a more foregrounded contemporary gender conception; Bachmann's victimized self-destruction of the female persona became a stronger accusation against her murderous ouster; Bachmann's utopian hopes were relegated more to an unending past than a foreseeable future; Bachmann's metaphoric imagery was reconceived in more expanded supplements due to the transposition into the filmic medium; and Bachmann's narrative ubiquity became even more strongly rooted in a Viennese/Austrian environment. Book, screenplay and film should therefore become an interactive reception process to fully appreciate the metamorphosis from source to cinema.

Rice University

Notes

1. Ingeborg Bachmann, *Malina* (Frankfurt: Suhrkamp, 1971); translation by Philip Boehm, *Malina: A Novel* (New York: Holmes and Meier, 1990).
2. Sarah Lennox, "The Feminist Reception of Ingeborg Bachmann," *Women in German Yearbook* 8 (1992): 73-111.
3. *Malina,* film adaptation made in 1991, color, 125 minutes, German with English subtitles. Directed by Werner Schroeter; script written by Elfriede Jelinek from Ingeborg Bachmann's novel; photography by Elfi Mikesch; art direction by Alberte Baracq; edited by Juliane Loranz; original music by Giacomo Manzoni. Main cast: Isabelle Huppert, Mathieu Carriere, Can Togay. A German-Austrian co-production.
4. Alice Schwarzer, "Die Hölle ist die Hölle," *Die Zeit* 4.25 (January 1991): 18. Alice Schwarzer, "Schwarzer über Malina," *Emma* (February 1991): 14-20. Iris Radisch, "Die Hölle ist der Himmel," *Die Zeit* 4 (January 1991): 17-18. Dorothee Römhild,

"Von kritischer Selbstreflexion zur stereotypen Frauendarstellung: Ingeborg Bachmann's Roman 'Malina' und seine filmische Rezeption," *The Germanic Review* 68.4 (Fall 1993): 167-175. Kathleen L. Komar, "'Es war Mord': The Murder of Ingeborg Bachmann at the Hands of an Alter Ego," *Modern Austrian Literature* 27.2 (1994): 91-112.

5. "Das sind Gründe, warum die Koketterie mit der Sexualerniedrigung und der Sexualgewalt—und der Pornographie, die sie propagiert!—eine so bitterernste Sache ist...Die Propagierung des weiblichen Masochismus ist ein Angriff, durch Frauen ist es Kollaboration mit dem Feind. Es ist der ewige Krieg" in: "Schwarzer über Malina," 20.

6. "Der Konflikt, der die Frau bei Ingeborg Bachmann innerlich zerreißt, wird bei Elfriede Jelinek zu einer Geschlechterkampf-Klamotte...Werner Schroeter hat eine Oper inszeniert, auf die er, meist aus den Tiefen des Orchestergrabens die Kamera hält. Von weit oben, vom Plateau der Opernbühne, reicht er die Todesschreie, die Oboenklänge und Nachtmahre mit großer, leerer Geste hinab. Die Ekstase, die im Roman aus dem mörderischen Zusammenspiel von Erinnerungen, Erlebnissen und Projektionen langsam ersteht, ist im Film immer schon da...Es zischt und kokelt in den Kulissen. Das ist der Krieg zwischen den Geschlechtern. Ungerührt, mit der Eleganz eines Kaufhausabteilungsleiters geht Mathieu Carriere durch die Flammen der leidenden Frauenseele hindurch. Das ist das Ende...Von dem Riss, der bei Ingeborg Bachmann durch die Welt und durch die Menschen geht, ist in diesem flammenden Dramolett nichts übrig," Iris Radisch, 18.

7. "Bei Schroeter erfährt dieses Bild eine mystische Akzentuierung: in Grossaufnahme ist die infolge einer selbst beigebrachten Kopfverletzung mit einem Wundmal auf der Stirn gezeichnete Frau zu sehen und gleicht damit spiegelbildlich jener Christusstatue, an die sie sich anlehnt. Indem er das weibliche Leiden der Heilsgeschichte integriert und es damit verklärt, nimmt Schroeter dem Motiv sein gesellschaftliches Potential...Darüberhinaus verschenkt der Film durch seine Ästhetisierung des Ekels, selbst da wo die Gewalttaten des Vaters in den Traumsequenzen durch eine deutlich sichtbare Hakenkreuzbinde augenscheinlich in Beziehung zur NS-Vergangenheit gesetzt werden, das gesellschafts-

kritische Potential des Stoffes." Dorothee Römhild, 174.
8. See Anton Kaes, ed., *Kino-Debatte: Texte zum Verhältnis von Literatur und Film 1909-1929* (Tübingen: Max Niemeyer, 1978).
9. A large amount of theory and criticism has been published on the topic of film and literature. The following list of the most important book-length contributions is selective: Franz-Josef Albersmeier and Volker Roloff, *Literaturverfilmungen* (Frankfurt: Suhrkamp, 1989). Andrew Dudley, *Concepts in Film Theory* (Oxford University Press, 1984). Wendell Aycock and Michael Schoenecke, eds. *Film and Literature: A Comparative Approach to Adaptation* (Texas Tech University Press, 1988). Sigrid Bauschinger, Susan Cocalis and Henry A. Lea, *Film und Literatur: Literarische Texte und der neue deutsche Film* (Bern/Munich: Francke, 1984). George Bluestone, *Novels into Film* (John Hopkins Univ. Press, 1957). David Bordwell and Kristin Thompson, *Film Art: An Introduction*, 4th ed. (New York: McGraw-Hill, Inc., 1993). Joy Boyum Gould, *Double Exposure: Fiction into Film* (New York: Universe Books, 1985). Seymore Chatman, "What Novels Can Do That Films Can't Do (and Vice Versa)," *On Narrative*, ed. W.J.T. Mitchell (Chicago/London: University of Chicago Press, 1981). Seymore Chatman, "Story and Discourse," *Narrative Structure in Fiction and Film* (Cornell University Press, 1978). Keith Cohen, *Writing in a Film Age: Essays by Contemporary Novelists* (University Press of Colorado, 1991). Keith Cohen, *Film and Fiction: The Dynamics of Exchange* (Yale University Press, 1979). Pam Cook, ed. *The Cinema Book* (London: British Film Institute, 1985). Gary R. Edgerton, ed. *Film and the Arts in Symbiosis: A Resource Guide* (New York/London: Greenwood Press, 1988). Harry M. Geduld, ed. *Authors on Film* (Indiana University Press, 1972). Robert Giddings, Keith Selby and Chris Wensley, *Screening the Novel The Theory and Practice of Literary Dramatization* (London: Macmillan Press, 1990). John Harrington, ed. *Film and/as Literature* (Englewood Cliffs, N.J.: Prentice-Hall, 1968). Harry Ross, *Film as Literature, Literature as Film: An Introduction to and Bibliography of Film's Relationship to Literature* (Westport: Greenwood Press, 1987). Andrew S. Horton and Joan Margretta, eds. *Modern European Filmmakers and the Art of Adaptation* (New York: Frederick

Ungar, 1981). Manfred Durzak, *Literatur auf dem Bildschirm* (Tübingen: Niemeyer, 1989). Gerald Mast, Marshall Cohen and Leo Braudy, eds. *Film Theory and Criticism: Introductory Readings*, 4th ed. (Oxford University Press, 1992). Gerald Mast, "Literature and Film," *Interrelations of Literature*, ed. Jean Pierre Barricelli and Joseph Gibaldi (New York: Modern Language Association of America, 1982). Richard W. McCormick, *Politics of the Self: Feminism and the Postmodern in West German Literature and Film* (Princeton University Press, 1991). Joachim Paech, *Literatur und Film* (Stuttgart: J.B. Metzler, 1988). Eric Rentschler, ed. *German Film and Literature: Adaptations and Transformations* (New York: Methuen, Inc., 1986). Robert Richardson, *Literature and Film* (Indiana University Press, 1969). Irmela Schneider, *Der verwandelte Text* (Tübingen: Niemeyer, 1981). John Simon, *Movies into Film*, Film Criticism 1967-70. ("Adaptations") (New York: Delta Books, 1971). Neil Sinyard, *Filming Literature: The Art of Screen Adaptation* (London: Croom Helm, 1986). Susan Sontag, *Against Interpretation* (N.Y.: Farrar, Straus and Giroux, 1966). Alan Spiegel, *Fiction and the Camera Eye: Visual Consciousness in Film and the Modern Novel* (University Press of Virginia, 1976). Geoffrey Wagner, *The Novel and the Cinema* (Fairleigh Dickinson University Press, 1975).

10. Jelinek, *Malina. Ein Filmbuch. Nach dem Roman von Ingeborg Bachmann* (Frankfurt: Suhrkamp, 1991), 157.

11. Jelinek, "Der Krieg mit anderen Mitteln," *Kein objektives Urteil—Nur ein Lebendiges,* ed. Koschel von Weidenbaum (Munich: Piper, 1989), 311-320.

12. Jelinek, *Malina. Ein Filmbuch*, 9-10. In the 83rd scene the woman says: "But I began to understand. It was then that I felt compelled to distort all words," 107. Anything that represents the canon of power or myth is investigated down to its detailed fragments to see its source. As Jelinek states herself: "My mechanisms of work function when I make speech speak itself, via montage of whole sentences, which confront different speech patterns, but also via changing words or letters, which reveal invisible meanings in idioms," in: "Ich schlage sozusagen mit der Axt drein," *Theaterzeitschrift, Berlin* 7 (1984): 14.

13. "*Malina* is a novel that ends in the inability to speak. Human

communication is seen as lost. Dialogue is reduced to monologue, self reflection ends in tautology. But one may not forget that it was exactly this painful realization which Bachmann considered her existential source for the creative act. According to her, literary language is obligated to search for the elemental qualities in social, political and personal experience. She therefore considered negative or tragic formulations not paralyzing or ineffective in the reception process. In one of her public speeches she declares in unmistakable terms that truth can be borne, by humankind, since our strength reaches further than our despair, since one is knowingly able to live with disappointment." Margret Eifler, "Ingeborg Bachmann: Malina," *Modern Austrian Literature* 12.3/4 (1979): 390.

14. For a highly negative judgment of Jelinek, see Irene Heidelberger-Leonard: "War es Doppelmord? Anmerkungen zu Elfriede Jelineks Bachmann-Rezeption und ihrem Filmbuch *Malina*," *Text und Kritik* 117 (January 1993): 78-83.

15. Jelinek explains: "Ich habe die Frauen sehr kritisch als die Opfer dieser Gesellschaft gezeigt, die sich aber nicht als Opfer sehen, sondern glauben, sie könnten Komplizinnen sein. Das ist mein eigentliches Thema, ob das jetzt die Sexualität oder die ökonomische Macht ist, sobald die Frauen sich zu Komplizinnen der Männer machen, um sich dadurch einen besseren sozialen Status zu verschaffen, muss das schiefgehen. Ich mache mich aber nicht über Menschen lustig um dessentwegen, was sie sind, sondern um ihres falschen Bewusstseins wegen." Kurt Bartsch and Günther Höfler, eds. *Elfriede Jelinek: Dossier 2* (Graz: Droschl, 1991), 13.

16. *Dossier 2,* 4: "Für eine Frau ist das Schreiben schon ein gewalttätiger Akt, weil das weibliche Subjekt kein sprechendes ist...Wenn sie es doch tut ist das eine Überschreitung, eine Art agressiver Akt."

17. Jelinek, *Der Krieg mit anderen Mitteln*, 319.

18. Jelinek, *Malina. Ein Filmbuch*, 12

19. His films were shown in North America in a rare retrospective coordinated by the Goethe-Institut in 1988-89.

20. Timothy Corrigan, *New German Film: The Displaced Image*, rev. ed. (Bloomington: Indiana University Press, 1994), 169-183.

21. German collection of articles by Peter W. Hansen and Wolfram

Schütte, eds. *Werner Schroeter. Reihe Film 20* (Munich: Hanser, 1980); French book by Gérard Courant, *Werner Schroeter* (Paris: Goethe Institut/La Cinémathèque Française, 1982).

22. See review "Erfolgreiche Lust am Untergang," *Der Spiegel* 47 (November 22, 1993): 259-261.

23. *The Death of Maria Malibran*, 1971, 16mm, color, 104 minutes, played by his favorite actress Magdalena Montezuma and set to the polyphonic music of Brahms, Ambroise, Thomas, Catarina Valente, Stravinsky, Beethoven, Mozart, Marlene Dietrich, Cherubini, Händel, Puccini, Rossini and others.

24. Schwarzer, *Die Zeit*: 18.

25. Regula Venske, *Das Verschwinden des Mannes in der weiblichen Schreibmaschine. Männnerbilder in der Literatur von Frauen* (Hamburg/Zürich: Luchterhand, 1991), 101-128.

26. Komar, 99.

27. *Inter Nationes* press release statement to the film.

Austria's Feminist Avant-Garde: Valie Export's and Elfriede Jelinek's Aesthetic Innovations[1]

Margarete Lamb-Faffelberger

I.

The aesthetic and philosophical trends of the "modern period" and the "Avantgarde" of the early twentieth century lay buried under the rubble which the years of fascism and national-socialism left behind. In search of a new national and cultural identity, Austria's leaders embraced the *Anschluß*-idea and the "victim"-concept. The newly achieved status of neutrality was well suited as political identity.

In order to define a cultural identity distinctly different from Germany, Austria proclaimed the *Anschluß*[2] to its own great era, the cultural heritage of the nineteenth century and the *fin de siècle* literature and art.[3] Thus, the 1950s and 1960s were dominated by conservative cultural politics which discouraged any artistic expression that voiced criticism against established art forms and current politics.[4]

In this restrictive and discriminating climate, progressive and aesthetically innovative artists and writers created provocative statements of rebellion directed against the political and the cultural atmosphere. These artists attempted to reestablish a link with the prewar avant-garde in order to create a theoretical foundation. The new art movements shared the same concern about the material basis of art. Both movements pursued the same fundamental goal, namely questioning the traditional concept of the art-object as an organic and autonomous form and thus attempting to close the gap between art and everyday life.[5]

During the late 1950s and 1960s Austria's art scene experienced a tremendous explosion of innovative art. Performance art, e.g., Hermann Nitsch's *Orgien Mysterien Theater* (Orgy Mystery Theater)[6] and Joseph Beuys' happenings;[7] the "Wiener Aktionismus"[8] with Otto Muehl, Gunther Brus and others; cinematic experimentations, such as expanded cinema;[9] the literary experimentations of the Wiener Gruppe[10] with Oswald Wiener, Ernst Jandl and others; and the "Forum Stadtpark Graz" with its trend-setting contributions published in the *manuskripte* (manuscripts) by Alfred Kolleritsch[11] came to be known as Austria's avant-garde art scene.[12]

With the rise of the women's movement in the late 1960s and early 1970s, out of the shadows of Austria's male-dominated avant-garde appeared a distinct feminist avant-garde art scene. It is defined by an innovative aesthetics aimed at a strong criticism of the social, economic and political situation of women in today's Austria. The problematic situation of excluding women from the socio-formative and creative processes within the male-dominated structure of society formed the basis and target for its feminist stand and art expression.

Language consisting of words as well as images became the feminist avant-garde's weapon in the fight against logocentrism and phallocratic order.[13] Its texts are respective expressions of an *écriture féminine* aimed against the traditional writing of "his-story" and the established social and cultural canons. Displaying distinctive features of feminist writing such as anti-linearity, anti-mimesis, and polylogic, these texts are created by the artistic methods of collage and montage, which involve arranging and rearranging of text-segments.[14]

II.

Two of the most innovative and most prominent representatives of Austria's feminist avant-garde are the internationally acclaimed multimedia artist Valie Export and the author Elfriede Jelinek. Born in the 1940s, they were strongly influenced by the women's movement in the 1960s as well as by the innovative art forms of Austria's avant-garde.

In the male-dominated artist-milieus, Valie Export and Elfriede Jelinek were confronted with the underrepresentation of woman in art and the indifference of their male colleagues as well as the art institutions as a whole towards their work. Both artists felt the need to strive beyond the playing fields of artistic indulgence and go "against the horizon"—as Jaqueline Vansant called it[15]—by asserting their feminist views and pleas.[16] Export and Jelinek understand the private sphere as a representation of public attitudes.[17] Their work presents the mechanisms that create oppression in a patriarchal society, mechanisms that "deform" a woman's life.

The scholarly discourse of feminism explored in France and the United States in the 1970s and 1980s contributed to the theoretical foundation for Valie Export's and Elfriede Jelinek's art in form and content.[18] The criticism of the dominance of logocentrism and its phallocratic order constitutes the center of the art-production by Austria's feminist avant-garde. Throughout their work, Export and

Jelinek reflect upon Freud and Lacan's notion of "the woman as the other" and her representation within the canons of society and the culture of art. In addition, Jelinek's texts are characterized by the author's critical relationship to language. For Jelinek language signifies the power structures and mirrors the dominance of logocentrism within a capitalist society.[19]

Jelinek's literature as well as Export's films are directed at undermining the fundamental concepts of our thinking. Traditional premises such as logic and causality are confronted critically to make translucent the established canons and the limits of their truths. In spite of Export's and Jelinek's doubt that art today can be used as a means for social change, their work nevertheless is directed towards social consciousness-raising.[20] Thus, Export's and Jelinek's feminist aesthetics is an aesthetics of resistance.

Austria's feminist avant-garde aesthetics attempts to illuminate the hidden truths shadowed within the deep structure of meaning. Export and Jelinek transform existing images by creating texts of association that chain the conscious to the unconscious—both in the act of art creation and in the reception process. The normative use of language disappears and a new form emerges by releasing meaning, images of the mind that are hidden within the semantic canons of western society.

Export and Jelinek developed a critical art of looking, a kind of seeing which resembles the camera-vision of a photographer.[21] The artistic eye is quasi directed through a photographic lens onto the surface structure of society in order to elucidate social processes. When one looks through a camera lens, one sees a view restricted to a topographic segment of the whole. If one zooms in on a particular segment, that section appears enlarged. Details become recognizable. The selected segment—in its "blown-up" character—can be an indication of the actual structure and the true nature of the "big picture." Creating their text-collages, the artists arrange and re-arrange their selected segments, segments of the surface. By capturing several different enlarged segments and arranging them anew, they deconstruct the whole surface.

It is this artistic technique of deconstructing and creating anew which is subversive. The technique of dismemberment of topographic structures gained through a selective photographic viewpoint inherent in Jelinek's literary and Export's film texts exposes the deep-structure of signifiers—or according to Roland Barthes, the notions of myths. The process of exposure is the process of excavating the deep structure by penetrating the topography of images, of language, of meaning. This artistic technique permits a close-up look at conditions normally overlooked. It causes us to alter our pattern of organizing impressions and perceptions. It is precisely this process of rearranging segments of a so-called photographic topography, the process of deconstructing the dominant surface structure and illuminating the deep structure, that can be termed anagrammatic aesthetics.

The word *anagram* has its origin in Greek. Anagraphein means to rearrange linguistic elements within a single word, to deconstruct a name in order to create a pseudonym. It also means to rearrange letters within the frame work of a poem to construct a new poem. The rearrangement of letters in a word, in a group of words or in a sentence will then create a new meaning within the new constellation—an anagram. Originally used by the cabbalists in the Middle Ages in order to release secret truths of their religious texts, it became a literary game for poets during the Baroque period.

No longer used as a literary method in the eighteenh and nineteenth century it reappeared about forty years ago. The surrealistic visual artist Hans Bellmer and the poet Unica Zürn, who lived together in Paris in the 1950s and 1960s, produced anagrammatic art.[22] The writer Zürn "fled" into the production of anagrammatic lyrics to find the appropriate artistic means to find her voice. The use of the anagrammatic literary technique proved to be the only way to deal with the hidden realities and meanings of her personal life, which she called "the forbidden rooms." Her anagrams demonstrate Zürn's attempts to unlock them.[23]

Bellmer, who introduced Zürn to the art of anagrams had made himself a name with his artistic dolls.[24] Bellmer's dolls were, namely, likenesses of a dismembered and newly recombined female body. Export explains the connection between Bellmer's visual and Zürn's textual art in her theoretical manifest *The Real and Its Double: The Body*:

> Bellmer [did] exactly the same thing in his visual art that Zürn [did] in her language. As the body is divided into organs and then repeatedly reconstructed, so is the sentence split up into letters and reassembled anew. Objectual or verbal anagrammatizing results from the inadequacy of the body as a social construction of woman. The interchangeability of the body parts and the sentence parts stands for the interchangeability of the Self of women as body.[25]

As Zürn's textual technique of anagrammatic aesthetics relates to Bellmer's visual art so does Jelinek's textual deconstruction and montage relate to Export's medial anagrams. The parallels of the aesthetic endeavors between Export's multimedia art and Jelinek's literature invite a comparison with Bellmer's artistic dolls and Zürn's poetry. Like Zürn and Bellmer, Austria's feminist avant-garde moves beyond the traditional definition of anagrammatic form. Anagrammatic aesthetics in the context of Austria's feminist avant-garde no longer limits the rearrangement of elements to individual letters, single words or word phrases but expands the traditional literary method to ideas, notions, issues and representations of language that reflect the canons of society. Export and Jelinek not only shift language expressed in words as well as images but also shift perspectives for the reader/viewer, rupture the surface and expose the hidden truths concealed within the structure of a phallocratic society and its language. What is of interest in the context of Austria's feminist avant-garde, therefore, is the deconstructive energy of the anagrammatic format.

III.

Valie Export's anagrammatic endeavor is an aesthetic attempt to visualize the repression and social codification of woman. The roots for her theoretic, artistic and cinematic work lie in the aesthetics of the historic and neo-avant-garde.[26] Embracing these backgrounds she developed a particular visual philosophy of decoding role-prescribed embodiments by countering all fixations with multi-medial ruptures. She developed the art of anagrammatization of gender:[27]

> In my films and in my photographic work I use body parts or segments of body expression which have largely been used when portraying women,...[however they] are not the norm for the traditional representation of woman...I give these body parts a new and different medial expression and bring them ...into a new and different context. By overlapping the first image with a second image, the first one is destroyed, by overlapping the second with a third the second is destroyed and so on. However, it still remains the same body with which I am dealing. Practically that means that I use video, slides, film within film and projections that relate to each other. Video-clips meet with film projections which show the same image.

> I use different media and bring content...into a new and different context.[28]

Medial anagrams determine the formal process of Valie Export's art production. Particularly in her films, she shifts visual and verbal images and ruptures the surface of preconceived notions of the viewer. A scene from her film *Unsichtbare Gegner* (1976; *Invisible Adversaries*, 1987) can best serve as an example for the application of Export's anagrammatic aesthetics. Dealing with the topic of "the image of women within the traditions of art," Export created one of her most innovative images. Situated in a film studio, the filmmaker projects a photograph of a painting by the Renaissance artist, Tintoretto on a screen. An actress stands in front of the painting and attempts to recreate the posture of the painted woman. She assumes uncomfortable positions to cover the projected picture with her body. Using video technology, Export overlaps the female images of the famous painting with that of the actress by fading the pictures in and out of the TV screen. Thus, Export's anagrammatic technique enables her to show clearly that the woman's body positions in the painting are merely idealized projections by the male artist.

Valie Export's avant-garde aesthetics is strongly connected with the art of photography, the art of still-framing. In the 1976 publication *Körperkonfigurationen* (Body-Configurations),[29] Export explains her photographic art as a means of showing the physical deformations of the female body, which she interprets as an expression of the woman's inner state of mind. The three photo images "Elongation" (1976), "Zupassung" (Adaptation; 1976) und "Auflegung" (Integument; 1972) demonstrate the physical deformations of the woman through role-expectations within the phallocratic society and expose the hidden conditions of her mind. Referring to the surrealist Dali and his explanation of the parallel between the condition of landscape and the condition of mind, Export describes feminist discourse as an organic relationship between the female body and its male dominated environment. For Export, this relationship has its origin in the ongoing confrontation of body and mind. As the condition of the landscape for Dali is a reflection of time and space, so is the posture for Export a reflection of the state of mind. Thus, her photographic images of selected body parts and their arrangements and rearrangements express the conditions of the mind.

In "Elongation" (the term is defined as the angle between the sun and the planet), the woman lies stretched out in the middle of a staircase that leads up to Neptune's fountain. A black pen mark drawn from Neptune's head to her face indicates the angle of the god's look down at her. The picture "Zupassung" shows a woman's body blending into the wall of a building in neoclassicist style. Lying on a step next to the majestic building, one hand touches the ground, one leg is extended straight up along the wall, and one leg lies in a ninety degree angle on the step. In "Auflegung," the woman's body lies across a cobblestone street facing the ground while the embankment rises high on both sides of the picture.

Still-frames of photo images such as "Elongation," "Zupassung" and "Auflegung" are repeatedly woven into the fabric of Export's film texts. For instance, in *Die Praxis der Liebe* (1984; *Practice of Love*), the male gaze is literally printed onto Judith's breasts. The dominant role of still photography does not appear only in the textual structure of Export's films. *Unsichtbare Gegner* demonstrates most clearly the dominance of photographic material within the anagrammatic format. The main character Anna is a photographer by profession and has to capture her environment in the literal sense of the word: "I have to capture my environment." Anna "still-frames" topographic segments of her environment. Export arranges these pictures of construction sites, vandalized properties, such as parks, telephone booths, but also quarrels between fellow citizens with clips from war documentaries. Thus, the filmmaker compiles a portfolio that exposes the deep structures of violence and its hierarchy.

IV.

Valie Export's socio-analytic photographic focus corresponds with Elfriede Jelinek's "Sehweise" (way of seeing)—which has been characterized as "kalter analytischer Blick" (a cold analytic gaze).[30] Jelinek herself compares her artistic approach to the sharp observations of a scientist who looks at social processes from a great distance in order to describe them accurately.[31] Her texts are constructs depicting an enlarged view of super-exposed segments as seen through the zoom-lens. By selecting and isolating images, Jelinek reduces the complexity of social structures to placard representations.

Jelinek maintains a scientific—and may we also say—a photographic distance that allows her to reframe from any psychological analyses. Her protagonists remain as distant as their images in a photograph. They remain prototypes expressing themselves in an archetypal language, a constructed meta-language, a hybrid comprised of existing language material. Jelinek explains her methodological approach:

> I do not write about real people, but about people who materialize as speech-patterns. I let the language speak...[I] use ...phrases where the language tests itself for its usefulness... [and I use] literary techniques such as the anagram where language if slightly changed to reveal a higher truth—almost against its own will.[33]

By applying the anagrammatic technique, Jelinek creates distortions of language-images. The nexus-forming energies inherent in them make the movement of signifiers transparent—signifiers that are submerged within the deep structure of language.

Jelinek has been called a social diagnostician[34] and rightly so, since her literature can be read as a socio-political blueprint. Like Zürn, Jelinek searches relentlessly for "forbidden rooms" to open them and expose their hidden content. However, unlike Zürn's privatized "forbidden rooms," Jelinek knocks on the doors of society's "forbidden rooms," e.g., the taboos of clichés such as love and marriage as means for a woman's rise within the social hierarchy in *Die Liebhaberinnen* (1975; *Women as Lovers*, 1994), the social taboo of a destructive mother-daughter relationship in *Die Klavierspielerin* and the political taboo of Austria's Nazi era in *Burgtheater* (1982, 1985) or the myth of a blessed "postcard-Austria" that is cashing in on its clichés of cultural traditions, friendly people, generous hospitality and natural beauty, as in *Oh Wildnis, oh Schutz vor ihr* (1985; Oh Wilderness, Oh Refuge from It). In her acceptance speech for the prestigious Heinrich-Böll-Prize entitled *In den Waldheimen und auf den Haidern*, Jelinek states: "We are nothing, we are only what we seem."[35] Applying the anagrammatic technique of shifting letters, syllables and phrases, the author creates connotations that open up "forbidden rooms," namely Austria's Nazi past and its never accomplished "Vergangenheits-bewältigung" (coming to terms with the past) as well as the myths of a "Sound of Music" fairy tale land.

Jelinek's anagrams penetrate the surface of clichés and myths that Austria's society has securely locked into its structural make-up and canonized. In the 1991 play *Totenauberg*, two Austrian natives, the

"Gamsbärtler," describe their attitude towards contemporary life in their home, today's tourist-Austria: "We who live here never observe our land, we experience it through its value that is determined by others...We are enough for ourselves. We do not have to destroy the opinions of the foreigners, they should exchange them into valuable currency. We print our own opinions and then postcards thereof."[36] Here, Jelinek's anagrammatic method succeeds in unmasking the milking of mass-tourism in Austria's mass-media dominated society with its profit-oriented economy. Already in the early 1970s, Jelinek had produced a TV documentary about the well-known recreational resort, Ramsau am Dachstein, where she shifted accents from nature's beauty and tourist attractions to the harsh lifestyles of the people living in this region. On TV, in her novels and in her plays, Jelinek consistently unmasks the "Austria-aesthetics" as a market-oriented show— or in her own words from the text *Oh Wildnis, oh Schutz vor ihr*: "Sickly moss, weak forest, nowhere the true stuff from the screen."[37]

Jelinek's anagrams expose the artificiality and hypocrisy of Austria's "nature lovers." In *Die Liebhaberinnen* Jelinek asks the reader: "Do you know this BEAUTIFUL country with its valleys and hills. At its far borders lie beautiful mountains. It has a horizon that not many countries have."[38] The word "horizon" connects the mind of the reader with Austria's mountainous landscape but also suggests the desire to strive beyond the horizons of determination. Paula and Brigitte, the two protagonists who try to escape their monotonous life and vicious cycle that have placed them at the bottom of society in a remote country village, do not (or perhaps marginally) succeed in striving beyond the horizons of their destiny. Also touching upon the notion of high culture, Jelinek's anagram links the well-read audience with Mignon's song and Goethe's travels to Italy. Since this anagrammatic text appears as "Afterword" of the novel, Jelinek created a powerful distorted picture.

"I am sick therefore I am" as anagram of "cogito ergo sum" from the play *Krankheit oder Moderne Frauen* (1987; Illness or Modern Women)[39] may be further developed to "I speak/create therefore I am," and as such, it may stand as a representation of Export's and Jelinek's artistic endeavor. The perseverance of both artists as active feminists stands out in Austria's conservative society. Austria's "feuilletonistic" art critics have until recently rigorously rejected Jelinek's and Export's contributions to the feminist avant-garde. In today's mass-media dominated society, critics by and large still display a social and cultural-political conservatism. A large majority of the media's art critics, most of them men, have shown a strong reluctance to look beyond the horizons of tradition.[40] Provocative art that attempts to raise the general public's consciousness towards the problematic situation of women today is interpreted as an attack against the existing social order. The fact that Austria's women in large part still succumb to their traditional roles underscores the importance of Jelinek's literature and Export's films as an artistic endeavor for consciousness-raising.

Lafayette College

Notes

1. I presented a preliminary version of this article at the Modern Language Association Conference in December 1993. The French translation of this study entitled "L'avant-garde féministe autrichienne. Innovations estétiques: Valie Export et Elfriede Jelinek" is published in *Continuités et Ruptures Dans la Litterature Autrichienne*, eds. Dieter Hornig, Georg Jankovic, Klaus Zeyringer (Paris: Éditions Jacqueline Chambon) Annales de l'Institut Culturel Austrichien, vol. 1 (1996): 231-245.

2. Cf. *Zwischenbilanz. Eine Anthologie österreichischer Gegenwartsliteratur*, eds., Walter Weiss and Sigrid Schmid (Salzburg: Residenz, 1976).

3. Cf. *Das Große Erbe. Aufsätze zur österreichischen Literatur*, eds. Otto Basil, Herbert Eisenreich and Ivar Ivask (Graz: Stiasny, 1962).

4. Cf. *TransGarde. Die Literatur der Grazer Gruppe, Forum Stadtpark und manuskripte*, eds. Kurt Bartsch and Gerhard Melzer (Graz: Droschl, 1990).

5. Cf. Harold Rosenberg, *The Anxious Object: Art Today and Its Audience* (Chicago: University of Chicago Press, 1966).

6. Cf. Ekkehard Stärk, *Hermann Nitschs 'Orgien Mysterien Theater' und die Hysterie der Griechen. Quellen und Traditionen im Wiener Antikebild seit 1900* (Vienna: Fink, 1987).

7. Cf. Ingeborg Hoesterey, "Postmodern Hybrids: Visual Text, Textual Art," *Intertextuality: German Literature and Visual Art from the Renaissance to the Twentieth Century*, ed. Ingeborg

Hoesterey and Ulrich Weisstein (Columbia: Camden House, 1993), 64-80.

8. Cf. Rüdiger Engerth, "Der Wiener Aktionismus," *Protokolle* 1 (Vienna: Jugend & Volk, 1970).

9. Cf. Roswitha Mueller, *Valie Export. Fragments of Imagination* (Bloomington: Indiana University Press, 1995).

10. Cf. *Die Wiener Gruppe,* ed. Walter-Buchebner-Gesellschaft (Vienna: Böhlau, 1987).

11. Cf. *literatur in graz seit 1960—das forum stadtpark*, ed. Walter-Buchebner-Gesellschaft (Vienna: Böhlau, 1987).

12. Cf. Robert Fleck, *Avantgarde in Wien. Die Geschichte der Galerie St. Stephan 1954-1982. Kunst- und Kulturbetrieb in Österreich* (Vienna: Löcker, 1982).

13. Anita Prammer, *Valie Export. Eine multi-mediale Künstlerin* (Vienna: Frauenverlag, 1988), 10.

14. Margret Brügmann, "Weiblichkeit im Spiel der Sprache. Über das Verhältnis von Psychoanalyse und 'écriture féminine,'" *Frauen Literatur Geschichte,* ed. Hiltrud Gnüg and Renate Möhrmann (Stuttgart: Metzler, 1985), 395.

15. Cf. Jacqueline Vansant, *Against the Horizon* (Westport, CT: Greenwood Press, 1988).

16. Cf. Valie Export describes "Feministischer Aktionismus" in *Katalog: Zur Definition eines neuen Kunstbegriffes* (Galerie Krinzinger: Innsbruck, 1979).

17. Sigrid Weigel, *Die Stimme der Medusa* (Dülmen-Hiddingsel: tende, 1987), 53.

18. Julia Kristeva, "Ideologie des Diskurses über die Literatur," *Theorie-Literatur-Praxis*, ed. Richard Brütting and Bernhard Zimmermann (Frankfurt: Athenaion, 1975), 172-173. "Avantgarde texts deconstruct...the fundamental categories of Western thinking and its metaphysical tradition...in which we speak with one another."

19. Cf. *Elfriede Jelinek: Framed by Language*, eds. Jorun B. Johns and Katherine Arens (Riverside: Ariadne 1994).

20. Johann Stangel, *Das annulierte Individuum* (Bern/New York: Peter Lang, 1988), 14.

21. Günther A. Höfler, "Vergrößerungsspiegel und Objektiv: Zur Fokussierung der Sexualität bei Elfriede Jelinek," *Elfriede Jelinek*, ed. Kurt Bartsch and Günter Höfler (Graz: Droschl, 1991), 157.

22. Zürn-scholar Sabine Scholl gives a definition of anagrammatic aesthetics: "Wo die Wahrnehmung des Realen 'stets als eine vom Mangel beherrschte vorgestellt wird: Mangel an Realität, Mangel an Sein,' wird dieser Mangel Voraussetzung für die Produktion von Signifikanten, die im Anagramm fortlaufende Veränderung erfahren, aber nicht festgestellt werden, sondern lediglich begrenzt durch die Entscheidung des Produzenten, den Textraum abzuschließen. Die Imagination ersteht aus der Lücke, dem Loch im sozialen Netz...Der Fehler bringt das Anagramm in Gang und hält das Denken in Spannung, bringt die Widersprüche zwar zusammen, doch entscheidet nicht." Sabine Scholl, Fehlen Fallen Kunst. Zur Wahrnehmung und Re/Produktion bei Unica Zürn (Frankfurt: Hain Meisenheim, 1990), 69.

23. Books by Unica Zürn appeared in the series "Die Frau in der Literatur," Ullstein: *Der Mann im Jasmin. Dunkler Frühling* (30143), *Das Weiße mit dem roten Punkt* (30208) and Brinkmann & Bose publishing: *Anagramme* (1988), *Prosa 1* (1989), *Prosa 2* (1990), *Prosa 3* (1990), *Aufzeichnungen* (1989).

24. Hans Bellmer, *Die Puppe* (Berlin/Vienna, 1983), 95: "Der Körper, er gleicht einem Satz, der uns einzuladen scheint, ihn bis in seine Buchstaben zu zergliedern, damit sich in einer endlosen Reihe von Anagrammen aufs neue fügt, was er in Wahrheit enthält."

25. Valie Export, *Das Reale und sein Double: Der Körper* (Bern: Benteli, 1987). Transl. by Kurt Sager, "The Real and Its Double: The Body" in *Discourse* (Bloomington: Indiana University Press, 1988), 10.

26. Roswitha Mueller, *Valie Export. Fragments of Imagination* (Bloomington: Indiana University Press, 1995), xiii-xx.

27. Margret Eifler, "Valie Eport's Iconography: Visual Quest for Subject Discourse," *Modern Austrian Literature* 29.1 (1996): 109-130.

28. This is my translation of Valie Export's interview published as "Mediale Anagramme," *Kunstforum* (Vienna, 11/12 1988).

29. Cf. Valie Export, Katalog *Körperkonfigurationen* 1972-76 (Innsbruck: Galerie Krinzinger, 1977).

30. Sigrid Schmidt-Bortenschlager, "Der analytische Blick," *Frauenliteratur in Österreich von 1945 bis heute*, ed. Carine Kleiber and Erika Tunner (Bern/New York: Peter Lang, 1985), 118. Cf.

Rudolf Burger, "Der böse Blick der Elfriede Jelinek," *Gegen den schönen Schein. Texte zu Elfriede Jelinek,* ed. Christa Gürtler (Frankfurt: Neue Kritik, 1990), 17-29.

31. Sigrid Löffler interviews Elfriede Jelinek, *Profil* (Vienna, 1989).

32. Riki Winter, "Gespräch mit Elfriede Jelinek," *Elfriede Jelinek,* ed. Kurt Bartsch and Günter Höfler (Graz: Droschl, 1991), 13.

33. "Elfriede Jelinek im Gespräch" in Margarete Lamb-Faffelberger, *Valie Export und Elfriede Jelinek im Spiegel der Presse. Zur Rezeption der feministischen Avantgarde Österreichs* (New York, Bern: Peter Lang, 1992), 191.

34. Gisela Bartens praises Jelinek's accomplishments at the 1988 award ceremony of Styria's prize for literature (*Kleine Zeitung,* Graz, March 25, 1988).

35. Jelinek, "In den Waldheimen und auf den Haidern," *Blauer Streusand,* ed. Barbara Alms (Frankfurt: Suhrkamp, 1987), 42.

36. Jelinek, *Totenauberg* (Reinbek: Rowohlt, 1990), 46.

37. Jelinek, *Oh Wildnis, oh Schutz vor ihr* (Reinbek: Rowohlt, 1985), 7.

38. Jelinek, *The Lovers* (Reinbek: Rowohlt, 1975), 155.

39. Jelinek, *Krankheit oder Moderne Frauen* (Cologne: Prometh, 1987), 44.

40. Cf. Lamb-Faffelberger, *Valie Export und Elfriede Jelinek im Spiegel der Presse. Zur Rezeption der feministischen Avantgarde Österreichs.*

The Prosthetic Womb: Technology and Reproduction in the Work of Valie Export

Roswitha Mueller

The abiding interest in Valie Export's artistic and intellectual production, which spans well over three decades now, is partly generated by her insistence on bringing together two seemingly disparate discourses: technology and the body. Traditionally, the avant-garde movements embraced one or the other and only rarely bridged these poles. As a consequence we have become familiar with dichotomies such as the one between the technophile pronouncements of the early Brecht and the psychosomatic concerns of Artaud; or the one between the machine enthusiasm of Italian Futurism or Russian Constructivism and the human-centeredness of Expressionism and Surrealism. And it seems that the more recent avant-gardes of the sixties have tended to reproduce this split, at least on the level of their means of production, mainly around the question of inclusion or exclusion of the techno-logical media in their presentations.

The group of artists who can be considered a kind of background experience in Valie Export's artistic genesis, the Viennese Actionists, had emphatically opted for the human body, exploring it in all its sensual and sexual codifications, to the exclusion of technological interferences. Export differentiated herself early on from the group's affairs by giving technology a fairly prominent place in her own work, without, at the same time, relinquishing the emphasis on the body. The sculptural use of the body, especially of women's bodies, in the context of the Viennese Actionists' performances struck Export as counter-productive in terms of the newly emerging feminist consciousness of that decade. Since the female participants of these performances were always acted upon as objects, without ever being considered subjects, it was clear to Export that a completely different conception of the body had to be put in place in order to avoid reinforcement of an already passive positionality of women in society.

Like so many of the heroines of her feature films, Export recog-nized the importance of technology in the shift from passive to active, in the regaining of mastery on the part of women over their own corporeality as well as over the redefinition of their image. Her counter-conception to the Actionists' implementation of bodies, which she termed "Feminist Actionism," thus included the prosthetic body, technology as an enabling extension of the organic body. In her early experimental films of the sixties, Export had tested the boundary between body and technological medium. One important aspect of her "expanded movies" had been to explore the body as an extension of the machine, or, more specifically, of the filming process. In this category, the torso of a man was used as the screen in a film projection, blending in, as it were, the organic body with the technical apparatus. The reverse conception, the machine as extension of the body, which corresponds to the more basic impulse behind the development of technology as such, figured centrally in Export's early film experiments. These instances tended to foreground the camera as an extension of the human eye, performing in ways inaccessible to the natural organ.

In "Adjungierte Dislokationen" (1973; Adjoined Dislocations), for example, a simultaneous view in opposite directions, normally not granted to natural vision, is afforded by tying two 8 mm cameras to the chest and back of the filmmaker's body, and by later projecting both filmstrips side by side onto the screen. The 8 mm filming was itself recorded by a 16 mm camera, whose footage was also included in the final simultaneous projection. What this filming of a filming brought to the viewer's attention went beyond the recognition that the capacity to see was augmented by the technical apparatus; it also showed the effect of this increased potential on the body as a whole and its relation to the environment: "What is demonstrated is not only the investigation of the environment on film, but a film of the investigation of the environment through the body, which turns the environment into a body, into the body's extension, into an environmental body."[1]

Similar explorations of the relation between body, machine and environment, whether sociopolitical, natural or architectural urban, can be traced through all of Export's work, her performances, her photography, and above all, her later films, where the use of the camera becomes the central trope in the protagonist's investigation of her position as a woman in patriarchal society. In most cases body and technological apparatus are not just played opposite each other in a bipolar tug of war but are placed in a field that includes the third term of the natural and cultural environment.

In this field the body displays its double determination not only as both nature and culture, but also as self and other: "The ontological experiencing of the body by woman is the simultaneous experiencing of the personal and the alien."[2] Again and again, Export emphasizes the body as boundary and gives personal expression to this concept. She also cites the experience of other women artists regarding the sense of "separation of the self from the outside world," a separation which implicates the body as the other to such an extent that it "ultimately becomes the outside world."[3]

Gender is all-important in this process of individuation. Coming to consciousness in Export's account is empowering to the male subject, but for women the same juncture in psychic development brings about their relegation to the world of objects. The twin project of mankind, to expand and enhance the natural strength and force of the physical body through tools and technology on the one hand and, secondly, to augment consciousness following the Freudian prescription "where id was, there ego shall be," does not pertain to women. Their position on the side of the unconscious, their merger with the body and the dimension of space and with nature, animals and objects, which is assigned to them "under the pressure of culture,"[4] precludes them at the same time from participating in the prevailing rational/technological, symbolic system.

Export's critical analysis of women's position in western patriarchal societies is matched and complemented by her artistic output which deepens this criticism viscerally but, more importantly, it continually invents new forms and means of confronting and countering the rigid determinants of this position. The confrontation itself centers on the female body and proceeds along two conceptually opposite lines of approach. It explores the traditional equation of body-woman-nature, not, to be sure, with the goal of verifying this equation, but aiming to reappropriate and redefine the relation thus established toward the articulation of new positions. In more recent feminist debates this approach has been characterized as "radical" due to its strategic essentialism and its insistence on the corporeality and sexual specificity of the rational, knowing, subject. Implied in this emphasis on the body, which seemingly supports essentialist concerns, is the recognition that the body/mind split, and its attendant ascription of the resultant poles to fixed gender positions, is itself a construction. Facing the body in this way as one's traditional domain is entertained with the full awareness that the "ideal type of the thinking and deliberating subject, as constructed in the Western rationalist tradition from Plato onward, has coincided with that of 'man,' a 'man' who recognizes himself as such in the measure that he succeeds in subduing what is feminine in himself."[5]

The domain of the body is scrutinized with great emphasis in Export's performances but also in her photography and in her films, particularly in her experimental film *Syntagma*. The point of departure for Export's investigations is the concept of the body as boundary, or, as she often describes it, as bearer of signs, of social inscriptions and codes. In this conception, the body is both mind and matter, nature and culture, which explains its pivotal position in the context of Feminist Actionism. The primary source of Feminist Actionism, as Export has pointed out, lies in the "history of female experience."[6] This experience is recorded and stored by the body both in the form of physical traces, scars, gestures, postures and sicknesses, as well as traces deposited in the psyche through the function of memory. The unconscious is the site of this history, not only of the repression of the individual psyche, but also of the history of the "dark continent" of female repression.

The engraved body in its most literal form is the tattooed body. The 1970 "body sign action" for which Export had a garter tattooed on her thigh is accompanied by the following text: "The garter is used as the sign of belonging to a class that demands conditioned behavior, becomes a reminiscence that keeps awake the problem of self-determination and/or determination by others of femininity." Here tattooing does not have the rite-of-passage connotation that it carries in tribal societies, for example, where it functions in some cases as a test and a badge of courage as the young person enters adulthood. Instead, in this action, it represents a kind of branding, a marking of property, of c[h]attel. And as such, it is a permanent stain on the surface of the body reminding it of its otherness.

A comic version of "branding" the body as a sign of its object status, its position as commodity in a relation of owner and owned, is developed in Export's contribution to the 1986 omnibus film *Sieben Frauen—sieben Sünden* (Seven Women—Seven Sins). This twelve-minute meditation on the modern meaning of voluptuousness or lust, in its ancient sense of moral transgression and capital sin, comes to the conclusion that if prostitution is the voluntary loss of ownership of one's body, i.e., the selling of the body, then the term applies not just to the old-fashioned whore, but also to the modern athlete who uses his body as a billboard for advertising certain "brands" of products. And, judging from the pornographic images on the female protagonist's wedding gown, the objectification of women in prostitution is extended also to the institution of marriage.

But not all traces are as literal as these direct inscriptions on the skin. In other cases the imprints on the body are left behind in posture and gesture. Three millennia of subjugation under patriarchal rule have cultivated a body language of humility and submission. The most striking findings from an investigation of the transmission of certain gestures and postures through the centuries are exhibited in a ten-minute video performance entitled "Stille Sprache" (Silent Language). After several years of developing, this piece found its way into Export's first feature film, *Unsichtbare Gegner* in 1976 (*Invisible Adversaries*, 1987). The possibility for video to retrace images in a process of superimposition and gradual blending of two distinct image levels allows for an experiment in which an actress in modern clothes imitates the posture of a woman in a Renaissance painting, e.g., Mary, mother of Christ, kneeling and embracing the foot of the cross. Gradually, the superimposition drowns out the background of the ancient painting and what emerges is the modern woman clutching a modern cleaning utensil in the ancient posture of the original female figure in the painting.

Similar concepts are at work in some of the photographic experiments dating from the same time. In a series of photographs of Madonnas modeled after Michelangelo's *Pietà*, the women posing for this experiment are adopting the body posture of the figure in the original art work, but retain their modern dress. Instead of the body of Christ extended across their lap, these latter day Madonnas are holding a knitting machine in their arms or a washing machine between their knees, as in the case of "Die Strickmadonna" (1976; Knitting Madonna) and "Die Geburtenmadonna" (1976; Birth Madonna), respectively. What is revealed in these photographic investigations is not only the persistence of certain gestures and postures as they are transmitted through the ages, but also the impact of culture on molding the body. Once again we are confronted with a view of the body as borderland between nature and culture, as the physical expression of cultural determinants. A repertoire of gestures typical of women such as kneeling, clutching, cradling is gleaned from these studies and becomes understandable as physical responses to historical, cultural phenomena rather than as biological givens.

This insight into the cultural-historical genesis of the very appearance of women is supported by other investigations that concentrate more specifically on the placement of the female body in its modern environment, the urban landscape. These studies are extremely important since they provide an arena for action, which is the third term in the nature-culture proposition, preventing the poles from becoming fixed opposites. Perhaps the most significant series in this respect is the 1972 "Körperkonfigurationen in der Architektur" (1972-1973; Body Configurations in Architecture). These images combine structural geometric concepts inspired by architectural forms and the female body. Accordingly, they explore both the body as ornament as well as its necessary adjustment and accommodation within its architectural environs. Some of the studies' titles, e.g. "insertion," "adaption" or "addition," underline the sense that these arrangements are also externalizations of internal states and that the adjustments are a form of marginalization. This sense is further heightened when these studies are placed in a narrative field. A whole cycle of "Körperkonfigurationen in der Architektur" was shot in 1976 specifically for *Unsichtbare Gegner*. By foregrounding the female protagonist's point of view, geometric form is permeated with emotional content, further emphasizing the aspect of externalizing internal states. An ornament at best, the protagonist demonstrates the qualities of "adaption" and "insertion" as she merges with the architectural forms, fitting herself into the gaps, hollows and corners of her environment in an attempt not to take up space.

The analysis of how the image of woman is constructed in patriarchal society is certainly a step toward its deconstruction. Yet, while Export has directed much of her artistic efforts toward breaking open the structure of representation and the codification of the traditional image of woman, her conception of Feminist Actionism is not contained by purely textual analyses. It goes beyond that by suggesting interventions in everyday life—strategies for ordinary women in their struggle to disassociate themselves from their social determination as nature and body. To this end, the implementation of technology and its rational stance can be seen as an attempt at redefinition and at a reaffiliation of entrenched gender positions.

In two of her feature films *Unsichtbare Gegner* and *Die Praxis der Liebe* (1986; *The Practice of Love*, 1989), the female protagonists are equipped with cameras and recording apparatuses in order to pursue their activities as photographer in the first instance, and as professional journalist in the latter. In the earlier film, the woman uses the camera almost as a defense against her environment and in an effort to extricate herself from her designation as ornament. As the object to be looked at, she is assigned the passive end of the specular relation. She wields her camera in order to reverse this relation and to make her the active subject of the gaze. In the journalist's case the subject-position is already well established, but she, too, can not take it for granted. Before long she learns that the gaze is a prescribed one that does not necessarily coincide with her way of seeing things. She recognizes that the very technological apparatus that has served her so well in building her career can just as easily be summoned for destructive purposes. This she comes to realize not only through her investigation of an illegal arms deal, which turns out to be supported by the government, but also as a consequence of retaliatory actions against her involving the use of surveillance equipment. In *Die Praxis der Liebe*, technology is more problematized than in Export's earlier films.

The question of domination and power in the implementation of technology is crucial to Export's concerns and explains her vigorous defense of the need to engage responsibly in the struggle over the direction given to these powerful extensions of the body. In this respect, I might also add, Export parts company with recent "radical feminism," for which the rational-technological project is hopelessly compromised. Instead she prefers "to engage in local, piecemeal critical inquiries into the effects of the sexual power structure on philosophy and other branches of learning,"[7] which is a position that has been described in contrast to the radical viewpoint as "reformist."[8] Export's impulse regarding technology can be situated in proximity to Donna J. Haraway's propositions in "A Cyborg Manifesto," where she asserts that "[c]ommunications technologies and biotechnologies are the crucial tool recrafting our bodies. These tools embody and enforce new social relations for women worldwide."[9] Such a momentous insight entails active intervention in the form of "seizing the tools to mark the world that marked them as other," and it also would seem to present "the task of recoding communication and intelligence to subvert command and control."[10] On one level, "seizing the tools" and "recoding" have been Export's project from the moment she had formulated the notion of "Feminist Actionism."

In her 1983 experimental film *Syntagma*, Export examines the notion of codification. In repeated series of staircases on which a pair of feet are descending or climbing upward, sometimes bare and sometimes

coded as feminine because of the high heels they are wearing, the look
of the feet is subjected to various constructions, including that which
points to the difference between the original and the copy. By blurring
the borderlines between the natural, the artificial, the authentic and the
copy, codification itself is seen as epiphenomenal and subject to
change. Change in *Syntagma* comes as a relief from the obsessive
staircase sequences. It comes in form of "seizing the tools"—the female
subject takes the camera and opens up her claustrophobic perspective to
a panoramic 360-degree view around the city's main square.

The film's final section deals in some detail with the question of
technology's usefulness for women in their quest for self-determination.
The female protagonist is sitting at a table writing by hand. Behind her
as a backdrop are the gigantic pages of a book (magnified to fill the
entire frame), which are periodically turned by an invisible hand. The
camera slowly pans to the left of this scene and focuses on the screen of
a video monitor, showing the same table and woman, only here the
woman is using a typewriter. Panning back again to the first writing
scene, the camera rests on the woman who is now using a typewriter as
well. These pans are repeated three times in different constellations. On
the last set the silhouette of a bicycle, which was a symbol of emancipation for the suffragettes, can be made out behind the woman's back.

This passage is not just a historical reflection on the importance of
technology for the emancipation of women, it also establishes technology as both mind and matter. Just as the body in Export's treatment is
the meeting ground of the mind and the biological, natural entity in
constant reciprocal exchange, technology bridges both material objects
and mental constructs. Technology has just as much to do with
language, writing and thought as it does with physical apparatuses and
equipment. The material-mental distinction has become particularly
inadequate for modern machines; as Haraway has observed, they are
"quintessentially micro-electronic devices: they are everywhere and they
are invisible. Modern machinery is an irreverent upstart god, mocking
the Father's ubiquity and spirituality."[11]

In her scrutiny of the significance of the female body in patriarchal
society, it was only logical that Export would sooner or later recognize
that "[t]echnologies of reproduction pose the question about the body,
and above all, about the female body, most radically."[12] Precisely
because of her insistence on the body as "the double of the real," the
question of disembodiment presents itself, especially with regard to the

crucial issue of reproduction. Both in her writing and in her artwork, but especially in her performances, Export passionately sketches a pessimistic prognosis of the possibilities of the female body within the confines of the real which "represents the power of the man."[13] Since Export does not understand the real to mean an ontological or biological reserve, separate from the social, but rather sees it mediated by the image, it is more aptly described in terms of Freud's "reality principle (of the logos)."[14] Her move toward disembodiment, therefore, is a move on the level of representation, "because for woman in the system of representation of our masculine culture, the image and the represented object have the same reality."[15]

Export's extreme position with regard to reproduction might best be seen on the same level as her body actions, or better, as a performance refusal. Having tested the body's capacity to endure and to overcome its many negative determinations in her performances and actions, one ultimate challenge remains, that of pulling the body out of circulation altogether. Like the anorexic's and the hysteric's attack on the physical body, the refusal of biological reproduction comes from an extremely weak position. Yet, as Export points out, since this is the position assigned to women in patriarchal society, the dissolution of the body may be the only way to sever the ideological identification of women with the biological functions of their bodies.

University of Wisconsin-Milwaukee

Notes

1. Valie Export, Export Archive.
2. Valie Export, "The Real and Its Double: The Body," *Discourse* 11.1 (1989-88): 17.
3. Ibid., 5.
4. Ibid., 17.
5. Sabina Lovibond, "Feminism and the 'Crisis of Rationality,'" *New Left Review* 207 (September-October, 1994): 75.
6. Valie Export, "Aspects of Feminist Actionism," *New German Critique* 47 (Spring-Summer 1989): 71.
7. Lovibond, "Feminism and the 'Crisis of Rationality'": 77.
8. See Lovibond.

9. Donna J. Haraway, *Simians, Cyborgs, and Women* (New York: Routledge, 1991), 14.
10. Ibid., 175.
11. Ibid., 53.
12. Export, "The Real and Its Double: The Body": 6.
13. Ibid., 24.
14. Ibid.
15. Ibid.

Out from the Shadows, into the Shadows: Kitty Kino's "Kino"

Jutta Landa

Kitty Kino (whose real name is Kitty Gschöpf) graduated from the Viennese Academy of Music and Performing Arts in 1975-76 with a diploma in editing and directing, even though her male colleagues had warned her that "as a woman [she would] never make a film."[1] Since then she has directed numerous shorts, TV series, and three feature films. The misogyny expressed by Kino's mentors assumes an even more cynical undertone when one ponders the layers of meanings behind "as a woman." Calling for male mimicry on the part of women who want to get involved in film, the phrase implies a deep mistrust in women's filmmaking abilities; their technical know-how, organizational skills, and leadership qualities are all questioned. In view of such a blatantly sexist attitude one really wonders how Kino and her fellow filmmakers such as Valie Export, Susanne Zanke, and Käthe Kratz, to name but a few, managed, at least temporarily, to break into the male-dominated Austrian feature film.

The answer to this question pulls together issues of financing, film tradition, and the filmmaker's personal signature. To understand the problems of financing one has to know that Austrian film is synonymous with subsidized film. In fact, Austrian film was on the verge of extinction, saved only by the somewhat overdue enactment of the Austrian Film Promotion Law in 1981. Since then a variety of money-granting institutions on the federal and state level have rescued an industry ravaged by its own output of low-quality films and the impact of TV. Women filmmakers benefited from this situation, as money became available to applicants of both sexes. Austrian Television, the ORF, participates in the subsidizing process by paying about a third of its budget to the Film Fund. However, the ORF's most valuable contribution no doubt consists in giving work to young filmmakers, including women. As a result of this policy Kino's *Nachtmeerfahrt* (1986; Sea Journey into the Night) was shot for TV.

Yet, in spite of the new money available to them, women would probably never have stood a chance in feature film had it not been for the avant-garde and underground film. In the late sixties and early seventies in particular, the years of the demise of Austrian commercial film, it was the avant-garde which kept film art in Austria alive. More importantly, the experimental films by artists such as Peter Kubelka, Valie Export, Ferry Radax, Peter Weibel, Kurt Kren, Ernst Schmidt, and Hans Scheugl contributed to the international reputation of Austrian film. Although the avant-garde film scene was, and is, unfortunately just as exclusionary of women as the commercial market—in the *Catalogue of the Austrian Avantgarde- and Undergroundfilm. 1950-1980 Retrospective* one counts 33 male names and only four women's names: Friederike Pezold, Valie Export, Maria Lassnig, and Lisl Ponger[2]—it nevertheless offers women a niche. In this context, one must credit Export with single-handedly opening avenues for women in film through her pioneering work. By challenging the demarcation of social roles and ingrained viewing habits, along with questioning the traditional representation of women in the media, her films have not only established a women's avant-garde tradition, but also paved the way for an increased participation in commercial film by and for women. In participating in the more commercially oriented film, feminist filmmakers had to face a new challenge. On the one hand, true to their calling, they had to circumvent and subvert the politics of the subjugating the male gaze so prevalent in mainstream film,[3] while on the other hand, they had to garner mass audience appeal. Kitty Kino attempted to solve the dilemma by instituting her "pop avant-garde" style: the fusion of avant-garde strategies with the populist practices of narrative film.

In the strictest sense of the word, Austrian avant-garde film of the sixties (like its international counterpart) meant non-narrative film given to technical experimentation. It was influenced by the visual arts and defined itself as "the other cinema" which steered clear of the factory-produced commercial cinema.[4] The low-budget *auteur*-style of avant-garde cinema with its resulting unfinished look was preferred over a high-gloss picture-perfect product. Another quality essential to Austrian avant-garde cinema was its tendency to subvert cinematic conventions by manipulating not only the medium itself, but its surrounding apparatus as well: the film celluloid, the screen, and even the movie-theater.[5] Austrian women's avant-garde film in the sixties and seventies pushed these parameters into the direction of female actionism, which according to Export "seeks to transform the object of male natural history, the material 'woman,' subjugated and enslaved by the male creator, into an independent actor and creator, subject of her own history."[6] Her films show an obsession with the female body as the site of regimentation and self-deformation. In addition, Austrian feminine avant-garde film is often an interplay of different kinds of discourses, including paintings, television, radio, advertising, videos, aiming at the deconstruction of the media's cultural coding of women. Assessed against this set of parameters, Kitty Kino's films *Karambolage* (1983; Carambolage), *Nachtmeerfahrt*, and *Wahre Liebe* (1989; True Love)[7] show only rudimentary connections to the Austrian feminine avant-garde tradition. Leaning towards pop culture fantasies, her films are largely based on narrative, the camera work is only occasionally innovative, and there is very little self-reflexivity or attention-calling to the apparatus surrounding production and distribution. Nevertheless her films, to a varying degree, retain the avant-garde impetus. This indebtedness is evident in several aspects of her work: her vision of film as a consciousness-raising instrument, her *auteur*-like status as a filmmaker, her inclusion of visual tableaus in the style of MTV music videos, her questioning of spectating processes, and last but not least her critical representation of the avant-garde circuit itself. There is circumstantial evidence to be found in the films as well: Kino's *Nachtmeerfahrt* quotes a scene from Export's *Unsichtbare Gegner* (1976; *Invisible Adversaries*, 1987) which focuses on a burning paper boat. The motif of the bearded woman, only briefly hinted at in Export's film, becomes the central metaphor for culturally conditioned gender roles in Kino's *Nachtmeerfahrt*.

In a statement entitled "Filmmaking as Consciousness-Raising Process—Consciousness-Raising Process as Film,"[8] Kitty Kino claims that the guiding star in her efforts as a filmmaker has been the attempt to depict processes which result in a changed consciousness. While Kino extends this concept of a heightened awareness to social and political as well as metaphysical issues, its reference to gender and sex is foregrounded in all her films. Additional space for serious cultural critique is opened up through the critical presentation of a designer world, inhabited by the with-it people whose social, political and sexual consciousness limps behind their professed enlightened lifestyles, and through the self-conscious depiction of the processes of looking. Kino's first feature film (released in 1983), aptly titled *Karambolage*,[9] explores in rather traditional film language the collision of male and female gender roles. The visual metaphor for this collision is a pool game, more specifically "Karambolage" or three cushion billiards. The film's protagonist, Judit, adopts the game as she looks for a way out of her male-dependent existence. In her own words, a woman "has to be able to do something better than men." As she fine-tunes her game to a competitive level, she increasingly encounters the hostility of a misogynist society that will not allow such transgressions into male territory. At the film's conclusion Judit challenges a brutal pimp from Hamburg, called the King, to a game she cannot win. He uses physical force to subdue her and in the end attempts to rape her. Owing to its Freudian imagery, the game of pool lends itself as a perfect metaphor for gender conflicts: the phallic connotation of the cue stick is several times referred to in the demeaning innuendo of the men who want to "teach" Judit how to handle the cue, but also by an angry Judit herself, who contends that "one plays pool with a cue not with a prick." The criss-crossing paths of the white and red balls and their clicking sounds are reminiscent of the gender collisions within the film. On the other hand, the billiards game offers the protagonist the possibility of surmounting female discrimination through a training of her visual capacities. Judit becomes an accomplished player by acquiring the sharpened vision of a Zen archer who wins by remaining completely free of intentions. As Judit avers, in such an ego-less state "one is not nothing, on the contrary, one is everything." Judit's second hobby serves to strengthen this emphasis on her superior gaze: she routinely rummages through second-hand furniture stores in search of undiscovered art treasures which she restores and resells. Again, as the art dealer Hans Seebaum freely admits, she is more successful at this game than her male competitors. Significantly, in a fusion of the film's gendered theme and the politics of the look, Seebaum is the man with whom Judit is in love and who fails to see the exceptional in her.

Like all of Kitty Kino's films, *Karambolage* takes place in a glitzy yuppie setting, replete with expensive designer clothes, extravagant apartments and elegant furniture, all of which serve to expose the avant-garde pose. Kino portrays the fashionable avant-garde as a heartless social clique, which ostracizes Judit as soon as she is dropped by her lover. At one of their trendy parties, Judit witnesses a performance-art show in which men and women exhibit a panoply of revolting animal costumes. Not only do these costumes externalize the evil behind the chic facade, but the shocking array serves as a comment on the ennui of a slick society which requires its provocative spectacle. Nevertheless, in spite of its critical impetus and its adept visualization of gender issues, the film's ending leaves behind an ambiguous message. The point is made that by adopting male qualities Judit has betrayed not only her friend Lilo, who is in love with the King and warns Judit to stay away from him, but also her entire gender. As Kino sums it up, Judit must learn to "distinguish between ego-trip and self-realization."[10] Such an account-taking buys into the long-held convictions that women should exercise constraint rather than follow their "blind" ambitions, otherwise they run the risk of provoking male violence. In a roundabout way the ending of the film, with its retreat of feminist positions fought for earlier, betrays Kino's internalization of the "as a woman" adage. It reflects the filmmaker's own difficulties in distinguishing between an ego-trip and the demands of a male-oriented profession—difficulties perhaps also implied by her adoption of a new name and thus persona. In this context, the pool game also serves as a metaphor for the filmmaker's professional goal: to become better at her métier than most men. *Karambolage* was indeed a critical success and did well at the box office. Incidentally, the film succeeded on another unexpected level: after its release Austrian women's enrollment in pool clubs increased.

In *Nachtmeerfahrt*,[11] Kitty Kino resolves her personal ambiguity by offering the concept of androgyny. This concept is embedded in a film which again draws its audience appeal from the world of high fashion and glamor, of discos and designer apartments in which the protagonist, the model Lilly, moves. Initially, gender roles are clearly defined in the film: Lilly is at the beck and call of Richard, a married man, who runs her modeling career and is involved in an affair with her. Their secured gender-specific positions unravel when Lilly discovers that she is growing a beard. Unable to hide her disfiguration any longer, she sets out on a dark journey into the "night side" of Vienna. The model's new identity as a man leads her through a string of encounters that help her shed her dependencies on the men around her. In an act of emancipation, she accepts an invitation to a fashion shoot against the will of her lover. To everyone's shock she appears at the session with a neatly trimmed mustache, displaying fanciful clothes that serve to underline the androgynous aspects of her appearance. Surprisingly, the star designer Bartolomeo, himself seemingly androgynous, is fascinated by Lilly and chooses her as his new star model.

The glamorous setting of the film *Nachtmeerfahrt* functions to signify the overall problem of female representation. The fashion milieu exemplifies the all-pervasive male gaze that is inextricably bound to the commodified aspect of femininity. The model Lilly is, in Laura Mulvey's sense, literally the object of the male gaze, her entire sense of identity based on it, making her in fact a non-entity. It is not coincidental that the film begins with Lilly and her agent Margret sifting through a stack of pictures in search of the one in which she looks the best, only to have their decision overturned by Richard. The male stands as the undisputed authority: "You just don't have the male eye."[12] The degree to which Lilly's narcissism is fueled by the approving male gaze is shown by her obsession with mirrors. In continual acts of self-torture, she nervously checks the growth of her beard in the mirror, plucking away with a pair of tweezers. The model's counterstrategy against the penetrating male gaze is withdrawal: she locks herself in her apartment. But even within her own four walls she allows herself the disintegration of her appearance only after she has covered up the mirror. In a gesture remindful of Export's female actionism, Lilly then regresses to infantile patterns: she gets her hands sticky with dough and rolls autistically on the floor. Richard's shocked reaction upon his return indicates to what degree he views Lilly as a mere component of her designer environment. Lilly's "Sea Journey" becomes her crucial eye-opening experience; Kino borrows a term from C.G. Jung for the journey into the "dark waters of one's unconscious, during which one encounters as a woman one's inner male counterpart—the animus—and as a man one's anima."[13] The various images of night, waves, boats, and an iconic moon, scattered through the first part of the film, beckon to Lilly to break out. Thus the very commercial props by which she is surrounded emerge as dreamy visions or signs of an impending freedom. Similarly, the pop tune of the film implores Lilly to journey into her own soul: "Have courage, find your soul, and then everything will be fine." In the course of her "Sea Journey," Lilly accepts the male and female positions within herself: "We do not exist without the other, we are two sides of the same coin. In other words, we are one. Just one."[14] In the last climactic and extensive fashion shoot, the video-like set designs, along with Lilly's cosmic clothes, incorporate symbolic contrasts that coincide with her new androgynous self-image. A desert scenery alternates with a seascape replete with birds, seastars, and fish. In the final take of the shoot, sun and moon are locked in an embrace, in a world where binary oppositions of male-female no longer exist. The ending of the film finds a "normal" Lilly smiling at her bearded alter ego in the mirror.

With *Nachtmeerfahrt* Kitty Kino advanced a process of self-realization which would result in the transcendence of gender divisions. Yet, Kino's approach is once again somewhat problematic. Although Lilly's androgynous look spells emancipation, it is in great danger of being absorbed as yet another commodity by the fashion industry, a danger indicated by a final view of Margret trying on different beards. The to-be-looked-at-ness is now enhanced—incidentally, the clothes Lilly dons at the photo session are made of revealing clear plastic and sheer veils—by the dimension of titillating bisexuality. Nevertheless, in her own pop-style, complete with pop music, Kino makes clever use of the possibilities of make-up and retouching, gestures and mimicry to break through the limits of the physical definition of gender.[15]

While *Nachtmeerfahrt* has been described as an "experimental, symbolic-archetypically designed women's film,"[16] *Wahre Liebe,* released in 1989,[17] is by Kino's admission the film most removed from avant-garde practices.[18] The gender conflicts in *Wahre Liebe* are presented in a much more muted way than in her previous films. Here, the filmmaker's use of car collisions, so typical in their evocation of the war of the sexes, loses its threatening aspect, and instead signals the beginning of romance: as Karl so poetically puts it, his and Roxanne's cars "have kissed each other." Moreover, women are shown as much more empowered: both Roxanne and Barbara, Karl's wife, are strong career-oriented women who design their own environment. The conflicts between Karl and Barbara, and Roxanne and her boyfriend Erwin are presented as eminently solvable, with Erwin finally assuming his responsibilities and Karl developing an understanding for his wife's career and emotional needs. In Kino's typical fashion, *Wahre Liebe* employs the extravagance of pop culture for its reflection of the processes of spectation. Interwoven with the story of two lovers who keep missing each other are Roxanne's problem-ridden preparations for a rock concert starring the colorful but contentious hard-rocker Terry Singer. Intercut in the film's beginning sequence is the shoot of a promotional music video. The video's sudden onset serves to confuse the spectator's sense of location within the film; in addition, its shifts of focus and special effects provide a blurred image. The film culminates in the rock concert itself, during which the multiple exchanges of looks of people on stage, backstage, and in the audience—enhanced by the glow of the fans' swaying cigarette lighters—result in a regrouping of the love constellations. In addition to rock music spectaculars, Kino makes use of the sun as an agent of visual contact. It is the glare of the sun which is to blame for the car collision of Roxanne and Karl. Another time the sun's impact is so strong that it explodes the window pane. But the sun not only attracts, it also separates. The only time when Roxanne actually walks into Karl's field of vision, a blinding sun literally obliterates her. The process of looking at and reproducing the object of the gaze is also thematized in Karl's attempt to draw a phantom image of Roxanne with the help of his computer.

Although Kitty Kino stays true to her objective of heightening her protagonist's, and by extension, the movie-goer's consciousness, *Wahre Liebe* does not reach the critical level of the much more experimental *Nachtmeerfahrt,* or of *Karambolage* for that matter. The film's message that true love can set thought processes in motion which result in a higher level of awareness is submerged in gestures of resignation; both Karl and Roxanne resolve to find fulfillment in their existing relationship. The one experimental impetus of the film, "that the construction of meaning in all the apparently chaotic and accidental events in life is a question of overview, just as the film spectator owns the overview which is lacking in the film's protagonists,"[19] is effaced by a narration which comes dangerously close to the "cute-meet" formula of many Hollywood films. Yet, by overstraining negative coincidence, the film strives not at replicating, but rather at exposing such plot manipulations. Furthermore, Kino deliberately deprives the audience of a happy ending. In the last instance, it is probably the combination of a purely decorative designer world with a rather conventional romantic story (in other words more pop than avant-garde) which accounts for *Wahre Liebe's* loss of critical acumen. However, when considering the film's shortcomings, one should keep in mind that with a six-week time limit for shooting and her highest budget so far—15 million Austrian schillings—the outside pressures on Kitty Kino had also increased. At the mercy of a "strong" cameraman, imposed upon her by the Film Promotion Board, Kino had difficulties realizing her female aesthetic. Her desire to subordinate the images to an emotional, dramaturgical need was all too often thwarted by a dictatorial "that's how we do it" or a contemptuous "I'm not going to perform exercises on the equipment."[20] How such problems (which the film-maker incidentally likened to marital discord) could be compounded is illustrated by the previously mentioned take into the sun, which was not only sabotaged by the gaffer and the camera-man who refused to pan the camera into the sun, but, even worse, it was later almost cut by the editor. Small wonder that, operating under such constraints, Kino only retains vestiges of avant-garde rebellion in *Wahre Liebe*. Ultimately, Kitty Kino's strategy of buying into pop culture by mixing the avant-garde impetus with a more commercial appeal proved too fragile not to be overrun by commercial pressures.

This downward spiral of Kino's film project opens up the question whether a progressive silencing of the filmmaker's voice has taken place. Such a conclusion is warranted by the fact that, in spite of the often benign attention given to her work by the press, repeated allusions are made to Kino's singular status as a female filmmaker who describes the emotional and career needs of emancipated women. A telling remark by the ORF's Gerald Szyszkowitz, who was responsible for commissioning *Nachtmeerfahrt*, sheds light on the nature of experimentation in Austrian film: "Who says we are not courageous? We have never made a film with Kitty Kino, that is an experiment."[21] Furthermore, one must not overlook the fact that Kino's official filmography contains a second, unofficial one: a list of rejected projects. Her theoretical concept of film as a four-dimensional medium, which is uniquely suited to retrace the "arrow of time" by remembering the past as well as the future, resulted in a number of projects which were rejected due to their "bizarreness." One of them anticipated, by some years, the theme of the American box office hit *Ghost*. In addition, the fact that "women's film" was no longer in vogue in the late eighties aborted other projects planned by the filmmaker. Under these circumstances, it seems quite feasible that a further sharpening of Kino's creative and experimental skills was also prevented by a self-imposed inner censorship. In 1992 and 1993 she was commissioned by the ORF to direct, as the first woman (!), two segments of the *Eurocop* television series, entitled "Operation gelungen" (1992; Operation Successful) and "Transit in den Tod" (1993; Transit into Death). Showing more confidence in her second assignment, the filmmaker introduced Bigi Herzog, a female detective, in "Transit", a reversal of ingrained gender patterns that was duly noted in the papers.[22]

Although the filmmaker professed interest in the psychological and logical unraveling power of the detective genre, her remarks betray a fear of being swallowed up by the routine serial work of television. At once happy that "she is needed," she speaks of future projects "into which I can transport more of myself."[23] None of these have been realized so far, at least not in film—her theater workshop *Der Gipfel von allem* (The Peak of Everything) presented at the "Styrian Fall" in Graz in 1994 was highly praised for its impressive "images and scenes of great intensity."[24] In fact, Kino's movie career seems to have come full circle, with another male-authored verdict—"She is pretty much passé"—hanging over her head.[25]

Granted, that the journey from out of the shadows back into the shadows is not one shared by all Austrian women who are feature filmmakers, especially those who work in documentary, Kino's story, unfortunately, seems to be representative of an ongoing struggle against marginalization and commercialization. Austrian women's feature film deserves continued unequivocal support—whether its allegiance is commercial or avant-garde—for its position overall is tenuous. Statistics show that whereas in the years 1981-1986 the ratio of feature films made by women as opposed to men was 1 in 5, it dropped to 1 in 8 for 1987 and 1988. In 1990 and 1991 not even one of the 30 feature films released was directed by a woman. This ominous trend continues with all 15 feature films in 1993 signed by male directors, and with only a slight upward trend in 1994-95.[26] Given these figures, one is inclined to perceive Austria's recent 1994 Academy Award nomination for best foreign film, Paul Harather's *India*, as mainstream film's backlash. With its predominantly male cast, its "odd-couple" bonding story, and its indulgence in slapstick and bathroom humor, it stands as a celebration of the return to the male-dominated film, away from the esoterica of Kitty Kino's *Kino*.

University of California, Los Angeles

Notes

1. Cited by Kitty Kino in a personal interview, August 6, 1992. All translations are mine, unless otherwise indicated. Further references to this interview are marked with "Int."
2. *Katalog: Österreichischer Avantgarde- und Undergroundfilm 1950-1980* (Vienna, 1980), 2.
3. Austrian women filmmakers, again with Valie Export in the forefront, anticipated and paralleled Laura Mulvey's critique of

male-oriented film, as explicated in her seminal article "Visual Pleasure and Narrative Cinema," *Screen* 16/3 in their work.

4. See Ernst Schmidt Jr., "Das andere Kino—ein Lexikon des neuen europäischen Films," *Film 1968* (Hannover: Velber, 1968). For a more extensive definition of Austrian avant-garde film also see Hans Scheugel and Ernst Schmidt Jr., *Eine Subgeschichte des Films—Lexikon des Avantgarde-Experimental- und Undergroundfilms*, edition suhrkamp 471 (Frankfurt: Suhrkamp, 1974).

5. Peter Weibel, *Filmgeschichte(n) aus Österreich*, Folge 10., ORF 1972, cited in Walter Fritz, *Kino in Österreich 1945-1983: Film zwischen Kommerz und Avantgarde* (Vienna: Österreichischer Bundesverlag, 1984), 145.

6. Valie Export, "Aspects of Feminist Actionism," *New German Critique* 47 (Spring/Summer 1989): 71.

7. These titles are the official translations of the Austrian Film Commission.

8. "Filmemachen als Bewußtwerdungsprozeß – Bewußtwerdungsprozeß als Film," an unpublished statement by Kino.

9. *Karambolage*, dir. Kino, Neue Studio Film Gesellschaft, Vienna, 1983.

10. "She finally learned to differentiate between egocentrism and self-realization." See note 8.

11. *Nachtmeerfahrt*, dir. Kino, Thalia Film Ges.m.b.H., Vienna for ORF, 1986.

12. "Euch fehlt halt der männliche Blick."

13. "Kitti [*sic*] Kinos Film vom doppelten Geschlecht," *ORF Pressedienst* (Vienna), (December 18, 1986): 4.

14. Emphasis is in the spoken film dialogue.

15. This practice puts her in the vicinity of female actionists such as Katherina Sieverding, who is mentioned by Valie Export in her article "Aspects of Feminist Actionism": 92, see note 6.

16. "Experimenteller, symbolisch-archetypisch aufbereiteter Frauenfilm." See catalogue *Austrian Films 1981-86* (Vienna: Austrian Film Commission, 1988), 57.

17. *Wahre Liebe*, dir. Kino, Wega Filmproduktionsges.m.b.H., Vienna/Julian R. Film, Munich, 1990.

18. "Kitty Kino: Kommerz fürs Herz," *Skytec* (November 1990): 14.

19. See Kino's statement (note 8): "Der Film ist so aufgebaut, daß der Betrachter mehr weiß als die Protagonisten. Er kann sich

deswegen ein besseres Bild über 'Zufall' oder 'Schicksal' machen und so wird ihm vielleicht bewußt, daß es nur eine Frage des Überblicks ist, ob man die Sinnhaftigkeit in all den scheinbar so chaotischen, zufälligen Ereignissen erkennen kann."

20. "So mach' ma's" and "ich mach' doch keine Übungen am Gerät," (Interview).

21. "Wer sagt, wir seien nicht wagemutig? Mit der Kitty Kino haben wir noch nie einen Film gemacht, das ist ein Experiment." Ditta Rudle, "Bartkraulen," *Wochenpresse* 5 (January 28, 1986): 41.

22. "Frauen dominieren," *Neues Volksblatt* (February 21, 1992).

23. "Wo ich mehr von mir rüberbringen kann." Susanne Heinrich, "Man fühlt sich gebraucht," *Kurier* (February 14, 1992): 40.

24. "Bilder und Szenen von großer Intensität." Frido Hütter in his review, "Bilder aus dem Holzvulkan," *Kleine Zeitung* (October 10, 1994): 43. The theater workshop *Der Gipfel von allem*, by Otto Zykan (who wrote the music) and Kino, was premiered as the indoor opening show of the yearly avant-garde festival "Steirischer Herbst."

25. "Die ist weg vom Fenster." This comment was overheard by the author on August 29, 1994 in the Austrian Film Commission.

26. See the respective catalogues of the Austrian Film Commission. The data for 1996 are more promising. Films by Käthe Kratz, Marjan Vajda, and Susi Graf are in production.

Ruth Beckermann: Re-Activating Memory—In Search of Time Lost

Renate S. Posthofen

Ruth Beckermann's works are in many ways exemplary for leaving the realm of darkness and moving beyond the shadows: they are situated within the context of contemporary feminist and minority discourse and present a noteworthy contribution to an interdisciplinary exploration of those questions that are related to the ethnic and cultural identity of today's Jewish Austrians from a woman's point of view. Beckermann has set out to examine the boundaries of the constructed somber and silent space in which the lost memory of her Jewish history has been placed. Her films and essays that bear the testimony of a search for identity combine visual elements with intercultural subtexts to analyze the situation of those Jews living in Austria, who are to this day victims of prejudice. Her work focuses on the rising consciousness of current historiographic positions in literature and film that embody creative approaches in dealing with the current debate about the "*Limits of Representation.*"[1]

Born in 1952, Beckermann's formative years were spent in Vienna in the 1950s and 1960s. During the 1970s and the 1980s she studied journalism and art history. The years 1970 and 1971 mark her study abroad experience in Israel. In 1975 and 1976 she spent time in New York, where she studied photography and filmmaking at the School of Visual Arts while producing her first 8mm films. After earning her doctorate in 1977 at the University of Vienna, she became a journalist, documentary writer and filmmaker, documenting her search for her Jewish ancestry and her displaced eastern European Jewish culture in its relations to her own identity. In 1977, Beckermann was instrumental in founding and organizing the "filmladen" in Vienna—a distribution, rental and production agency for lesser known 16mm films and videos.[2]

In 1978 and 1982, Beckermann's first two films premiered.[3] In 1983, the documentary about the life and memories of Franz West (alias Franz Weintraub) became her first widely recognized production.[4] The title of this film, *Wien Retour* (Vienna Revisited), indicates the journey which the Jewish social-democrat, communist, and emigrant Franz West had to undertake to save his life from his National-Socialist adversaries in Austria during the fascist rule of the Nazis. Franz West's powerful closing statement reminds the viewer of the necessity and actuality of representation and remembrance of the Holocaust.[5] After he narrates and presents the story of his life, he concludes:

> There are many people today who don't want to know anything anymore about THAT, and precisely because of this it is nevertheless important to talk about IT every now and then, to remind everyone what kind of times these were that one was living in back then.[6]

The film deals with the fate of Franz West through his personal recollection and detailed memory. As he himself tells his life story, powerful images from archival footage and documentaries appear on the screen; thus intertwining his personal recollections with historical facts. The focus rests specifically on the transitional period between 1924 and 1934 which marks the shift from the liberal to the Austro-fascist government. The film presents Beckermann's basic concern—namely, to use film as a medium to preserve the memory of Franz West as a representative of his time. The filmmaker demonstrates with Franz West's testimony that the rise of Austro-fascism was the result of Austria's own economic and political concerns and that anti-Semitism was not simply a German import.

Beckermann addresses this issue not only in her films but in her documentary writings as well. In 1984, she edited and published the documentary, *Die Mazzesinsel, Juden in der Wiener Leopoldstadt 1918-1938* (The Island of Mazzes, Jews in the Viennese Leopoldstadt), a compilation of historical photographs as well as socio-cultural and literary essays which reflect upon and recount Jewish life in the Viennese Leopoldstadt.[7] Numerous literary and historical memories by such well-known writers as Joseph Roth, Manès Sperber, Friedrich Torberg, Otto Abeles, Bruno Frei, Egon Erwin Kisch, and Elias Canetti contextualize and situate the photographs within the cultural sphere of Vienna in the twenties and thirties. In her introductory essay "Die Mazzesinsel," she crosses the boundaries between collective and individual memory—between the public and the private dimensions of remembrance.[8] As she brings to light the memory and history of the Jewish people, Beckermann's difficulty in locating a place that she herself can call home emerges. Therefore, her filmic journeys become the vehicle to establish her own identity as an Austrian Jewish woman artist living in contemporary Vienna.

In 1985 Beckermann's cinematographic contributions were officially recognized: she received the "Förderungspreis für Filmkunst." The year 1987 marks the debut of Beckermann's critically acclaimed film *Die Papierene Brücke* (Paper Bridge)[9] which links her own existence and search for her family's history to the fate of several old Jewish communities in Bukovina.[10] Like Franz West, Beckermann is motivated by her own personal connection with the Jewish history to render her version and interpretation of events within the frame of a specifically Jewish historiography. She writes:

> Since the completion of *Wien Retour* I deal with the possibility of finding forms in the vicinity of the documentary genre, which would make it possible to employ language not simply as a commentary and the images not alone as alibis. The connection between image and language should be made on a different, deeper and more complex level. I not only wanted to follow the few single traces of my family history, but I also wanted to find out how the proven and told stories would mix with my own experiences and feelings.[11]

The film documents Beckermann's quest for a virtual and spiritual home, and the recovery of her cultural and historical roots. It leads the filmmaker to explore the reality of her life in Vienna and how it relates to her Jewish heritage. She hopes to find a connection with the past and present life of Jews, whose numbers are declining, in eastern Romania and the former Soviet Union. Her journey from her home in Vienna brings her to Seret in Romania, and to Czernovitz[12] and Satagura in the Ukraine: "I traveled to the East, because I was simply curious if there still existed those images of the stories with which I grew up." (PB).

Beckermann journeys to her father's hometown, but contrary to her expectations, she realizes that "the closer to the destination I was, the more inaccessible it became" (PB). Her father's stories about the miraculous rabbi in Satagura, the markets and the traveling stages and theater-groups from Galicia which performed in Vienna function as geographic and ethnic markers and illustrate the once flourishing and harmonious multicultural society in Bukovina. Yet, the geographical and temporal distance between her generation and that of her parents becomes evident: "What my parents related to us about former times sounded as remote and as far away as the Middle Ages" (PB).

Beckermann's search for remembrance and identity establishes not only geographic and temporal but also mythical markers of Jewish existence, and thus significantly alters the traditional (predominantly non-Jewish) historiographic representation of the Shoah. She weaves stories from her childhood with narratives, tales, symbols and myths. This reveals her openness and acceptance of the multi-dimensional conditions under which her personal search for identity as well as the collective memory of the Jewish fate after the Holocaust must occur. The allegorical tale of the "Paper Bridge," narrated by Beckermann in the film herself, was once told by the mystical figure Hagazussa:

> The inhabitants of a small city on the river had an iron bridge over which they used to cross the river, from one border to the other. At the same time they dreamed of a second bridge, not made out of iron, wood, or stone, but made out of cigarette paper. Of course those who are doubtful and proud will laugh about those dreams, and they will continue to use the iron bridge, which will ultimately fall and they will drown. But the others who are not fearful and believe, will not hesitate to cross the river via the Paper Bridge and will walk into life while singing. (PB)

Hagazussa serves in the film as a symbol for memory; she has seen many things and relates this powerful parable. Her presence as a symbolic persona functions as a vehicle for remembering those who crossed the "Paper Bridge" and were redeemed. Beckermann's reference to Hagazussa's flight, as she is chased away by the villagers, may be interpreted as the villagers' attempt to force the memory of the Holocaust's victims into a sphere that is seemingly inaccessible to those who seek the truth. The filmmaker tries to find and occupy a permanent space for the Holocaust victims when she says, "the people who knew bridges made out of cigarette paper are already dead" (PB).

The intertextual dimension suggests connections to the Old Testament such as the Jewish mass exodus from Egypt which points to the mythical redemption that is associated with crossing the "Paper Bridge." With the biblical allusion, Beckermann elevates the importance and immediacy of memory and history into the realm of a universal presence. The film underscores the importance of the historical presence in a commemorative way. In this context, Beckermann quotes the Russian fiction writer Ilya Ehrenburg: "The less there is being remembered about the past, the easier it is to pass through the events" (PB). Beckermann's intention is to reclaim and establish the memory of the dead as a part of the living and to illustrate "how much the fear of the death of the parents is connected to the fear of forgetting, and vice versa; the fear of forgetting with the death of this generation" (PB).

Her visual strategy of bringing to light almost invisible and long forgotten events points to the potential for the elimination of collective and individual memory. This is again evident as Beckermann meets with Herbert Gropper, an elderly Jewish gentleman, in Soutceava. He shows her the Jewish cemetery of Seret and gives her a lesson in Jewish cultural history.[13] The images of the cemetery function symbolically, in the same sense as the people who cross the "Paper Bridge." The cemetery remains as a sign of the resistance, an intricate part of the memory of the once flourishing Jewish community. In Yiddish and German Herbert Gropper explains that it will be fenced in for the purpose of preserving the memory of the Jews who are buried here. Thus, the parable of the "Paper Bridge," as well as the names on the concrete tombstones, function as allusions to the Jewish flight from death which must remain in our conscience.

Beckermann aims at establishing a critical and complete memory. Thus, after having visited the stage for the American film production *War and Remembrance* in Osijek,[14] she contemplates:

> Maybe our fate is that of the wandering Jew who got lost in the forest. He walked around for days until he finally found another forest dweller. "Please help me," he screamed. But the other dweller answered: "I can't help you. I've been living in this forest for a long time, and I look like a forest dweller but in reality I'm only a Jew like you." "What shall we do?" asked the other in despair. "I don't know," the first one responded. He went on to say: "After all these years, which I spent living here in the forest, I only managed to find all the ways one is *not* able to get out of the forest."[15]

In subverting the stereotypical image of the lost and wandering Jew by placing it in a specific historical context and attaching virtual significance to it, this sentiment is again echoed when Beckermann asks: "Who are we? The children of the survivors? The children of the second generation?" (PB). As the filmmaker traces her family's history and searches for clues and recognition of her identity, it becomes obvious that she is partially successful in uncovering her personal past. Home for Beckermann and her family is the former apartment of her parents in Vienna's inner city in the former Jewish textile quarter where she herself had grown up. In the film her journey ends here with the realization: "I will never know any other place as well as this one. You will be so happy about every stone, about every glance which you can find when you come back" (PB).

The year 1988, the fiftieth anniversary of the events in March 1938, sets the time to look at contemporary Austrian society at large to assess the relationship between Austrians and Jews, in particular their attitudes towards tolerance and understanding each other. In her essay with the telling title *Unzugehörig* (Not Belonging), Beckermann examines the relation of Austrians and Jews after 1945 from a socio-cultural perspective.[16] Her text is an eloquent combination of facts and persuasive arguments which expose the anthropological connection between presumptions and suspicions as they constitute prejudice and misperception. Beckermann writes against silence[17] and takes an active part in the postmodern discourse about the Holocaust and its consequences. She explains: "The children of the survivors are indeed not willing anymore to remain silent; to have long discussions with anti-Semites or to request compassion. However painful their childhood experiences proved to be, they recognize in retrospect that the feeling of not belonging finally opened their eyes" (U 11). It is again her childhood images which lead her to inquire about the hidden and seemingly buried traces that continue to shape the personal, historical, and cultural elements of her existence. *Unzugehörig* presents her findings and systematically reveals the disturbing fact that the attitudes of many Austrians toward their Jewish neighbors are still characterized by disrespect, prejudice and a lack of critical interest in constructively confronting and analyzing their past and present relationship. Beckermann's examination is directed toward finding and establishing a common point of departure from which ethnic marginalization and xenophobia can be understood.[18] Beckermann documents that the Jewish population in Austria is developing a consciousness regarding the ambivalent and problematic nature of their existence in Austria today:

> In dealing with the dilemma, to be part of it and to feel extraneous, two tendencies can be distinguished: The attempts to establish a certain continuity by reconstructing or renovating synagogues which were destroyed in 1938, and cultural activities that are thought to have an enlightening effect by their organizers. On the other hand, the tendency to make the rupture noticeable, which was brought about in 1938 and the following years, in order to expose it accordingly. (U 106)

She points out that establishing a contemporary Jewish identity manifests itself in a polarized division of historiography, in which a discussion about Auschwitz and a Jewish perspective have no space (U 108). The lack of open discussion about the past—and the renewed call from the political right wing for a homogeneous Austria—makes it hard for Austria's Jews to address their needs within the historic perspective (U 21).

As Beckermann documents the rise of fascism in Austria from 1934 to March of 1938 in great historical detail and makes transparent the misbeliefs that led to the great pogrom in Vienna with sudden vicious anti-Semitic fervor, she also traces the psychological conditions of anti-Semitism at the time. She argues that anti-Semitism empowered the weak and gave them the illusion of an identity, a powerful social position and a political voice. The continuity of Austrian anti-Semitism in conjunction with the formation of a national consciousness after 1945 has been instrumental in establishing a lasting uncritical attitude in the postwar Austrian Republic (U 68-69). This national consciousness was founded upon the exclusion of "the outsiders": ethnic minorities and Jews. Since Austrian patriotism has been constructed as a concept based upon homogeneity, the Jews were and are to this day excluded from it, Beckermann argues.

In all of her films and documentary writings, Beckermann, who is part of the second generation of Jewish Austrians whose parents survived the Holocaust and now live in Vienna, focuses on the connections between historiographical representations and her own personal history and identity. As such she attempts to highlight less obvious elements of Viennese Jewish history. She also traces eastern European Jewish traditions in order to establish a contemporary discourse on Jewish identity (U 105).[19] Ruth Beckermann's *Unzuehörig* adds a divergent, yet convincing voice to the monocausal historiography that deals with Austro-fascism: "The remembrance of the severity and the dimensions of the killings also challenge the very purpose and meaning of one's own existence for the children of the survivors. After all, the survival of the parents was ultimately a coincidence" (U 127).

In the last chapter, "Youth in Vienna," (U 117-129) Beckermann traces her childhood and feelings back to life in Vienna in the 1950s, when Israel was seen as the ultimate homeland and America as its protector (U 117). A seemingly new form of anti-Semitism among her politically liberal friends constituted for Beckermann a different catalyst to continue her deep-rooted search from yet another angle (U 126). The search for an exploration of a "homeland" as the unifying place for all lost and wandering Jews, and other "displaced persons" of Jewish origin (U 80-84) has taken Beckermann to Israel on a number of occasions.

In 1990 the filmmaker produced the last part of her filmic "trilogy." The title *Nach Jerusalem* (Towards Jerusalem) signals the correlation of space and time. The English translation, "Towards Jerusalem" for *Nach Jerusalem*, does not make reference to the temporal dimension that is implied in the German film title. Beckermann explains in an interview:

> The film is called "Towards Jerusalem" which has a double meaning in the German language. The word "towards/after" has a spatial as well as a temporal meaning—one can well be on the way to a specific place, but in one's consciousness already have progressed past that. That is why I chose the title, because it is clear to me that I can never arrive in a real, depicted Jerusalem; on the one hand, as a European Jew with a conscience that has been formed by the Shoah, and on the other hand, with a positive Diaspora-identity. It is clear to me that Jerusalem is a place and a metaphor for yearning from afar: from the distance of two thousand years as much as from the far European perspective.[20]

"Towards Jerusalem" fits the genre of a documentary "road movie,"[21] which captures the five weeks / sixty-kilometer journey from Tel Aviv, on the Mediterranean Sea, to Jerusalem that Ruth Beckermann and her camera woman, Nurith Aviv undertook.[22] In an interview the filmmaker stated:

> The challenge was to make a political film that ignored the preconceived expectations. It was not my intention to reproduce those televised images about thrown stones and shootings and broken bones that we are exposed to on a daily basis, which constitute of course part of the reality as well. The point for me was specifically to film on a road, where things are relatively quiet, although it is located approximately twenty kilometers from the occupied territories.[23]

The evolving representation of Israel reflects Beckermann's impressions as a western European Jew. The camera captures the background of local architecture, into which Beckermann blends interviews with people whom she meets on the road who represent diverse ethnic origins and credos. Largely improvised and unrehearsed, the film presents the diversity of the people who live in Israel today. Beckermann's aesthetic format highlights the evidence of harmony as well as tensions between the multi-cultural people, among them the Jewish and Arabic population, that exist side by side.

Yet, *Nach Jerusalem* does not reflect Beckermann's particular opinion of today's Jewish and Arabic affairs in Israel; rather it attempts to show a representative segment of contemporary life in Israel. Beckermann pursues intercultural comparison and transnational representation of Jewish life-styles in the Diaspora. Thus, *Nach Jerusalem* constitutes the filmmaker's creative attempt to address the multitude of images and impressions of Jewish life and to deal with divergent identities within our postmodern world.

Dagmar Lorenz refers to this specific character of Beckermann's works in her recent article "Austrian Jewish History and Identity after 1945": "In Beckermann's case, clarity about her situation does not lead to a permanent 'solution,' but only to a recognition that solutions are relative and at best temporary."[24] Elfriede Jelinek points out yet another dimension in Beckermann's work: "If one is a member of a suppressed group—which women are in any case—then one is basically forced to look at the collective fate of the group as such, and beyond the individual fate."[25]

With her work, Beckermann not only claims her existential right to a personal history and identity, but also overcomes the predicaments and taboos that are associated with being Jewish in today's Austria.[26] Through her films, she undertakes the effort to break the silence of the victims and brings to the screen a modified and annotated historiography. She engages in an ongoing effort to change the traditional perceptions and stereotypes arrayed against contemporary Austria's Jewish citizens. Her work commemorates those who have lost their homes and lives forever, and whose children to this day feel ignored and deeply offended. For these children and their faint memories, she creates a voice and a space in which her critical observations force the audience to rethink and reassess their memory about and attitude towards misrepresentation of the Jewish cultural heritage. At the same time, she continues to voice her concerns on a variety of other issues. Her most recent articles, entitled "Du, gemütliches Österreich...der Blick auf ein Land, das sich selber gerne anders sieht" (You, nice Austria...the view of a land that likes to see itself differently),[27] and "Die Wegbereiter. Wenns drauf ankommt, ist Zigeuner wieder Zigeuner und Jud wieder Jud" (The Scouts. When it comes down to it, a gypsy is a gypsy and a Jew is again a Jew)[28] are her answers in exposing Austrian xenophobia and racism in the killings in the Austrian town of Oberwart, Burgenland early in 1995. Through her woman's point of view and her analytical perspective, the audience experiences, discovers, and rediscovers Jewish history in its contemporary dimension in Vienna, Bukovina and Israel.

Utah State University

Notes

1. *Probing the Limits of Representation: Nazism and the "Final Solution,"* ed. Saul Friedländer (Cambridge: Harvard University Press, 1992).

2. At the same time she also finished the production of the film *Arena Besetzt* (Arena Occupied). Information contained in the biographical information leaflet to Beckermann's film *Die Papierene Brücke* (Vienna: INFO filmladen, 1987).

3. Ibid.; *Auf amol a Streik* (Vienna, 1978); *Der Hammer steht auf der Wies'n da draussen* (Vienna, 1980).

4. Ruth Beckermann and Josef Aichholzer, *Wien Retour* (Vienna: filmladen, 1983). The film was shown at film festivals in Berlin, Florence and Paris.

5. *Holocaust Remembrance: The Shapes of Memory*, ed. Geoffrey

Hartman (Oxford, UK: Blackwell, 1994); Patrick H. Hutton, *History as an Art of Memory* (Hanover, NH: University of Vermont Press, 1993).

6. Franz Weintraub in *Wien Retour*. Weintraub's recorded memories represent a common account of a Jewish experience during Nazi Austria. The film constitutes an important contribution to the materials that deal with Holocaust testimony, and deserves more attention in light of current debates about the construction and formation of Jewish identities and autobiographies. English translations from the original German filmscript are mine.

7. *Die Mazzesinsel. Juden in der Wiener Leopoldstadt*, ed. Ruth Beckermann, 4th ed. (Vienna: Löcker, 1992).

8. Beckermann, "Die Mazzesinsel," *Die Mazzesinsel, Juden in der Wiener Leopoldstadt*, 9-21.

9. The film was awarded the prize of "Das goldene Einhorn" at the avant-garde film-festival in Vorarlberg, Austria. Subsequently it was well received at various European film festivals in Berlin, Edinburgh, Mannheim, Paris, Vienna and Wels. For her contributions to the "Austrian Film," Beckermann also received the "Österreichischer Staatspreis für Filmkunst" in 1989.

10. Beckermann, *Die Papierene Brücke* (Vienna: Fima Schlappenhut/filmladen, 1987). Further references to this film will be marked with PB in the text.

11. Beckermann, "Zur Produktion" (Vienna: filmladen, 1987).

12. Beckermann describes her first impressions and experiences from her trip to the former Russian town in her article, "Die Verhaftung," *Profil* 34 (August 19, 1985). It is during her first short visit in Czernovitz that she realizes that filming at her father's birthplace would be impossible because of the unstable political climate at that time. This article was orginally entitled "Erdbeeren in Czernovitz" (Strawberries in Czernovitz).

13. Beckermann filmed in Seret in Rumania instead of Czernovitz in Bukovina due to the unstable political climate.

14. Osijek on the river Drau is in the former Yugoslav Republic. The American Television Corp., CBS network, rebuilt the former concentration camp Theresienstadt for the filming of *War and Remembrance*. On the set, Beckermann meets and films the Viennese writer, Robert Schindel, who acts as an "extra" in this film. Cf. *Gebürtig*, 3rd ed. (Frankfurt: Suhrkamp, 1992). In this

novel, Schindel provides a semi-documentary account of this episode in the epilogue "Verzweifelte," 341-353.
15. Beckermann's family background also inspired her to undertake this film project. The personal history of her parents becomes part of her film: Betty and Salo Beckermann lost a large part of their respective families in different concentration camps. The fate of her grandmother "Oma" Rosa, who survived the Holocaust by hiding, and passed away in 1957, when Beckermann was five years old, is also mentioned as an important part of the filmmaker's past.
16. Beckermann, *Unzugehörig—Österreicher und Juden nach 1945* (Vienna: Löcker, 1989). Further references to this publication are marked with U in the text.
17. Cf. Neva Slibar, "Anschreiben gegen das Schweigen. Robert Schindel, Ruth Klüger, die Postmoderne und Vergangenheitsbewältigung," *Jenseits des Diskurses, Literatur und Sprache in der Postmoderne*, ed. Albert Berger and Gerda Elisabeth Moser (Vienna: Passagen, 1994), 337-356. Slibar asserts that the postmodern discourse has yielded the result of successfully verbalizing themes such as National Socialism and dealing with the past in such a way that the ability to differentiate becomes more complex not only in form and style, but also in matters of content of those literary texts in question as well (350).
18. Cf. the first chapter entitled "Davor, Danach," 9-16. The controversial memorial "Fascism and War"—created by the Austrian sculptor Alfred Hrdlicka located at the Albertinaplatz in Vienna for the 50th anniversary of the Austrian "annexation" to Nazi Germany—becomes an example to analyze the public misperception regarding Austrian-Jewish relations. For her, the Jew who is depicted sliding along the ground still demonstrates the inequality, weakness and defeat of the Jews.
19. In her notes about the production of the film, Beckermann comments on the elements which form her Jewish identity: "The eastern Jewish traditions with their stories..., the annihilation of the Jews, which will remain inconceivable..., my specific situation in Austria..., finally Zionism, as a prewar yearning for normality." Beckermann, "Zur Produktion" (Vienna: filmladen).
20. Beckermann is interviewed by Christa Blümlinger on January 11, 1991, *INFO filmladen* 121 (Vienna, April 1991).

21. "Dem Zufall eine Chance zuviel gegeben. Beckermann's Israel-Film *Nach Jerusalem* im Kino," *Die Presse* (April 10, 1991): 10.
22. Ibid. and "Sechzig Kilometer im gelobten Land," *Der Standard* (April 10, 1991): 13.
23. Blümlinger Interview.
24. Dagmar C.G. Lorenz, "Austrian Jewish History and Identity after 1945." Special Issue, *Modern Austrian Literature* 27.3/4 (1994): 12.
25. Cf. leaflet with biographical information for *Die Papierene Brücke* (*INFO filmladen*).
26. For a detailed analysis of the contemporary context within which Beckermann's work is situated, the following article offers additional insight: Jacqueline Vansant, "Challenging Austria's Victim Status: National Socialism and Austrian Personal Narratives," *The German Quarterly* 67/1 (1994): 38-57.
27. Beckermann in *Tagesanzeiger* (Zürich, June 28, 1995).
28. Beckermann in *Profil* 9/27 (Vienna, February 1995): 83-84.

From the Shadows into Silence:
What Remains of the World of Milena Jesenska: Nadja Seelich's Film *Sie saß im Glashaus und warf mit Steinen* in Context[1]

Dagmar C. G. Lorenz

The filmmaker Nadja Seelich left her native Prague during the suppression of the "Prague Spring" and the Russian occupation in 1969.[2] Since that time she has lived in the West, for the most part in Austria. For her films of the 1980s, including *Kieselsteine* (1981; Gravel), a work examining the interaction between children of Holocaust survivors and Austrian and German Gentiles, and her children's movies, the language is German, the setting Austria.[3] The works reflect the filmmaker's own experience of marginality in a serious, but not a didactic or tragic manner.[4] Seelich's protagonists are set apart from the mainstream and engage in a quest for alternative realities. Her films include absurd elements which create ambiguity. Her flair for tempering disaster with introspection and irony, observed by Ursula Kubes-Hofmann,[5] is particularly obvious in *Sie saß im Glashaus und warf mit Steinen* (1992; She Sat in a Glass House Throwing Stones), a documentary film that is also a carefully composed work of art.[6]

Sie saß im Glashaus examines Seelich's cultural, aesthetic and moral frame of reference in conjunction with Prague's transformation from Socialism to Western-style democracy. The film pays tribute to the dissenters who were affiliated with *Divoke Vino* (Wild Wine), the literary magazine of *Klub Mlada Poezie* (New Poetry Club), for which Seelich worked as an editor in the late sixties during her student years at the Charles University in Prague. It was at this time that she met Jana Cerna (1928-1981), the daughter of Milena Jesenska and the Jewish architect Jaromir Krejcar (Kubes-Hofmann: 17).

Seelich and her co-producer Bernd Neuburger commemorate the vanishing culture of Prague's dissenters. Personal narratives, objects, and locations such as Cerna's first desolate hotel room and her former apartment, now a cozy middle class home, document Prague's physical and ideological transformation. The current gentrification is not represented as positive, as a statement in the film brochure reveals: "The Potemkin villages of post-industrial society are more hideous than their archetypes, since they are no longer merely facades. MC-DONALD'S is also MCDONALD'S on the inside: the mice flee into the hamburgers and are sold along with them."[7] As early as the postwar era, Cerna seems to have felt ambivalence towards the West, in spite of her dream to join André Breton's Surrealist circle in Paris. Bondy's account of a failed attempt to escape suggests that she was held back by psychological rather than external obstacles, including her hesitation to emigrate to Austria where former Nazis enjoyed prominence.[8]

Seelich and Neuburger describe the intent of their film as follows:

> To record the surrealist aesthetics of the sordid, the desperate and the true, elements from which Jana Cerna drew her existence, and to fulfill this aim before Prague finally becomes a cheery backdrop for the hectic bustle of assorted travel agencies. To quote Milan Kundera: "Kitsch is the negation of trash." (Film brochure)

Underground dissenters who remained outsiders, compared to the now "respectable" democrats, are the heroes of *Sie saß im Glashaus*. By examining the world of the poet and critic Jana "Honza" Cerna, Seelich, who prepared Cerna's most notable book *Adresat Milena Jesenska* (Addressee Milena Jesenka) for publication, explores her own roots as well. Cerna's biography emerges from the accounts of others, but Seelich's emotional involvement is obvious from her impassioned reading of Cerna's works on voice-over.[9]

That the film is in German rather than in Czech is of cultural and political significance. With the exception of Cerna's former neighbors and the prison matron,[10] the interviewees speak Prague German, the *lingua franca* of once cosmopolitan Bohemia. Along with this lost language the images suggest alienation, defining the featured intellectuals as members of a generation suffocated by war, revolts, and dictatorship. Indeed, now that their works can and do appear, their message may have become obsolete.[11] Yet, they may still speak to future readers, once the excitement of the "Velvet Revolution" has died down.

The picture of Cerna, the absent protagonist, can only be found on the program cover. Although she died in a car crash eleven years before the production of the film, her memory was kept alive by her friend and alter-ego Johana Kohnova,[12] a writer and expert in Russian literature, by the philosopher Egon Bondy, the poets Ludvik Hess and Ivo Vodsedalek, and by Seelich, who elicits their memories in interviews. Cerna is the unifying element for these vastly different personalities.

Cerna's image as conveyed by the individual speakers lacks consistency; the men pride themselves on their intimacy with her, Bondy describes her as a *femme fatale* and a guru, and Kohnova reflects upon her capacity for friendship. Ultimately Cerna's true identity remains an enigma—her own texts do little to synthesize the disparate impressions. The abrupt ending of one of the film's central sequences involving Hess carrying a heavy casket reinforces the sense of mystery. When he puts the crate down in front of the camera, he states that it contains Cerna's stories, and leaves the viewers to speculate on specifics.

As early as *Kieselsteine*, Nadja Seelich had thematized otherness, in part as the result of the long-term effects of the Holocaust. While they are too young to have been Nazi victims or perpetrators, her protagonists are still influenced by the past. The film suggests that the Holocaust produced different collective memories on the part of Jews and Gentiles, and that it is the cause of Central Europe's cultural fragmentation.[13] The direct and aggressive articulation of biases which German and Austrian bigots express only to people who share their point of view, lends a remarkable quality to Seelich's film. The secret rhetoric of everyday Fascism and neo-Nazism are exposed from the perspective of an unconventional Jewish woman who is neither religious nor assimilated. Seelich's Hannah Stern has no intention of forgiving and forgetting the crimes of the past, nor does she have the desire to leave Austria.[14] In contrast to most Jewish protagonists in contemporary German literature, Hannah is neither a victim nor a villain. Struggling to gain respect as a woman and as a Jew, she turns the tables on her opponents, making Germans and Austrians the objects of her unmerciful gaze, and stereotyping them as radically and unfairly as anti-Semites would Jews. Seelich's detachment from German and Austrian culture enables her to diagnose the intolerance which poisoned Vienna in the pre-Waldheim era: proto-Fascist tendencies, xenophobia, and the abuse of Jews, women, transients, disabled persons, homosexuals, and animals.

In *Kieselsteine*, Seelich establishes her critical approach, which is to evaluate society by the condition of those who live on the margins. Her children's films also portray the point of view of the underprivileged.[15] *Jonathana und die Hexe* (Jonathana and the Witch), for example, thematizes the friendship between an orphan girl and a bona fide witch who helps her little friend to escape from her petty-bourgeois home and a hideous prospective stepmother into a fantastic alternative reality. Physically and psychologically this benevolent witch resembles Johana Kohnova in *Sie saß im Glashaus*.[16] *Sie saß im Glashaus* was produced in Prague, a city with whose Jewish tradition Seelich strongly identifies.[17] Her and Cerna's background, Prague's modernism with Kafka as its most significant representative, is evoked through images of buildings, paintings, and interiors. Despite the fact that Kafka had died well before Cerna was born, she was so intensely identified with him that she considered him to be her father, and, indeed, like him, she became an icon of individualism. Among the many divergent forces in her life, her affinity to the Jewish fate and the Holocaust is preeminent. Although she died a devout Catholic, Cerna had herself cremated and her ashes scattered, finding, as in Celan's *Todesfuge* (Fugue of Death), "a grave in the breezes."[18]

Sie saß im Glashaus accentuates Cerna's defiance of every bureaucratic system and her connection to pre-Nazi and pre-Stalinist anarchism. It is implied that commemorating Cerna is synonymous with commemorating Central European modernity, whose legacy seems threatened by extinction, now more than ever. The fall of Stalinism ushered in cultural indifference, which is as destructive to intellectual life as cultural dictatorship. Cerna's entire life appears like a paradigm of the repression suffered by Bohemia's intellectuals caught between two totalitarian regimes ("Film, Staat und Gesellschaft": 3). Inscribed with the terror of Nazism, World War II, and the chaos within her own family, Cerna's body and mind become sites of resistance against imposed norms.

There is a parallel between Cerna's plight and the tenuous position of the women poets of the World War I era, who were torn between bourgeoisie and bohème, Socialism and individualism, Jewish and Gentile culture—as was the case with Else Lasker-Schüler and Claire Goll. Like Cerna, none of them fit the mold. Cerna's ideas and way of life challenged the ideologies of her time, to a large extent because, as a woman, her experiences were distinct from those of men. Her existential loneliness is conveyed in haunting motifs, for example the figure of a lonely girl standing underneath Prague's bridges, cut off, as it were, from nature and the city alike, or in the image of white birds, swans, gulls, and geese, taking off in flight, leaving behind only a black duck—a loner like Cerna. The latter image also contains one of the numerous allusions to Kafka, whose last name signifies "blackbird" in Czech. Another such allusion is embedded in Bondy's account of the ravens who refuse to leave the old Jewish cemetery, which he tells, ironically, in a latrine overlooking Prague's ghetto complex.

The interwar bohème—Kafka, Lasker-Schüler, Brecht, Klaus and Erika Mann, degenerates according to Nazi doctrine—became subject to persecution. Stalinist Czechoslovakia continued to oppress anyone who attempted to revive the legacy of the twenties with a cultural program that closely resembled Nazi aesthetics. *Sie saß im Glashaus* juxtaposes Fascist and Socialist Realism with Surrealist aesthetics. Vodsedalek, for example, exhibits crude Soviet posters depicting wholesome men and women, Madonna-like mothers, and Lenin as a father-figure and contrasts them with Cerna's philosophy of art which was opposed to such reductionist simplicity. The mentality expressed by these posters, which were intended as models for the artists of postwar Czechoslovakia, is the same as that of the naively aggressive fighting song *Katyusha*, playfully parodied by Bondy.

The images of aging Johana Kohnova dancing in a homemade red dress, black stockings, and silver shoes, all remnants of her work as a designer for the professional attire of prostitutes, Cerna's painting of Kohnova as "an old cat," and Bondy's obscene nonsense verses in the tradition of Morgenstern, are antithetical to Fascist and Socialist Realism. They represent attempts to come to terms with twentieth-century reality. In the context of a dictatorship, Bondy's frivolous puns and Cerna's and Kohnova's spontaneous "happenings," as well as their bizarre flights of imagination, represent ideological statements.[19]

In a more theoretical vein, Egon Bondy tells about the Prague Surrealists' projects to protect modern art, including their clandestine removal of prints from library books to safeguard them from government censorship and preserve them for other intellectuals. To counteract the anti-Semitism of the Socialist state, the group members, including Bondy, whose original name was Zbynek Fiser, assumed Jewish-sounding names and, as a result, came under severe attack. As the daughter of a Jewish Surrealist and an anti-totalitarian woman journalist, who denounced Communism once the goals and methods of Stalinism were comprehended, Cerna was a misfit from childhood on and subject to oppression.

Sie saß im Glashaus is a subjective film, replete with associations, symbols, and objects with particular significance to those who knew Prague's Cold War scenery. In her anti-hierarchical cinematographic approach Seelich integrates prominent and obscure personalities and places. Her first husband Ludvik Hess, once a brilliant poet, turned horse breeder, the founder of *Klub Mlada Poezie*, and editor-in-chief of *Divoke Vino*, provides some of the most powerful leitmotifs. His appearances—alternately on a black and a white horse—reinforce the film's structure that is based on the pendulum motion of Prague's Metronome, a giant structure erected at the former location of a Stalin monument which was destroyed during the revolution. The Metronome's red hand is shown as it moves from left to right and, then, during the retrospective segments, in the opposite direction.

The Metronome and the sinister horseman, who claims to have no recollection of the past, illustrate Bohemia's seesawing between right wing and leftist extremism, between Western and Eastern Europe. The seemingly perpetual movement precludes a metaphysical order or a teleology. The reaction every action engenders is automatic, and all conditions are temporal, including the present move toward democracy. The same dialectic pattern governs Cerna's fate who observed that, as the daughter of leftists, she had to reject Communism, but, if she had been born as Marie Antoinette, she would have supported the revolution. Finally, in conjunction with the pendulum motion, colors, particularly black, red, and white, the colors of the Habsburg monarchy, and yellow, the color of the Jewish star, are also employed to concretize historical processes and to support the major themes.

Seelich assigned to the late Cerna the function of a force field, of an invisible center. All that remains of the real person are texts, paintings, poetry, and anecdotes, submitted to the viewer for interpretation. None of these fragments amount to a coherent story. Instead, they form a mosaic from which the viewer can gather certain details, for example, that Cerna stayed with her overbearing grandfather Jan Jesensky, a dandy and university professor, after her father's departure into exile and her mother's deportation.[20] According to Bondy, Cerna's childhood was overshadowed by neglect, poverty, her mother's sickness, and by incest involving her father who had returned from England for a short period of time. Bondy reports that Cerna grew up in foster homes without formal education, and that she embarked on a life as a survivor/victim without any social skills. To illustrate her ineptitude in practical matters, he relates how she squandered her grandfather's estate in a few months, got married four times, and had five unplanned children.

Cerna's disregard for the Stalinist bureaucracy which might have offered her a modicum of stability is discussed by Kohnova, who stresses that her friend became the center of a subculture, in spite of the fact that she depended on welfare support for her survival. Both women seem to have been proud of not having "sold out" to the system, even though this resulted in having to eke out a living as transients and petty criminals. Poverty, drunken brawls, substance abuse, imprisonment, promiscuity, and botched abortions were a part of their everyday existence. Seelich portrays this milieu from an insider's point of view. Without underestimating the problematic aspects of Cerna's existence, she is sensitive to its liberating qualities which account for Cerna's *joie de vivre*.

The tragicomic, grotesque, and pornographic stories told by the interviewees reveal a hedonism which put them at odds with the "productive" members of society. Their tenets are most clearly expressed in Bondy's bawdy anecdotes which demonstrate the interconnectedness of body and intellect, sex and philosophy. Cerna's statements shed light on the reasons for her refusal to lead a structured life—her yearning for freedom, her vulnerability and naiveté, but also her resilience in her struggle against authoritarian structures. Cerna's commentary on her first sexual experience suggests that she remained aloof from the men in her life. She concedes that her first lover may have felt like a conqueror, but to her the encounter was a rite of passage. In another episode, she characterizes heterosexual activity as a social event and, in contrast, auto-eroticism as the actual source of a woman's pleasure. The image of one black and one spotted panther engaged in a courtship ritual accompanies the text, suggesting that men and women are members of different subspecies.

As a radical individualist Cerna has considered her own desires first priority, and she engaged in an uncompromising search for love and affection—even those closest to her criticized her solipsism. Bondy complains about her tendency to withdraw without prior notice and other types of willful behavior, Kohnova remarks on her inordinate need for validation—one of the reasons, according to her, why Cerna never found a proper father for her children. It is amusing to compare Cerna's enraptured statements about sensuality and ecstasy with the bourgeois disapproval of her fellow anarchists.

While Kohnova dwells on Cerna's incompetence, Bondy interprets her life choices within the context of Existentialism and the hippie movement, with one significant distinction: in contrast to the freely-evolving Western movements, he defines the Prague bohème as the necessary expression of a prolonged state of emergency.[21] Indeed, Cerna was willing to pay a high price for her nonconformism. As a result of her "asocial" behavior she was frequently imprisoned, and she attributed her existential isolation to the emotional trauma of incarceration which, the way she describes it, can be compared to her mother's concentration camp experience. It is no coincidence that the image of the women's prison in *Sie saß im Glashaus* resembles that of the concentration camp Mauthausen in *Kieselsteine* (Lorenz: 78). To express the "cruel frivolity," as Bondy calls it, of Cerna's fate, the prison is juxtaposed to a luxurious Baroque castle, where Cerna's family caroused, unconcerned with their relative's plight.

Cerna accepted no authority but her own; in contrast the systems under which she lived, National Socialism and Stalinism, demanded total surrender. She was surrounded by tyranny, even within her family—like her mother she suffered from Jesensky's despotism. In defiance of social and private constraints, Cerna took charge of her own body, thoughts, and productivity. Carefully selected images illustrate the forces which shaped her attitude: a military cemetery in Russia evokes World War II and Nazi aggression, the Jewish cemetery and the *Altneuschul* portray Jewish culture and its annihilation in the Holocaust, the polluted industrial landscape in the outskirts of Prague, an emblem of the Communist legacy, and the statue of a lion, half wrapped in plastic, which could represent either the lion of Judah or the Bohemian lion.

Cerna's excesses must be interpreted against this historical background. Only then does it become obvious that she reflected back at the world what the world had offered her, and that her achievements were considerable: against all odds and not always consistently, she turned pain into pleasure and hatred into love. She rejected the work ethic and the murderous secondary virtues championed by Nazis, Communists, and capitalists alike; cleanliness, cashier's honesty, and neatness. Her innate pacifism and her passion for life and the human body made her a hero in an era of oppression, even if by default, as is suggested by the anecdotes about her inability to perform upon command.

In contrast to Bondy's cerebral analysis, Kohnova approaches the phenomenal Honza Cerna on an intuitive level, acting out her stories, for example the account of one of Cerna's abortions. Kohnova reenacts the event and demonstrates how she carried Cerna's placenta down a flight of stairs in a bunt cake pan. The old woman holding an imaginary cake pan while reiterating the onomatopoetic words "blah-blah-blah-cup-cup..." is the film's most pathetic scene. The absurd chant expresses tragedy, insanity, a grotesque kind of pragmatism and a magic, all of which underlie Seelich's work, especially the disquieting universe of *Sie saß im Glashaus*. Prague's spectacular scenery emerges as if through the eyes of a well-informed outsider who is too familiar with the sights to be taken in by their glamor, and yet not familiar enough to avoid them. The opening scenes suggest chaos and unrest; historical architecture clashes with the stark edifices of the Socialist era and with the new concession stands and advertisements for Western products. The soundtrack includes noise of drilling and detonations, thus reinforcing the images of rapid change. Amidst the ruins of the past and the debris of the present, history is erased even more efficiently than after World War II. The business of laying the past to rest is conducted with an uncanny speed. The music underscores the merging of different cultures; the French folk song "La Blonde," first whistled as if by a breathless man, then played on a piano, and then rendered in a jazz version, alludes to elements of French, American, and Eastern European culture. The love song of the Moldavian mariners, sung by Bondy, introduces Bohemian folk tradition, and *Katyusha* and the *Marseillaise* allude to Europe's major revolutions.

"La Blonde" in conjunction with the young woman by the river suggests that Cerna was a delicate blonde woman. This notion, like many others, is playfully dismantled. Upon closer look, the girl is a brunette and quite dissimilar to Cerna, whom Bondy describes as tall, strong, chestnut-haired, cross-eyed, and "somewhat syphilitic." Nadja Seelich remembers her as "a large, solid woman, with a fat stomach and sagging breasts, dressed in men's trousers, with straggly dark hair, soft full lips, a squint, and wearing spectacles" (Cf. Film brochure), and Vodsedalek depicts her as a passionate, revolutionary-minded woman in men's clothes, "definitely not a lady."

The complicated interplay of visual images, text, and music reflect the complexities of the postmodern condition. For example, the saxophone music of the Prague Gypsies, which combines elements of jazz, klezmer, and folk music, establishes a link with pre-Nazi culture, but it also transcends the boundaries between East and West today, illustrating the obsolescence of the traditional categories of ethnicity and culture.[22] It is the music of a cosmopolitan mass culture which has been associated with decadence and non-conformism in the former Eastern Bloc countries. The Russian film *Taxi Blues* for example uses jazz as a manifestation of Western decadence to characterize a Jewish saxophone player as the counterpart of a traditional Russian man.[23]

Acoustically and visually Seelich's film characterizes the mentality of the aging beatniks and Surrealists who seem unaffected by the material blessings of the new commercial culture. The image of a subway tunnel is an apt metaphor to describe their submergence during Fascism and Stalinism and their continued life on the fringes. The notion that these intellectuals have been defeated is gradually revised. Although a supposedly global culture and economy have canceled the traditional right-wing and left-wing politics, the intellectuals continue on their quest for alternatives—even now after the liberation has taken place.

As is the case in Leonard Cohen's vitriolic song about the reorganization of the former Eastern Bloc, *The Future*,[24] *Sie saß im Glashaus* implies that the appreciation for intimacy, remembrance, and history can only thrive among individuals with love as its driving force. Kohnova's friendship, Bondy's passion, and Seelich's admiration for Cerna ensure continuity on the basis of personal memory. Hence, there is an emphasis on sexuality throughout the film—its celebration as the ultimate source of pleasure and its discussion in philosophical terms. In keeping with Wilhelm Reich's *Massenpsychologie des Faschismus* (1933; Psychology of the Masses during Fascism), a cult book of the sixties movement, Cerna regarded sexuality as the key to a person's innermost being and the primary instrument of perception. She viewed the world in sexual terms, but she criticized the traditional gender roles, for example in her statement that eyes are genitals which only men are allowed to use.

Cerna and her friends were aware of the revolutionary potential of sexuality as well as its opposite, the deformation of character and the creation of authoritarian structures through sexual repression.[25] In *Massenpsychologie*, Reich maintains that whoever controls a person's or group's sexuality has gained control over their entire existence. This political view of sexuality pervades Seelich's film, as it establishes a correlation between free sexual expression, the freedom from materialism, and the ability to oppose tyranny. The importance Cerna attributed to loving and being loved constituted a rebellion against her society's mechanistic view of sexuality and denial of pleasure. Her rebellion against rationalism was motivated by her resolve to resist domination by the desires and demands of others. It is in this way that Cerna added a feminist dimension to Reich's Marxist psychoanalysis which comes across in Seelich's film on a multitude of levels.

Ultimately the dimension of hope prevails. The image of the Metronome, framed by two of the angel statues, alludes to and refutes Benjamin's concept of the Angel of History. Seelich's image suggests that in order to come to terms with history, it takes two angels communicating with one another, rather than a single one surveying past and present. More likely, however, it takes no angel at all, but human beings, to watch over history—the Angels guarding the Karlsbrücke between the city of Prague and its ominous castle are old, and they are made of stone.

Ohio State University

Notes

1. I am indebted to Jeni Cushman for her editorial comments.
2. Seelich published poetry, short stories, and radio plays while a student in Prague. Her poetry anthology, *Akdar Ajdan Leporello*, written in 1969, was prepared for publication but did not appear in print. It is scheduled for publication in Prague in the near future.
3. The reactions to *Kieselsteine* were mixed, cf. Robert Streibel, *Volksstimme* (January 20, 1984): 9, and Horst Christoph, *Profil* (January 23, 1984): 58. Seelich's films for children, liked by young and adult audiences alike, received international awards, for example *Jonathana* at the International Festival for Children's Film in Chicago and at Bratislava. See also: Dagmar C.G. Lorenz, "Three Generations Remember the Holocaust. Hilsenrath, Becker, and Seelich," *Simon Wiesenthal Center Annual* 5 (1988): 77-96.
4. Seelich's change of medium from poetry to film can be explained in part by the necessity to adjust to the German-speaking

environment. In the files at the Literaturhaus in Vienna, she is referred to as a "Wahlösterreicherin" (Austrian by choice).

5. Ursula Kubes-Hofmann, "Die Macht der Poesie," *Stimme der Frau* 2 (1991): 17. The ambiguous treatment of Jewish identity and the Holocaust in *Kieselsteine* was criticized particularly by leftist publications, such as "Moskauer Film-festival: Diskussion um *Kieselsteine*," *Volksstimme* (July 17, 1983): 9 and others. Among Seelich's works not discussed here are the screenplays *Ein Spielfilm für 2 Berge* (A Film for Two Mountains), *3 Schauspieler und ein Feuersalamander* (1983; Three Actors and a Salamander) and *Nett* (1984); the films *Mein Name ist Egon* (1988; My Name is Egon), *Who Is Who in Mistelbach* (1989), the four-part TV series *Mein Zuhause, dein Zuhause* (1989; My Home, Your Home), and *Lisa und die Säbelzahntiger* (written in 1992, in preparation; Lisa and the Saber-toothed Tigers).

6. *Sie saß im Glashaus und warf mit Steinen*, written by Nadja Seelich; produced by Seelich and Bernd Neuburger. Vienna, Extrafilm 1992. In 1993 the film received the "Österreichischer Dokumentarfilmpreis Wels" and was nominated for "FELIX." In 1993 it was featured at the following film festivals: Rivertown, Montreal Nouveau Cinema, Duisburg, and in 1994 at the Berkeley Women's Film Festival, and the Munich and Karlsbad film festivals.

7. Quoted from the English version of the film brochure accompanying the subtitled version. Seelich, Bernd Neuburger, "She Sat in a Glasshouse Throwing Stones," Vienna: Extrafilm, 1992. The brochure contains Seelich's "Farewell to Jana Cerna," as well as short biographies of Johana Kohnova, Egon Bondy aka Zbynek Fiser, Ludvik Hess, Ivo Vodsedalek, Nadja Seelich, and Bernd Neuburger.

8. Prior to their expedition together, Bondy had walked to Vienna several times. He ate, drank, and had odd encounters with actors such as Attila Hörbiger and Ilse Werner. Cerna seems to have had ambitious dreams of going from Vienna to Paris and tried to turn the escape into an adventure. Ultimately they surrendered to the Russian soldiers, went back to Prague, and relinquished their hope for the "free world."

9. In "Die Macht der Poesie": 17, Kubes-Hofmann observes that the

opening of the borders inspired Seelich's greater freedom of expression. Peter Wallner, who criticizes the film's constructedness in *Der Standard* (October 30, 1992): 9, emphasizes the film's Prague Jewish atmosphere.

10. In some of the Czech-language portions techniques better known from silent films are applied. Captions explaining the goings-on are interpolated between individual scenes.

11. Works such as Jana Cerna, *Clarissa a jine texty* (1990) and *Co cist z torby spisovtely Jihomoravskeho kraje 1990* (1991). Cerna's Jesenska book was widely received, for example: *Adresat Milena Jesenska* (Prague: Club Mlada Poezie, 1969) and (Prague: Concordia, 1991). Translations: *Vie de Milena: de Prague à Vienne* (Paris: Maren Sell, 1988); *Kafka's Milena* (London: Condor, 1988), (Evanston, Ill.: Northwestern University Press, 1993), (University of Michigan: Slavic Languages and Literatures, 1982); and *Milena Jesenska* (Frankfurt: Neue Kritik, 1986). Egon Bondy's rich production since 1990 includes *3x Egon Bondy* (Prague: Panorama, 1990), *Lesbicky sen* (1993), *Bez pameti zilo by se lepe* (1990), *Cesta ceskem nasich otcu* (1992), *Indicka filosofie* (1992), *Orwelliada* (1990), and many others. Seelich states in an unpublished lecture manuscript, "Film, Staat und Gesellschaft in Ost- und Westeuropa und ich," n.d.: 7-8. "Unfortunately, the screenplays which were written in the past 20 years, but whose filming was prohibited, are now, for the most part, outdated; the desire to make movies out of them no longer exists." She believes that the situation is different in the case of books.

12. The symbiotic quality of Kohnova and Cerna becomes obvious when Kohnova states that because of her friend's experience she did not need to act on her own impulses.

13. Ruth Beckermann, in her perceptive study *Unzugehörig. Österreicher und Juden nach 1945* (Vienna: Löcker, 1989), 17f. without mentioning Seelich as the author of the script, criticizes the polarization of the Jewish woman-German man *Kieselsteine*, correctly pointing out that the Austrians were anything but innocent bystanders.

14. Unlike Deborah Lefkowitz' *Intervals of Silence. Being Jewish in Germany*, 1989, Cambridge, MA: Lefkowitz Films, which remains within the bounds of polite discourse. Most critics were

uncomfortable with *Kieselsteine*. Reinhard Tramontana, for example, calls it an "uninforming film" and oddly enough perceives Hannah's desire for revenge as "masochism." In: "Gemischte Gefühle," *Profil* 5 (January 30, 1984): 50-52. Gottfried Distl, on the other hand, described the work as "responsible" and praised the outstanding performance on the part of the actors. In: "Kieselsteine," *ÖH-Express* (February 1984): 43.

15. Seelich contextualizes her children's film in terms of the Bohemian literary tradition. "The phenomenon, 'child,' traditionally has high value in Czech culture and society...Most of the important Czech authors have also written for children. Children's literature was not considered of lesser value, just as children are not lesser human beings. The fact that it is different in other countries, e.g., in Austria, was a major part of the culture shock that I suffered in the West" ("Film, Staat und Gesellschaft": 1).

16. Seelich discusses Kohnova's influence on her in the interview; Kohnova and Cerna introduced the young motherless woman to the bohème and Surrealism.

17. Cf. *The Jews of Bohemia and Moravia. A Historical Reader*, ed. Wilma Abeles Iggers (Detroit: Wayne State University Press, 1992).

18. Paul Celan, "Death Fugue," tr. Lowell A. Bangerter, *Austria in Poetry and History* (New York: Frederick Ungar, 1984), 306-309.

19. In some ways these forms of expression can be compared to the production of the *Wiener Gruppe* and the *Aktionisten*. Cf. Horst Kurz, *Die Transzendierung des Menschen im bio-adapter. Oswalds Wieners 'Die Verbesserung von Mitteleuropa, Roman,'* Diss., Ohio State University, 1992.

20. Milena Jesenska died at Ravensbrück, a concentration camp for women.

21. He points out that his and his friends' rebellion resulted in their being considered enemies of the state. He refers to *On the Road* by Kerouac, an author whom Seelich mentions as well. She describes her life in Prague during the sixties as follows: "We wrote, published, acted, discussed for hours, listened to jazz. Jean-Paul Sartre came to Prague and told us about Marxism and

we laughed and laughed" ("Film, Staat und Gesellschaft": 3).

22. "Black jazz musicians in the Weimar Republic belonged to the category of 'the Other,' a stereotypic construction intended to reinforce the hegemony of European identity over all non-European peoples and cultures...The concrete specificity of jazz disappeared into geographic, racial, and historical vagueness," observes Cornelius Partsch in "Jazz in Weimar," *Dancing on the Volcano. Essays on the Culture of the Weimar Republic*, ed. Thomas W. Kniesche and Stephen Brockmann (Columbia, SC: Camden House, 1994), 111.

23. *Taxi Blues*, directed by Pavel Lounguine, USSR: Lenfilm Productions, 1990; New Yorker Films Artiwork, 1992.

24. Leonard Cohen, *The Future*, CBS Sony Compact Disk, 1993.

25. See also Theodor W. Adorno et al., *The Authoritarian Personality* (New York: Harper, 1950).

Interview with Nadja Seelich:
August 29, 1994 at 7:30 p.m.,
Café Museum, Vienna, Austria

Dagmar C. G. Lorenz

DAGMAR LORENZ: What was it that prompted you and Bernd Neuburger to make a film about the remnants of the bohème around Milena Jesenska, now that the so-called Iron Curtain has fallen?

NADJA SEELICH: Just to clarify, our film does not focus on Milena Jesenska, but on her daughter, Jana Cerna. One of the reasons for making *Sie saß im Glashaus und warf mit Steinen* (She Sat in a Glass House Throwing Stones) was that a host of documentary films about Prague was produced after the Velvet Revolution. I looked forward to each new film with great anticipation and was shocked after watching them, because all these films dealt with the Prague Baroque, beer, and Kafka. So Bernd suggested that we make a film of our own—a film about me, but that struck me as a completely obtuse idea.

The deciding factor was a film entitled *Milena Lover* which we saw when we attended the Munich film festival that year. It was an awful piece based on a novel by Jana Cerna which appeared in Prague in 1968 in the publishing house where I worked at the time. I knew Jana Cerna personally and had had frequent discussions with her about her work. In Czech, the book is entitled *Adresat Milena Jesenska* (Addressee Milena Jesenka). When it was translated into German a few years later, it appeared under the title *Milena Jesenska*. When a film was finally produced, its title was *Milena Lover*. I consider this the epitome of the commercialization of Czech culture, of culture in general, during the last twenty-five years.

Then I told myself, make a film about Jana Cerna, something that relates closely to the spirit and atmosphere of Bohemia and Prague as I see them. For that reason we produced a film about Jana's Prague.

DL   You mentioned that you knew Jana Cerna personally. How did you meet her?

NS We published a journal entitled *Wilder Wein* (Wild Wine), a literary journal, and Jana Cerna wrote for this publication.

DL In which language was this paper published?

NS In Czech, of course.

DL I was not quite sure since you referred to it as *Wilder Wein* and because the language of *Sie saß im Glashaus* is German with a few exceptions.

NS Well, yes, that's a long story. When I came to Vienna twenty years ago and had such difficulty with the German language, particularly written German, and people ridiculed me because of my accent, as they customarily do with non-natives, I promised them, one day it will be extremely "in" to speak like I do, one day I will belittle them. And in 1989 when the opening between East and West occurred and the hatred of foreigners was rekindled at the same time, I wanted to show that a person can be intelligent and witty even if he or she talks like a dolt.

DL Which does not apply to you under any circumstances.

NS You'd be surprised.

DL How do you assess the situation of Prague intellectuals at this point and of the intellectuals whom you have known in your own Prague past?

NS I have the impression that the wonderful Velvet Revolution was a mass psychosis like any other revolution, just think of 1968. Only this time it happened miraculously, without violence. Such revolutions occur with regularity every twenty to thirty years and reflect the turnover of the majority of the population. And once again, intellectuals found themselves in the position which they occupy in all societies, Socialism included: some of the dissidents became successful and began to establish themselves careerwise, while others quickly abandoned this notion, and, well, that's democracy. The intellectuals are a minority, and they are treated gently but they make no difference.

DL What I found particularly interesting in your and Bernd's film are the many images which, in my opinion, suggest how western materialism with its values and products has entered Prague and swamped it with its values and priorities, including consumer goods. How do you view the chances for a future autonomous, intellectual Czech culture considering this lopsided influence?

NS I believe that in Central Europe every nation will attempt to maintain its own culture. However, I have no comment about Czech culture at this point in time. Everywhere in the world culture seems to stagnate—for decades there has been nothing new. This is also the case in the Czech Republic with the distinction that some amazing books have appeared there after the revolution; these are books, however, which have been barred from publication for twenty years.

DL You mean that these books were withheld all this time waiting to be published?

NS Precisely. Only a couple of authors appeared on the scene recently, authors who did not write before 1989—even among the Eastern Europeans . . .

DL How about the two central characters of *Sie saß im Glashaus*, namely, Egon Bondy and Johana Kohnova?

NS As far as Bondy is concerned, he teaches Philosophy in Preßburg [Bratislava, DL]. In the course of his life he wrote seventy-eight books which kept appearing one by one after the Velvet Revolution. And Johana, who is, was, and always will be a survival artist, works with an incredible enthusiasm as a sales clerk in an Asia shop.

DL You don't say. A little while ago I asked you about sound effects and the music which is so essential for the overall artistic composition of your film. I am unfamiliar with some of the scores and songs you chose, as I said. Would you say a few words about the choice of music and the production?

NS A Czech poet named Machar wrote a marvelous poem about Prague in which the writer envisions Prague at the crossroads between Russian melancholy and French lightheartedness. I agree with him and feel that his ideas can be applied to the earlier revolution. I think that Jana Cerna and her friends had envisioned a revolution of French character but the revolution they were given was the Russian revolution. This concept is integrated into the film by first playing the *Marseillaise* in many different variations and then *Katyushka*, a Russian folk song which is primarily known as a revolutionary song. The long melancholy solo piece spontaneously sung by Bondy is a traditional song of Moldovan fishermen containing a declaration of love. The third element is the French folksong "La Blonde" which was Jana Cerna's song, a leitmotif and a signal. People whistled the tune of this song to her all the time, and lovers of Jana Cerna whistled it, standing under her window—sometimes she let them in.

In the film it is played by Prague Gypsies who are not actual professional musicians but carry coal for a living; they refuse to play commercially, because they claim that music exists to bring joy, not to make money.

DL   They carry what?

NS   Coal. In the United States you're probably not familiar with that, coal for heating. In Prague coal is transported on trucks, unloaded and taken to people's basements. That's what these men do.

DL   And they play music extraprofessionally?

NS   Yes, they do it for fun and play at weddings and the like. And they play everything, not only this kind of music, but everything they are asked to play, only with their very own rhythm. The saxophonist in particular creates very special sounds...

DL   Let's take a little break since food and coffee have arrived.

NS   Very well.

DL   The last issue we discussed were the coal carriers who are actually musicians or vice versa. You told me earlier that they are considered the Black people of Prague which is an interesting observation. What did you imply?

NS   We were at their place, at the house of these musicians, together with our sound specialist who was greatly interested in ethnology and ethnography and knew everything about Roma, Sinti, and other tribes. When he asked them if they were in fact Roma or Sinti one of the gypsies looked at him with great surprise and replied that they were actually from Karlin, a district of Prague. And then they referred to a percussionist whom they wanted to play with as "White," but stated that he could play like a "Black" person. What I wanted to say with all this is that they do not consider themselves some exotic, romantic ethnic group, but as people of Prague, Black people of Prague.

DL   This is fascinating. With regard to the current ethnic situation in Prague, these reactions suggest that the city culture may be diverse, but not in a traditional sense. The old ethnic divisions no longer apply, and what is at stake is privilege, which generates a sense of integration.

NS   That is entirely the case.

DL   I wanted to ask you also about your own artistic creativity as a woman, a Jew, and as someone born in Prague who commutes between Prague and Vienna. How do you envision your work between the languages, cultures, and traditions?

NS   That is a good question. I consider myself to be a Central European first and foremost and presuppose that every educated Central European must master several Central European languages. In Prague, Czechs, German-speaking Jews, and Germans have lived side by side, just as there are people in Vienna, immigrants, who understand and write Czech and German as a matter of course. That is part of the Prague tradition. You know for example that Milena Jesenska translated Kafka into Czech, but Kafka corrected her translations and was continually dissatisfied because he recognized immediately when this or that was not rendered properly.

DL   Which new Central European traditions do you think will arise in the next few years? Do you have any idea based on your first-hand experience in your two cities of residence, of the course things will take? Do you predict a cultural dissociation or an increasing homogenizing?

NS   I have a sense that the situation can best be described as treading water, culturally speaking, and that this has been the case for quite some time now everywhere in the world, including Vienna and Prague. I am very curious to see what the future will bring. About one thing I am sure, namely, that both cities will somehow develop in tandem. To my great delight Prague is right now a most dynamic place. Approximately 30,000 young Americans live there, students or graduates, who at some point want to become painters, artists and the like. It makes me happy that Prague is today what Paris was in the 1930s and that it is necessary to live there at some point in one's life, even if only to record this experience in one's biography.

DL   This intense energy, this tension, characteristic of today's Prague, emanates from your film.

NS   But it is important to note that the people who contribute to it primarily have come after 1989, particularly these young Americans who come to live there for four years and help to shape student life.

DL   Nadja, a couple more questions. First, if you were to characterize yourself, which important influences would you mention and which artists inspired your work?

NS I fell into the hands of Jana Cerna and Johana Kohnova at the age of eighteen. These two witches took charge of me and began to teach me all about life since I had no mother at that time. You can imagine what that meant—both of them influenced me vitally at this important phase of my life. For some reason both of them felt that I had a striking resemblance to Kafka. This was one of the reasons why they loved and pursued me so inordinately and wanted to entrust me with their legacy, because of this physical resemblance to Kafka.

DL Do you suppose that there was an intellectual or psychological affinity as well?

NS Oh well, you know that to make such an assumption would be exaggerated. At any rate, I am happy to say that I was lucky and I got away pretty much unscathed at the age of twenty. However, after this education, which you can well visualize, having seen our film, I arrived in middle-class Vienna—I was married or rather, married into a cute little kitchen painted yellow and white, complete with kitchen towels in a yellow and white plaid pattern. That was quite a culture shock.

DL You just mentioned two terms, witch, a concept which plays a central role in contemporary feminism, and middle class in the sense of petty bourgeois, a milieu which you found too confining.

NS Yes. My background was the *haute bourgeoisie*, more or less.

DL What is your view of the women's emancipation movement? Do you consider yourself a feminist?

NS Under no circumstances. Probably because I grew up in a matriarchal family. My grandmother was venerated by everyone and her advice was respected because she was in fact a very wise woman. All the clever and strong men of this family followed my grandmother's advice and as a child I never had the feeling that a woman might possibly be inferior to a man. My particular education had certain advantages as far as the so-called battle of the sexes is concerned. A girl in my family had equal rights and could not fathom not having them. It is possible that things were different in professional life. Until then I had no notion of women's inequality, I had only read about it. The first time I was confronted with the problem that women were considered inferior was in the West at the age of twenty, but at that age one no longer buys into it. I understood that women faced this issue over here, but I did not identify with it.

DL   As a young co-editor of *Wilder Wein* did you not feel discriminated against?

NS   No. I worked with the publication when I was a student, all of us were students, even the editor-in-chief.

DL   These are the questions I wanted to ask you, Nadja. If there are other issues you would like to address, something you consider important in view of our conversation or with regard to your film, please do not hesitate to mention it. Perhaps there are also issues with which you would like to familiarize your film and reading public, or people who want to get to know your work?

NS   With regard to the latter I have nothing to say at this time, but I realize that I gave a completely idiotic answer when you inquired about personalities who influenced me. I would like to talk about this in more detail. Kerouac was terribly important for me, also Ginsberg who was in Prague in 1965, but I had read his poems prior to that. Then there was Karel Capek,[1] and of course Franz Kafka, who intended his works to be witty, which is a little-known fact.

DL   I cannot but agree, that's exactly my opinion as well.

NS   Quite in contrast to Kafka, Hasek intended his good soldier Schwejk as a critical realistic novel and people find it insanely funny while everyone ascribes alienation and depression to Kafka, while he was really humorous. I read Kafka for the first time when I was sixteen and he remained truly important for me. Another very significant author was Meyrink as far as I was concerned, not everything he wrote, to be sure, but particularly *Golem* and his feuilletons. I read one of his feuilletons after completing *Glashaus* and came across a statement which describes exactly what I wanted to express in the film. I am not sure if I can quote it without the text, but I'll send it to you.

DL   Let me add a question as well: at one point you mentioned your attitude towards the Prague Jewish Community (*Kulturgemeinde*) and your interest in making an active contribution to Prague Jewish life, and perhaps becoming an official member.

NS   It can hardly be called a question that I can or want to contribute to Jewish life in Prague, but I do feel an affinity and a sense of belonging especially as far as the cultural life is concerned. I can be a participant in it, much more so than in religious matters.[2]

DL Nadja, I want to thank you for giving me the opportunity to conduct this interview.

The interview was conducted in German and translated by Dagmar Lorenz.

Ohio State University

Notes

1. A representative of Czech Humanism, and author, dramatist, and writer of children's literature (1890-1938). Cf. Seelich, "Film, Staat und Gesellschaft": 1.
2. As of October 1995, Seelich no longer considers taking this official step. She is currently working on a short film based on her grandmother's account of Theresienstadt, taped immediately after the latter's liberation, and is reviewing the documents and letters of her relatives' Holocaust experience.

Contributors

Beth Bjorklund is Associate Professor at the University of Virginia and has published extensively on modern and contemporary Austrian literature. Her translations include: *Contemporary Austrian Poetry: An Anthology* (Cranbury: Associated University Presses, 1986), Friederike Mayröcker *Night Train* (Riverside: Ariadne, 1992), Renate Welsh *Constanze Mozart: An Unimportant Woman* (Riverside: Ariadne, 1997).

Maria Luise Caputo-Mayr is Professor at Temple University in Philadelphia. She is the co-editor of the ACSAL series *Österreich in amerikanischer Sicht*. Her numerous publications include extensive studies on Kafka, exile literature, postwar Austrian literature, 19th and 20th century poetry, Anton Fuchs, Christoph Ransmayr, Elfriede Jelinek, Anna Mitgutsch, and Florian Kalbeck.

Linda DeMeritt received her Ph.D. from Michigan State University in 1982. She is Associate Professor of German and Chair of the Modern Language Department at Allegheny College, Pennsylvania. Her interest in Austrian literature was kindled by a Fulbright scholarship to Graz, Austria. She has published on Peter Handke, Elfriede Jelinek, Elisabeth Reichart. Other works include a book on the literature of New Subjectivity and a textbook on German grammar.

Margret Eifler is Professor of German Studies at Rice University in Houston, Texas. Her research and teaching concentrate on the Modern/Postmodern Novel and Theory, Feminist Writing and Criticism, European Women Filmmakers, New German Cinema, Contemporary German Culture Studies. She has published several books and numerous articles on the socio-aesthetic constructs of predominantly 20th-century German and Austrian writers and filmmakers.

Nancy C. Erickson received a Ph.D. in 1989 at the University of Minnesota with a dissertation on Günter Grass's *Der Butt*. Her research interests have expanded to include Ingeborg Bachmann, Elfriede

Jelinek, Christa Wolf, Ingeborg Drewitz, and Irmtraud Morgner. In 1991 she led a team of language professionals to establish second-language competencies for high school students entering the Minnesota State University system schools. She lives with her husband and their two children in Bemidji, where she teaches all levels of German language and literature at Bemidji State University, Minnesota.

Konstanze Fliedl, Dr. Phil. from the University of Vienna, has been a Professor in Germanistik since 1991. Publication on Austrian literature and on women's writing. Her recent publications include *Arthur Schnitzler—Richard Beer-Hofmann: Briefwechsel 1891-1931* (Vienna: Europaverlag, 1992), *Österreichische Erzählerinnen. Prosa seit 1945* (Munich: Deutscher Taschenbuch Verlag, 1995), *Arthur Schnitzler: Der Weg ins Freie. Roman* (Co-authored with Karl Wagner; Salzburg: Residenz, 1995), and *Peter Rosegger—Ludwig Anzengruber: Briefwechsel 1871-1889* (Vienna: Böhlau, 1995).

Kristie A. Foell is Assistant Professor at Bowling Green State University, Ohio. She received her B.A. from Yale University, and her M.A. and Ph.D. from the University of California at Berkeley. She has been the recipient of several DAAD research grants. Currently, she is a Fulbright Scholar in Berlin, Germany. Her publications on Austrian and German literature and film include the book *Blind Reflections: Gender in Elias Canetti's "Die Blendung"* (Riverside: Ariadne, 1994).

Margarete Lamb-Faffelberger is Assistant Professor of German at Lafayette College, Pennsylvania. She received her Ph.D. from Rice University in Houston, Texas. Research interests include modern and contemporary Austrian and German literature, film studies, feminist theory. She has published on the Austrian feminist avant-garde, Elfriede Jelinek, Valie Export, Julian Schutting, Peter Turrini. Her book *Valie Export und Elfriede Jelinek im Spiegel der Presse* (Bern, New York: Lang, 1992) deals with Feuilleton-reception.

Jutta Landa, Ph.D., is Lecturer at the University of California, Los Angeles. She teaches German and Austrian film, literature, and Business German. In 1992, she was recognized with the *Distinguished Lecturer Award*. She has published numerous articles and authored *Bürgerliches Schocktheater* (Frankfurt/Main: Athenäum,1988).

Dagmar C. G. Lorenz is Professor of German at the Ohio State University in Columbus and a member of the Executive Board of the Melton Center for Jewish Studies. Her books include *Wiener Moderne* (Stuttgart: Metzler, 1995) and *Insiders and Outsiders. Jewish and Gentile Culture in Germany and Austria* (Detroit: Wayne State University Press, 1994). Her current research centers on 19th and 20th century Austrian, German Jewish and women's literature.

Margaret McCarthy completed her Ph.D. at the University of Rochester. Presently she is Assistant Professor of German at Davidson College in North Carolina. Her dissertation "Bodies, Beautiful Souls, and 'Bildung': Reconstituting the First-Person Singular 'I'" reassesses the concept of 'Bildung' in autobiographical texts written by German women during the 1980s. Her research interests include German film, feminist and literary theory, and post-WWII German literature by women. She has received Fulbright and DAAD grants. Currently she is conducting a study on Jutta Brückner's film *Years of Hunger*.

Edward R. McDonald is Professor of German at Lafayette College, Pennsylvania. He received his M.A. and Ph.D. in German Studies at Columbia University. In Germany he has conducted studies and research at the Goethe Universität in Frankfurt/Main, the Ludwig Maximilian Universität in Munich, and the Regensburg Universität. He has published on Franz Grillparzer, Adalbert Stifter, Theodor Fontane, Fritz Hochwälder, Friedrich Dürrenmatt, Heinrich Böll, Paul Heyse, Peter Schneider, and Wolfdietrich Schnurre.

Roswitha Mueller is Professor of German and Comparative Literature at the University of Wisconsin-Milwaukee, Wisconsin. She is the author of the books *Brecht and the Theory of Media* (Lincoln: University of Nebraska Press, 1989) and *Valie Export / Fragments of the Imagination* (Bloomington: Indiana University Press, 1994). She is co-founder and editor of the journal *Discourse* and co-editor of a series on "Women Artists in Film" published by Indiana University Press.

Renate S. Posthofen, born in Wuppertal, Germany studied Germanistik and history at the Albert-Ludwigs Universität in Freiburg. She earned her M.A. at the University of Pittsburgh, Pennsylvania and received her Ph.D. from New York University in Albany, New York.

She is Assistant Professor in the Department of Languages and Philosophy at Utah State University. Her publications include articles on Robert Schindel, Gertrud Kolmar, Geörgy Sebestyén and her book *Treibgut. Das vergessene Werk George Saikos* (Vienna: Böhlau, 1995).

Pamela S. Saur is Associate Professor at Lamar University in Beaumont, Texas, where she has been since 1988, teaching German, applied linguistics, and a variety of literature courses. She holds an M.A. and Ph.D. from the University of Iowa and an M.Ed. from the University of Massachusetts. Her publications are primarily in modern Austrian literature, but include other literary and pedagogical topics. She is the editor of *Schatzkammer* and the *Texas Foreign Language Association "Bulletin."*

Gerd K. Schneider, born in 1931 in Berlin, received his B.A. degree from the University of British Columbia (1962), his M.A. in German from the University of Washington (1963) and his Ph.D. in German Literature from the same institution (1968). He has been teaching at Syracuse University since 1966 where he is Professor of German. He has published a number of pedagogical articles and studies on F. Nietzsche, J. Amery, T. Horst, W. Heinrich, J.M. Simmel, P. Turrini, and D. Wellershoff. His latest book is entitled *Die Rezeption von Arthur Schnitzlers Reigen, 1897-1994* (Riverside: Ariadne, 1995).

Jennifer Taylor is Assistant Professor at the College of William and Mary in Virginia. Born in 1961 in Chapel Hill, North Carolina she grew up in Lexington, Virginia. She received a B.A from Grinnell College in 1983. From Cornell University she received an M.A. in 1988 and a Ph.D. in 1995. Her current research deals with the German-Jewish question in Jurek Becker's and Ruth Klüger's work.

Klaus Zeyringer, Dr. Phil. habil., was born in 1953 in Graz, Austria. He received his "Habilitation" at the Karl-Franzens-Universität in Graz. Since 1987 he is Professor at the Institut de Perfectionnement en Langues Vivantes of the Université Catholique de l'Ouest in Angers, France and heads the Department of German since 1991. His publications deal with Austrian literature of the 18th, 19th, and 20th century, e.g., *Innerlichkeit und Öffentlichkeit. Zur Österreichischen Literatur der achtziger Jahre* (Munich: Francke, 1992).

Name Index